TRADITIONAL
FAVORITES

THE ART OF SEWING

TRADITIONAL FAVORITES

BY THE EDITORS OF TIME-LIFE BOOKS

TIME-LIFE BOOKS, NEW YORK

TIME-LIFE BOOKS

FOUNDER: Henry R. Luce 1898-1967

Editor-in-Chief: Hedley Donovan
Chairman of the Board: Andrew Heiskell
President: James R. Shepley
Chairman, Executive Committee:
James A. Linen
Group Vice President: Rhett Austell

Vice Chairman: Roy E. Larsen

MANAGING EDITOR: Jerry Korn
Assistant Managing Editors: David Maness,
Martin Mann, A. B. C. Whipple
Planning Director: Oliver E. Allen
Art Director: Sheldon Cotler
Chief of Research: Beatrice T. Dobie
Director of Photography: Melvin L. Scott
Senior Text Editor: Diana Hirsh
Assistant Art Director: Arnold C. Holeywell

PUBLISHER: Joan D. Manley
General Manager: John D. McSweeney
Business Manager: John Steven Maxwell
Sales Director: Carl G. Jaeger
Promotion Director: Paul R. Stewart
Public Relations Director: Nicholas Benton

THE ART OF SEWING
SERIES EDITOR: Carlotta Kerwin
EDITORIAL STAFF FOR
TRADITIONAL FAVORITES:
Assistant Editor: David L. Harrison
Designer: Virginia Gianakos
Text Editors: Kathleen Brandes,
Gerry Schremp
Chief Researchers: Wendy A. Rieder,
Gabrielle Smith (planning)
Staff Writers: Sondra R. Albert,
Marian Gordon Goldman, Angela D. Goodman,
Joan S. Reiter, Sandra Streepey
Research Staff: Rhea Finkelstein,
Nancy J. Jacobsen, Ginger Seippel,
Cinda Siler, Vivian I. Stephens,
Reiko Uyeshima
Art Staff: Robert McKee
(design assistant); Patricia Byrne,
Catherine Caufield, Sanae Yamazaki
Editorial Assistant: Kathleen Beakley

EDITORIAL PRODUCTION
Production Editor: Douglas B. Graham
Assistant: Gennaro C. Esposito
Quality Director: Robert L. Young
Assistant: James J. Cox
Copy Staff: Rosalind Stubenberg (chief),
Susan B. Galloway, Mary Orlando,
Florence Keith
Picture Department: Dolores A. Littles,
Jessy S. Faubert

Portions of this book were written by Helen
Barer, Mary Batten, Don Earnest, Margaret
Elliott, Katie Kelly and Harriet Van Horne.
Valuable assistance was provided by these
departments and individuals of Time Inc.:
Editorial Production, Norman Airey; Library,
Benjamin Lightman; Picture Collection, Doris
O'Neil; Photographic Laboratory, George
Karas; TIME-LIFE News Service, Murray J. Gart.

THE CONSULTANTS:
Gretel Courtney is a member of the staff of the
French Fashion Academy in New York. She has
studied pattern making and design at the Fashion Institute of Technology and haute couture
at the French Fashion Academy in New York.

Annette Feldman is a knitting and crocheting
designer, for both clothing and interior decorat-
ing. She is the author of *Knit, Purl and Design*
and *Crochet and Creative Design.*

Tracy Kendall has worked in many capacities
for various fashion firms in New York. She is
now a freelance costumer and set designer for
television commercials and print advertising.

Toni Scott teaches needlework and quilting
techniques at The New School for Social Research in New York. She is also Special Educational Projects Consultant for the Singer
Company, as well as a freelance for numerous
sewing and needlecraft publications.

Julian Tomchin is a textile designer who has
been awarded the Vogue Fabric Award and the
Coty Award of the American Fashion Critics. A
graduate of Syracuse University's Fine Arts College, he has been chairman of the Textile Design Department at the Shenkar College of
Fashion and Textile Technology in Tel Aviv and
currently teaches at the Parsons School of Design in New York City.

CONTENTS

1
A BRILLIANT
RENAISSANCE

Sometime in the year 1887, Emily Smith, the future Viscountess Hambleden, announced in London that she could stand it no longer. The bustled, broad-skirted, furred, feathered, gloved, booted and extravagantly hatted fashions of the day, elegant and ultrafeminine though they might be, were simply too bulky, restrictive and troublesome. And that was not all.

"Petticoats," she said, zeroing in on the

THE FRESH APPEAL OF OLD STYLES

most frivolous and symbolic item of traditional women's dress, "are exhausting, unhealthy, dirty and dangerous. The trouser is not only more comfortable, healthy and clean, but also more decent."

Henceforth, trousers it would be, at least for her and all other sensible, independent-minded ladies. Horrified Victorian gentlemen could jolly well expire by the regiment if her pioneering notion did not suit them —which, of course, it most distinctly did not.

Nor, truth to tell, did it suit very many 19th Century women, whose daily habits, whose thinking, whose very lives—let alone clothing—were firmly based on tradition.

Today we who are trousered, trim and emancipated acknowledge the good sense of Lady Smith's words and applaud her freeing spirit. Nevertheless, there is hardly a one of us who does not feel more than a touch of longing upon seeing a picture of a beautifully caparisoned Victorian woman, or reproductions of other traditional—and equally feminine—fashions from bygone times. For what could be more flattering, or more demurely ladylike and charming, than a ribboned and ruffled blouse, snugged to the waistline and set off by billowing skirts? And no matter how much we may owe by way of liberation to the likes of Lady Smith, what woman's ankles wouldn't look pretty when framed by a turn-of-the-century petticoat described in a contemporary journal as: "Apple green silk . . . with deep scalloped edges placed over an accordion pleated flounce. . . . The rounded points of the upper skirt were edged with chiffon ruching in the palest . . . pink, and true lovers' knots of a slightly deeper shade of pink ornamenting each scallop."

One's no-cling sheath slip seems pretty unexciting by comparison, doesn't it? But more than that, the sight of such elegant and frivolous clothing generates a very personal appeal. One wonders, "How would I look in that?" And then comes the impulse, "I would love to try it on."

The latter is as honest a tribute as any style can have. And it is a tribute that is be-ing heard more and more as the emancipated woman of today finds herself looking toward the traditions of yesterday in order to add—in fact, to recapture—that special touch of femaleness, of individuality and even of lush indulgence that can give so much meaning to the freedom and convenience of modern living.

Bound up in that style and feeling are the truly marvelous needlecraft skills that were at the fingertips of virtually every American woman from the beginning of our history right up to the turn of the century. For us today, mastering some of their basic stitches, and a few simple but elegant embellishments, can be as exciting as the fashions themselves. But to our female forebears, needlecraft was much more than just a means of achieving style. In colonial times, and for many years afterward throughout rural America, a woman's needle was vital to her family's welfare. Not only the ladies' blouses and petticoats, but her husband's pants, her daughter's dress, her son's socks and underwear and mittens depended on her ability to sew, knit and crochet. So did her curtains and quilts, chair covers and pot holders. Thriftily, she would turn her worn, hand-sewn bedsheets into drawers, shirts and nightgowns, and would save mounds of odd fabric pieces to join into bed quilts (a proper wife never threw away a single scrap). She even created pictures for her walls with embroidery or needlepoint.

Besides being a matter of utility and survival, mastery of needlecraft became a point of feminine pride and a symbol of virtue, a mark of the goodwife demanded by husbands and much urged even from the pulpit (the warning "Stick to your knitting" is still very much with us, though not, mercifully, in the total Victorian sense). To ensure such virtue, and a continuing supply of useful talent, little girls were taught to sew and even to embroider shortly after they learned to walk. Stitchery of all kinds became part of the standard curriculum in the most refined female academies. And in case there was any doubt in the minds of upcoming generations that such skills were to be continually counted among a young lady's necessary accomplishments, Queen Victoria herself provided an unmistakable example, being a renowned creator of fancywork.

Thus, though a handful of rich and sometimes dilettantish ladies sent off to Paris or New York for their clothes, or relied on a local dressmaker, most women made their own things, every stitch. And though the labor might indeed be loving, it was, nonetheless, labor. For the full and flowing dresses of the past required the cutting, basting, pleating, tucking, fitting and stitching of as much as 20 to 25 yards of fabric. It was a rare —and usually rich—female who had more than six basic costumes.

But each costume was remodeled many times, in styles like those shown in Section 2 with leg-of-mutton sleeves to replace, perhaps, bishop sleeves; with a cascading

Five antique dolls, children's cherished possessions of the late 19th Century and now owned by a private collector, display miniature versions of Victorian fashions. The 100-year-old doll at left, standing next to an antique

doll-house chair, wears a deeply ruffled skirt of madras cotton, topped by a lace-edged peplum of the same material. The second doll, posed in front of a miniature sewing machine, is garbed in an everyday dress of

jabot ruffle instead of an old high-standing collar; with a new peplum and top or spaced tucks to transform a skirt. And between re-stylings each costume was endlessly varied with accessories of all kinds.

There were, for example, shirred and em-broidered sacques, or basques (fitted blous-es flounced at the waistline), to be worn with skirts in summer. The popular 19th Century periodical *Godey's Lady's Book* describes a simple one as being "in two shirrs, or draw-ings, on the shoulder with a deep ruffle, edged in needlework embroidery." To wear beneath the sacques, there were lace-edged camisoles or embroidered chemises. As a modest covering for the whole ensem-ble, a woman might fashion a sleeved pe-lisse, or a hooded mantle. And for a final fil-lip she would carry a reticule—a small purse artfully attached to a long silken cord.

The bureau drawers of the 19th Century lady overflowed with fine handkerchiefs, sashes, fichus, frilled aprons, lace mitts, pantalettes, knee warmers, bertha shawls and dozens of undersleeves, or *enga-geantes,* which extended from wrist to elbow, where they disappeared under the flowing sleeves of the dress. Making these fancy undersleeves could have been a ca-reer in itself, since practical ladies wore them to brighten and vary their loose-sleeved costumes of basic purple, gray, rus-

cotton dimity. The third doll wears an outfit considered à la mode for afternoon tea parties—a brown taffeta dress trimmed in lace and ruffled at the hem. Demure tucks end in an elaborate yoke ruffle on the fourth doll, whose cinched waist and ruffled skirt were children's fashions of the day. The fifth costume was appropriate for morning engagements: the long, tucked dress reveals a modest glimpse of a printed underskirt.

set or black. The undersleeves were run up with rows of ruching, tiers of ruffles or cascades of downfalling lace. And like so much else in traditional dress, they looked enchantingly feminine, fussy and, if one had pretty hands, very sexy.

Beyond the prodigious quantity and variety of needlecraft that went into her clothing, the goodwife kept her sewing basket bulging with the special tools—embroidery silks and other brightly colored yarns—of what she feelingly spoke of as "my work." That is, the meticulous and enchanting fancywork with which she embellished everything from cigar boxes to the Holy Bible. (Sewing for her own clothes was too routine to be mentioned as "work.") She lovingly generated hand-crocheted lace, ready to be sewn onto camisoles or baby dresses. She fashioned Berlin-work ottoman covers illustrating favorite passages from the Scriptures. Victorian ladies even put so-called dresses on table legs, ruffled slipcovers on wastebaskets and padded cozies or bonnets on smelling salts and ink bottles, teapots and bird cages.

In many Victorian households any item left uncovered was emblazoned with crewel, that is, with designs executed by needle in bright wools. (The origin of the word crewel is obscure, but may be rooted in the old English word *crull,* meaning curl, referring to wool yarn which is characteristically twisted.) The most comely petticoats were trimmed in crewel, and practical women wore embroidered sashes with hanging pockets at both ends in which sewing, keys or coins might be carried. Pincushions, fire screens, wall pockets, framed pictures and

blankets gave further testament to the goodwife's skill with the needle.

Perhaps the most eloquent testimony to that skill, however, were the handmade quilts, many of them preserved as cherished heirlooms—and museum pieces—to this very day. Sophisticated sewing critics see these cozy, colorful quilts not simply as bed coverings but as works of art. And indeed they are. Taking their inspiration from the world around them, colonial wives arranged triangles, strips and squares of leftover cloth into myriad designs with such names as Bear's Paw, Duck Paddle or, less happily, Drunkard's Trail.

Besides being an art form, some quilts are a revealing source of social history. "As the caravans of covered wagons rolled across the plains," wrote one student of this needlecraft, "the old quilt patterns recorded their progress. The Carolina Rose became the Prairie Rose when it reached Western soil, and in Texas the Star of the East became the Texas Star or Lone Star. And what could speak more poignantly of the hardships those women braved than the names they gave their quilts: Rocky Road to Kansas, Crosses and Losses, Indian Hatchet, Texas Tears, Kansas Dugout."

At about the time the wagons were rolling westward, carrying their burden of history, some drastic changes invaded the world of needlecraft. In the 1850s Isaac Singer perfected and marketed his marvelous new sewing machine. Simultaneously, standardized paper dress patterns began to replace the magazine illustrations, hand-me-downs, and the plain old imagination that had been a woman's only guides in creating her dresses. A Victorian-era New York dressmaker, named Ellen Demorest, had the brilliant notion of putting her tissue patterns into the mass market, and by 1873 her annual sales exceeded two million patterns.

Such corruptions of the needlewoman's art were no more welcome than ladies' pants to some gentlemen. (Besides, a Singer machine cost the ungodly sum of $50.) "The very best sewing machine a man can have is a wife," harrumphed one husband, in a scolding essay published in *Godey's Lady's Book.* "It is one that requires but a kind word to set it in motion, rarely gets out of repair, makes but little noise, will go uninterruptedly for hours, without the slightest trimming, or the smallest personal supervision. . . . It will make shirts, darn stockings, sew on buttons, mark pocket handkerchiefs, cut out pinafores and manufacture children's frocks out of any old thing you may give it. . . . Of course, sewing machines vary a great deal. Some are much quicker than others. It depends in vast measure, upon the particular pattern you select. . . . In short, no gentleman's establishment is complete without one."

So much for the well-sewn male chauvinist. Women, however, quickly (and blissfully) discovered that everyday sewing chores could be done more easily by machine. Even elegant fripperies like pin tucks and ruffled furbelows no longer demanded painstaking handwork. Unfortunately, as machine-created readymades grew more available, many of the old-fashioned skills of needlecraft began to disappear.

To restore the lost arts of the needle, to rediscover the joys of traditional fashions, we now need instruction, the wisdom of our great-grandmothers brought up to date. Many of the traditional fashions described in this book can be achieved more simply than ever by today's finely engineered sewing machines. Others, however, like the smocking in Section 2 and some of the quilting and appliquéing in Section 3, are best accomplished by hand.

Whatever work they might involve, needlecrafts hold a revived promise of artfulness and beauty that now seems irresistible, bringing the lovely fashions of yesteryear to today's wardrobe. And many women have already taken up the adventure. Crewel embroidery and needlepoint are in vogue. Smart shops in the best neighborhoods offer instruction as well as supplies. Knitting and crocheting have been taken up by the young, including some who once scorned to thread a needle.

As they do so, a strange and wonderful thing is beginning to happen. New heirlooms of needlework are beginning to take shape, each of them as lovely and intriguing in their special way as the delicate crocheted lace, the appliquéd blouse or the knitted afghan resurrected from a trunk in the attic. These aged artworks—and their modern counterparts—carry with them a sentimental and highly personal warmth. There is the warm touch of a vanished hand in Grandmother's Wedding Ring quilt. There are the giddy color sense and the dropped stitches of sweet Aunt Lulu in that skating scarf your little boy now wears. And there will, someday, be a similar link to another age in the handiwork that is stretched into your own embroidery hoop now.

A look of enduring elegance

Gowns may have disappeared with buckboards, but the decorative features that distinguish the traditional look—ruffles, peplums and leg-of-mutton sleeves—have never gone out of style. And neither have old-fashioned techniques like piecing fabrics, crocheting granny squares or embellishing plain cloth with tucks. These techniques, though born of frugality, produce such handsome effects that designers now choose them for beauty instead of thrift. The splendid dress at left, for example, is pieced—but with imported silk. The skirt above is appliquéd with velvet flowers, the quilted vest at far right is satin. And the brown velvet smoking jacket is set off by a patchwork cummerbund.

Today's dress from yesterday's handcrafts

Whether duplicated exactly for the sake of authenticity or redesigned to suit contemporary taste, the motifs and methods of traditional handcrafts are being turned to decorative advantage in ways that grandmother's generation never dreamed of. As the crewel bands on the caftan at left show, classic embroidery patterns are versatile enough to complement dress styles of all kinds. Crocheted granny squares that were once saved for coverlets and afghans now become the makings of a vest, a cape or a skirt like the one at right. Even so venerable a knitting motif as the snowflake is a modern pattern when used for a cummerbund (*far right*).

Decorative details

The seamstresses of long ago decorated clothes by sewing them in fanciful ways that can still turn a plain dress into a thing of beauty. Pin tucks, such as those in the bodices and skirts of the two dresses at far left, produce striped effects. Honeycomb smocking, like that adorning the apron waistband at left, gives cloth a three-dimensional diamond design. For an extra fillip, strips of fabric can be gathered into ruffles, or laces or braid can be used for outlines. Today only the smocking is handwork; the other effects can be achieved by machine, following the instructions in Section 2.

19

2
A LEGACY OF SEWING TECHNIQUES

Much of the charm of the clothes we consider traditional stems from old-fashioned, romantic details that lend themselves to any number of modern variations and improvisations. When these details—such as tucks and smocking—are worked on equally traditional fabrics, the look is borrowed straight from the past.

Because their links to fashion usually have more to do with nostalgia than with

THE CHARM OF ROMANTIC DETAILS

present-day definitions of what is chic, traditional clothes are regarded as timeless. But to be that successful, to be worn for many years, they must start with the right fabric. The ones best suited are simple—mainly ginghams, calicoes, corduroys and velvets—and most of them are easy to sew.

Cotton is still best for creating a truly authentic old-fashioned look. Over the years, the names of the various types of cotton have hardly changed at all. And delightful names they are: calico, gingham, percale, cambric, dimity, chambray, lawn, homespun. The difference between the cottons of yesterday and those of today is chiefly in their quality. The quality of the material that was woven at home from homespun thread or manufactured in the mills of the early days was unpredictable. The threads could be uneven, the weave too tight or too loose. Dyeing also was less dependable. Natural dyes varied greatly in quality and were not always fixed properly. And early synthetic dyes were not as resistant to light and laundering as those now in use.

Many modern cottons, in contrast, are virtually trouble-free. Soft and smooth, regular in weave, they are both colorfast and guaranteed against shrinkage. And, when blended with synthetic fibers, they are permanently crisp and crease resistant. Thus it is probably easier today to achieve an old-fashioned look than it was when these styles were created.

The tufty look of homespun, once the chance result of uneven spinning, now can be achieved on demand. It appears in handsome cotton, cotton-and-synthetic blends or a lovely soft wool. One blended cotton of this type is made to have a slightly washed-out look, and many of its designs are copied from old calico patterns.

Calico, probably the grandmother of all small-patterned prints, used to be a fairly poor grade of cotton. Today calico-type prints can be found on everything from fine cottons and cotton blends like challis and Viyella, to pinwale corduroy and velveteen.

Gingham, with its dainty checks some-times splashed with embroidered flowers, and chambray, with its faded look, are usually available today in cotton-and-synthetic blends. Flower-sprigged Liberty of London prints, available in either the classic fine lawn or a slightly heavier, more versatile weave, provide particularly attractive choices for period-look styles. And for more formal clothes, both lightweight taffeta and richly colored velvet are as appropriate now as they were in the past.

Many of the three-dimensional details of traditional styles—puffed sleeves, for example, or fichu or shawl collars—depend on classic fabrics for their shape. Crisp lightweight cottons like dotted Swiss are the best insurance that puffed sleeves will stay perky. The choice of a soft material such as challis simplifies the graceful folds of a bishop sleeve, and a mediumweight material like velvet ensures the graceful drape of a shawl collar and the Elizabethan elegance of leg-of-mutton sleeves.

Additionally, much of the success of the traditional styles comes from using these fabrics with the appropriate old-fashioned decorative techniques—hand smocking for the front of a chambray bodice, pin tucks on a high-neck calico band or a wide row of self ruffles along the bottom of a homespun skirt. These extra touches are all versatile, so that once you understand their techniques, you can develop your own uses for these effective details.

Tucks, for example, offer a variety of applications. Ranging from tiny pin tucks (as the name implies, they are no wider than a pin) to the flat, wider-spaced tucks, they have a tailored air and are most effective when made of a plain-colored fabric. Try pin tucking a white piqué yoke for a printed granny dress; or add tucked pockets to a simple calico apron. Spaced tucks can be arranged either vertically or horizontally. You might, for example, select vertical tucks for the front of a bodice and choose horizontal ones for the cuff of a long sleeve.

Edgings—which might be embroidered ribbon, lace or braid—brighten any garment. But be sure to use them properly, and avoid placing them where they will emphasize the wrong body features or break up a garment's fluid lines. Attach lace or plain-colored ribbon to prints; sew embroidered ribbon primarily to a plain-colored fabric.

Ruffles provide still more opportunities for decoration. They can even be added to a garment after it is finished. No doubt ruffles are a legacy from thrifty pioneer women who made them to use up leftover strips of fabric, as well as to decorate their clothes. Almost any light- or mediumweight fabric —either patterned or solid color—can be used for ruffles.

It is important, however, in deciding when and where you will add ruffles, to gauge proportions. You should not, for example, add five-inch ruffles to a short sleeve. Nor should a high neckband be finished off with a higher ruffle—if you have a short neck, the band

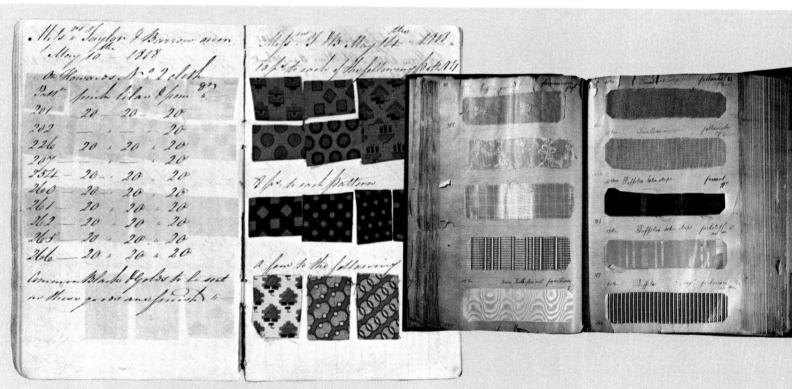

Fabrics that ranged from simple cottons to luxurious taffetas had to be imported to America prior to the establishment of the textile industry there. Swatches of printed cotton and scrawled figures in the book at left describe material ordered from a British mill's representative in 1808. The well-thumbed book at right, used by dressmakers and their clients in the 1890s, shows formal silks available from a French textile firm.

and ruffle may hide your neck altogether. If your pattern calls for this combination, change it by eliminating the neckband and then finishing the edge of the bodice neckline with only the ruffle.

Similarly, rows of ruffles or a jabot running vertically down the front of a bodice are attractive on a slender, narrow-shouldered figure; for a fuller figure, it is preferable to strive for the flat look of spaced tucks. The jabot was originally designed—in the time of Louis XIV—to disguise the buttons on men's dress shirts. Today it is a feminine fashion detail that is best used to soften the lines of tailored or formal pantsuits or dresses made of satin or velvet.

Another flatteringly feminine traditional style is the peplum. It trims the waist and accentuates the hips—and for that reason is not advisable if you have broad hips. Try combining a muted-color velvet bodice and peplum with a bright, flowered calico skirt. Or mix and match a variety of other patterns and colors for a fashionable eclectic look.

Few of the details that give traditional styles their flair now require the hours of painstaking handwork they demanded a century or more ago, when the fashion illustrations shown in the following section were new. With the instructions that accompany them, you can use your sewing machine to get the effect of hand-sewn heirlooms.

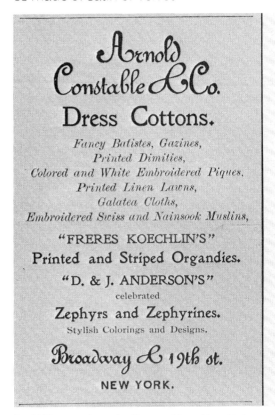

An 1897 magazine advertisement for a New York department store promotes imported special-occasion fabrics like the printed and striped French organdies shown in the sample book above at right. The book at left displays inexpensive American-made cottons of the same era; these fabrics, with floral and geometric patterns on somber backgrounds of red, blue and black, were typical materials used for everyday wear.

Adjusting patterns for perfect fit

There are two basic steps in sewing that are essential to attractive, well-fitting garments. The first is adjusting the pattern to fit the figure. To do this begin with the basics—lengthening or shortening and enlarging or reducing as shown at right. (Other more complicated pattern adjustments applicable to specific styles are discussed in the sections that follow.) In all cases compare your measurements with the ones printed on the pattern envelope: do not measure the pattern pieces themselves since they often vary from the printed measurements to allow for style and movement. Then adjust each piece, making all vertical changes before making the horizontal ones.

The second key procedure is transferring all pattern markings —seam lines as well as notches and circles—to the fabric as illustrated on the opposite page. All pattern markings, here and in the sections that follow, are indicated in white.

MAKING PATTERN ADJUSTMENTS

TO LENGTHEN THE PATTERN

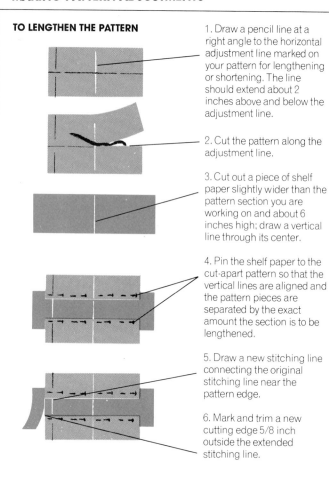

1. Draw a pencil line at a right angle to the horizontal adjustment line marked on your pattern for lengthening or shortening. The line should extend about 2 inches above and below the adjustment line.

2. Cut the pattern along the adjustment line.

3. Cut out a piece of shelf paper slightly wider than the pattern section you are working on and about 6 inches high; draw a vertical line through its center.

4. Pin the shelf paper to the cut-apart pattern so that the vertical lines are aligned and the pattern pieces are separated by the exact amount the section is to be lengthened.

5. Draw a new stitching line connecting the original stitching line near the pattern edge.

6. Mark and trim a new cutting edge 5/8 inch outside the extended stitching line.

TO SHORTEN THE PATTERN

1. Draw a pencil line above the horizontal adjustment line marked on your pattern for lengthening or shortening. The distance should be exactly equal to the amount the pattern section is to be shortened.

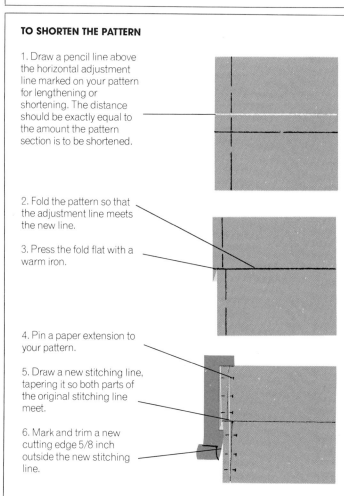

2. Fold the pattern so that the adjustment line meets the new line.

3. Press the fold flat with a warm iron.

4. Pin a paper extension to your pattern.

5. Draw a new stitching line, tapering it so both parts of the original stitching line meet.

6. Mark and trim a new cutting edge 5/8 inch outside the new stitching line.

TO REDUCE THE PATTERN

1. At the point where you need to reduce your pattern piece, measure in from the stitching line and mark 1/4 of the total amount to be reduced on each side seam.

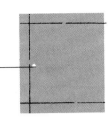

2. Draw a new stitching line, making a graduated curve from the point of reduction to the original stitching line.

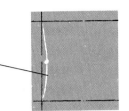

3. Mark and trim a new cutting edge 5/8 inch outside the new stitching line.

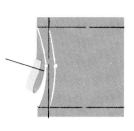

TO ENLARGE THE PATTERN

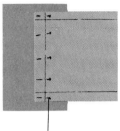

1. Lay your pattern piece on a strip of shelf paper cut to extend about 2 inches underneath the pattern and about 2 inches beyond the edge. Pin the pattern to the shelf paper.

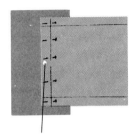

2. At the point where you need to enlarge your pattern piece, measure out from the stitching line and mark 1/4 of the total amount to be enlarged on each seam. Measure onto the seam allowance or beyond it onto the shelf paper, if necessary.

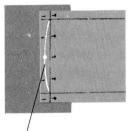

3. Draw a new tapered stitching line from the point of enlargement into the original stitching line.

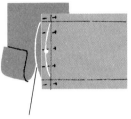

4. Mark and trim a new cutting edge 5/8 inch outside the new stitching line.

TRANSFERRING PATTERN MARKINGS

A

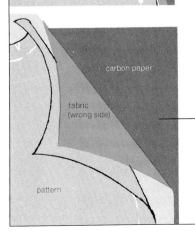

PREPARING TO MARK TWO LAYERS OF FABRIC

1A. After the pattern has been pinned to the fabric and the fabric pieces have been cut, remove just enough pins, from one piece at a time, so you can slip dressmaker's carbon paper between the layers of fabric and the pattern. Place one piece of carbon paper —carbon side up—under the bottom layer of fabric. Then place another piece of carbon paper—carbon side down—over the top layer of fabric. Pin the pattern back into position.

PREPARING TO MARK ONE LAYER OF FABRIC

1B. Place one piece of carbon paper—carbon side up—underneath the fabric.

B **MARKING THE FABRIC**

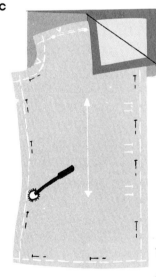
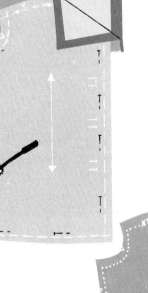

2. Run a tracing wheel along all stitching lines. Use a straightedge ruler as a guide for straight lines; trace curves freehand.

3. Trace the notches with a dull pencil.

4. With the dull pencil, draw an X through the center of all circles.

5. Remove the pattern from the fabric and baste along any markings that must show on both sides of the fabric—for example, the center front line and the placement lines for buttonholes, pockets and trimmings.

Tucks for ornamenting and shaping

Tucks are stitched-down pleats that serve ornamental—and sometimes structural—purposes. They occur in two main forms: visible tucks, in which the folds are sewn onto the outside of the garment so that they can be seen when the garment is worn; and hidden tucks, in which the folds are sewn on the wrong side so that only the seams of the tucks will show. Both kinds may be stitched the full length of the garment piece, from seam to seam, or they may stop short and be left open at one end. Those that are left open—called released tucks—shape a garment as well as decorate it.

The three most common types of visible tucks are pin tucks *(right)*, spaced tucks and blind tucks. Pin tucks are so called because each tuck is less than 1/8 inch wide. Spaced tucks are separated by a space equal to the width of each tuck. And blind tucks are arranged so that each one overlaps the stitching on the tuck next to it. With all of them, uniformity is the key. Not only must each row be perfectly spaced, but the stitches that form them must be small and as even as possible.

Tailored pin tucks—subtly reminiscent of a bouffant 1895 fashion—add a decorative touch to a contemporary shirtwaist dress.

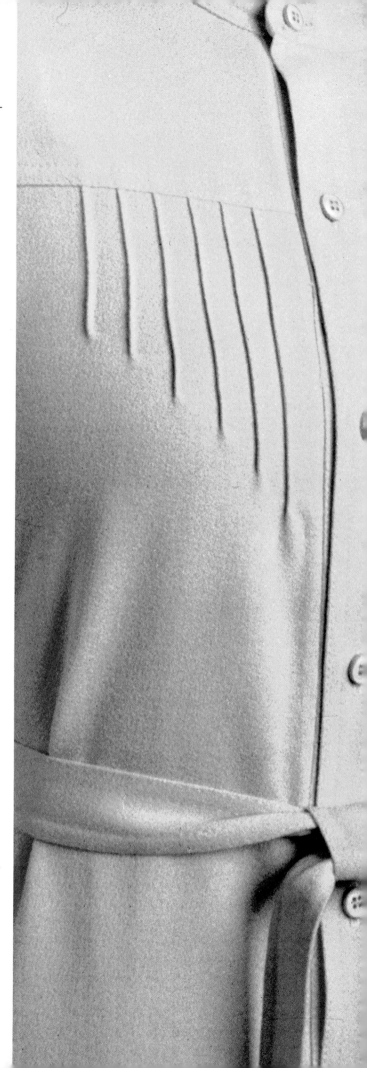

29

VISIBLE TUCKS

A — MARKING THE TUCKS

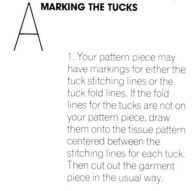

1. Your pattern piece may have markings for either the tuck stitching lines or the tuck fold lines. If the fold lines for the tucks are not on your pattern piece, draw them onto the tissue pattern centered between the stitching lines for each tuck. Then cut out the garment piece in the usual way.

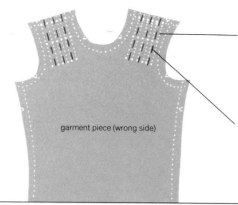

garment piece (wrong side)

2. Transfer the pattern markings for the stitching lines and the fold lines of the tucks to the wrong side of the garment piece. Remove the pattern from the garment piece.

3. Run a line of basting stitches along the fold lines so that you will be able to see the lines when the garment is placed wrong side down.

B — PINNING AND BASTING THE TUCKS

4. Measure the distance between the marked fold line and one of the tuck stitching lines on the pattern piece. This will give you the width for each tuck.

5. Mark this width on a small piece of cardboard such as an index card, and cut out a notch at the mark.

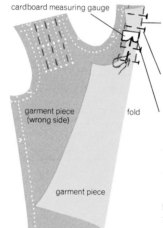

cardboard measuring gauge

garment piece (wrong side)

fold

garment piece

cardboard measuring gauge

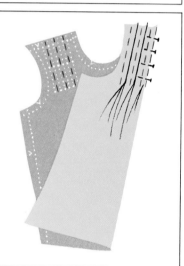

6. Fold the garment piece along the basted fold line of the first tuck so that the wrong sides are together.

7. Pin the tuck at 1-inch intervals.

8. Align the edge of the cardboard measuring guide with the basted fold line and baste the tuck, using the straight edge of the notch as a guide. Remove the pins.

9. Repeat Steps 6-8 for each tuck.

C — STITCHING THE TUCKS

10. Before machine stitching the tucks, experiment with the stitch length on a scrap of garment fabric as follows: fold the fabric and stitch through both layers; then adjust the stitch length until the stitches are small and look attractive. For lightweight fabrics the stitch length should be about 12-14 to an inch, for mediumweight fabrics 10-12 to an inch, for heavyweight fabrics 8-10 to an inch.

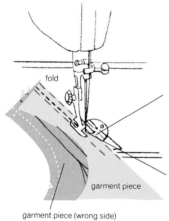

fold

garment piece

garment piece (wrong side)

11. Align the fold line of each tuck with a guide line on the throat plate of your sewing machine to make sure that the stitches will be perfectly straight. If no guide line equals the width of your tuck, measure the width from the sewing machine needle and mark it on the throat plate with masking tape.

12A. Machine stitch along the basting line of each tuck.

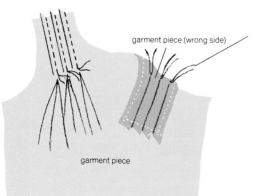

garment piece (wrong side)

garment piece

12B. If you are making tucks that will be open at one end, machine stitch as in Step 12A, leaving a few inches of loose thread at the open end of each tuck. Pull the loose threads through to the wrong side of the garment piece with a pin, tie a knot close to the stitching and cut off the excess thread.

13. Remove the bastings.

D — PRESSING THE TUCKS

14. Using a pressing cloth, press the tucks from the right side—the side that will be visible in the completed garment—in the direction your pattern instructs. If the tucks are open at one end, do not press beyond the end of the stitching.

15. Turn the garment wrong side out and press the tucks again.

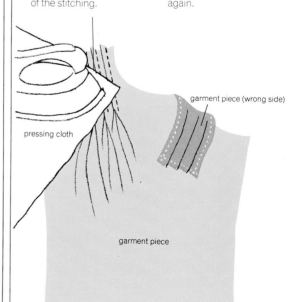

garment piece (wrong side)

pressing cloth

garment piece

HIDDEN TUCKS

A MARKING THE TUCKS

1. If you have not already done so, transfer the pattern markings for the stitching lines of the tucks to the garment piece. Remove the pattern from the garment piece.

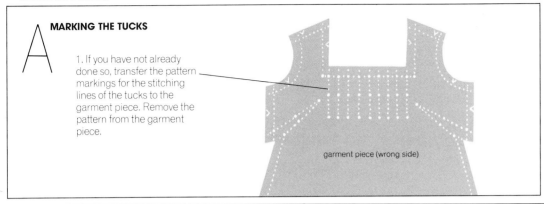

garment piece (wrong side)

B PINNING AND BASTING THE TUCKS

2. Fold the garment piece wrong side out, aligning the stitching lines of the first tuck.

3. Pin the tuck along the stitching line at 1-inch intervals.

4. Baste just outside the stitching line. Remove the pins.

5. Repeat Steps 2-4 for each tuck.

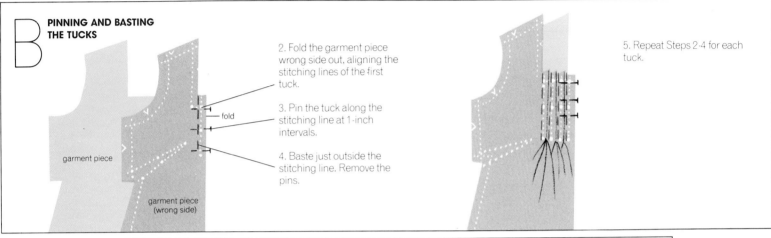

garment piece

fold

garment piece (wrong side)

C STITCHING THE TUCKS

6A. Machine stitch on the stitching line of each tuck.

6B. If you are making tucks that will be open at one end, secure the end of the stitching line by backstitching 2 or 3 stitches when you come to the open end of each tuck.

7. Remove the bastings.

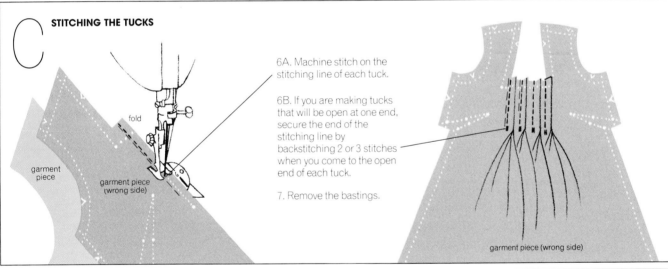

fold

garment piece

garment piece (wrong side)

garment piece (wrong side)

D PRESSING THE TUCKS

8. Press the tucks from the wrong side in the direction your pattern instructs. If the tucks are open at one end, do not press beyond the end of the stitching.

9. Turn the garment piece right side out and press again, using a pressing cloth.

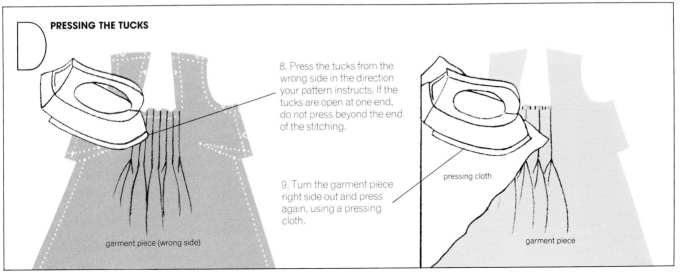

garment piece (wrong side)

pressing cloth

garment piece

Feminine ways with ruffles and edgings

Ruffles and ribbons, braids and laces make almost any sort of garment look deliciously—and traditionally—feminine. Ruffles, like the ones described on the following pages, usually form part of a garment's design and are most frequently made from the same fabric as the garment. Edgings, on the other hand, can be added as extra touches; and many of the prettiest—embroidered ribbons, woven braids, crocheted-type laces—are available ready-made.

Fabric strips cut on the crosswise grain become crisp and perky ruffles. Strips cut on the bias produce soft ruffles that drape gracefully. If the ruffle is more than two yards long, gather it in sections to avoid breaking the basting thread.

Ruffles can be attached in a seam, that is, with one edge hidden inside the garment, or attached on the outside with both edges hemmed and visible. Edging may be used as part of a hem, or as decoration for any part of the garment. When a ruffle is hemmed with an edging, as shown at right, the edging is attached before the ruffle is gathered.

A rim of lace outlining a ruffled cuff is a modern-day echo of fashions past, like those worn by the decorous ladies in the background.

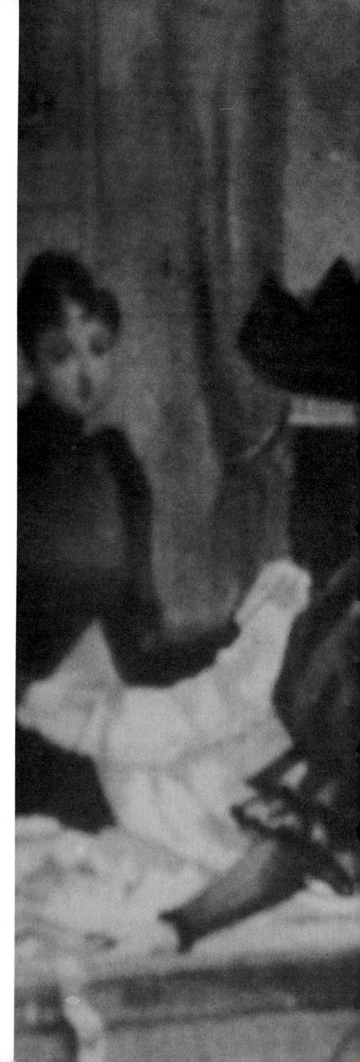

DETERMINING THE SIZE OF THE RUFFLE

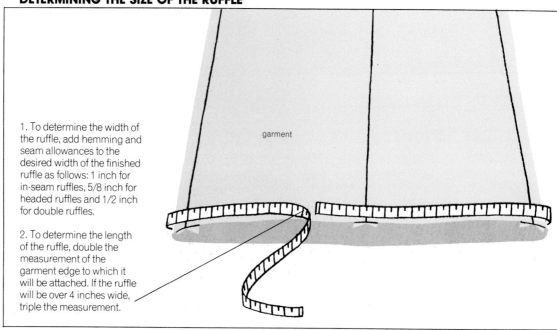

1. To determine the width of the ruffle, add hemming and seam allowances to the desired width of the finished ruffle as follows: 1 inch for in-seam ruffles, 5/8 inch for headed ruffles and 1/2 inch for double ruffles.

2. To determine the length of the ruffle, double the measurement of the garment edge to which it will be attached. If the ruffle will be over 4 inches wide, triple the measurement.

MAKING A RUFFLE STRIP CUT ON THE GRAIN

A STRAIGHTENING THE FABRIC

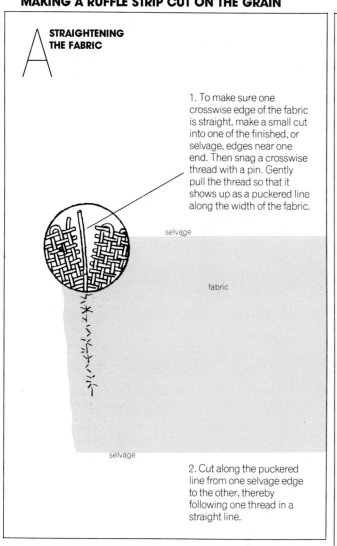

1. To make sure one crosswise edge of the fabric is straight, make a small cut into one of the finished, or selvage, edges near one end. Then snag a crosswise thread with a pin. Gently pull the thread so that it shows up as a puckered line along the width of the fabric.

2. Cut along the puckered line from one selvage edge to the other, thereby following one thread in a straight line.

B MARKING AND CUTTING THE STRIPS

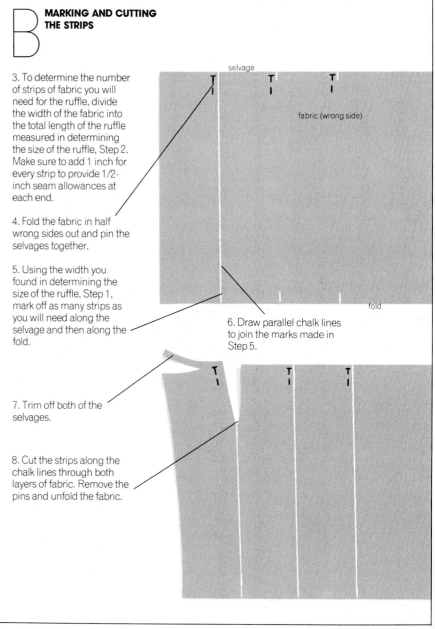

3. To determine the number of strips of fabric you will need for the ruffle, divide the width of the fabric into the total length of the ruffle measured in determining the size of the ruffle, Step 2. Make sure to add 1 inch for every strip to provide 1/2-inch seam allowances at each end.

4. Fold the fabric in half wrong sides out and pin the selvages together.

5. Using the width you found in determining the size of the ruffle, Step 1, mark off as many strips as you will need along the selvage and then along the fold.

6. Draw parallel chalk lines to join the marks made in Step 5.

7. Trim off both of the selvages.

8. Cut the strips along the chalk lines through both layers of fabric. Remove the pins and unfold the fabric.

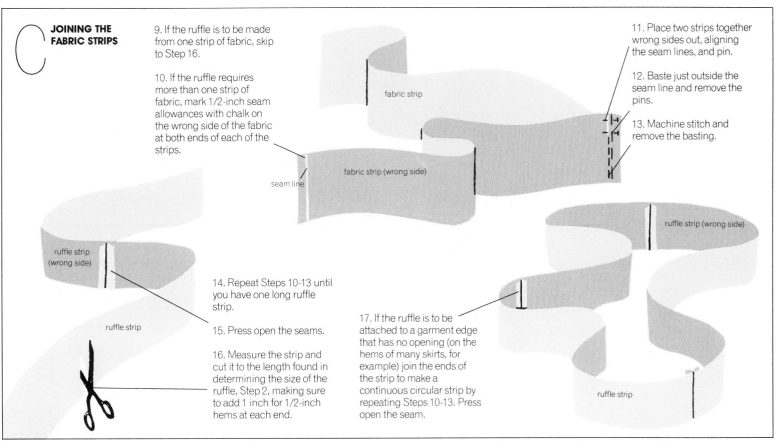

C. JOINING THE FABRIC STRIPS

9. If the ruffle is to be made from one strip of fabric, skip to Step 16.

10. If the ruffle requires more than one strip of fabric, mark 1/2-inch seam allowances with chalk on the wrong side of the fabric at both ends of each of the strips.

seam line

fabric strip

fabric strip (wrong side)

ruffle strip (wrong side)

ruffle strip (wrong side)

ruffle strip (wrong side)

ruffle strip

ruffle strip

11. Place two strips together wrong sides out, aligning the seam lines, and pin.

12. Baste just outside the seam line and remove the pins.

13. Machine stitch and remove the basting.

14. Repeat Steps 10-13 until you have one long ruffle strip.

15. Press open the seams.

16. Measure the strip and cut it to the length found in determining the size of the ruffle, Step 2, making sure to add 1 inch for 1/2-inch hems at each end.

17. If the ruffle is to be attached to a garment edge that has no opening (on the hems of many skirts, for example) join the ends of the strip to make a continuous circular strip by repeating Steps 10-13. Press open the seam.

MAKING A RUFFLE STRIP CUT ON THE BIAS

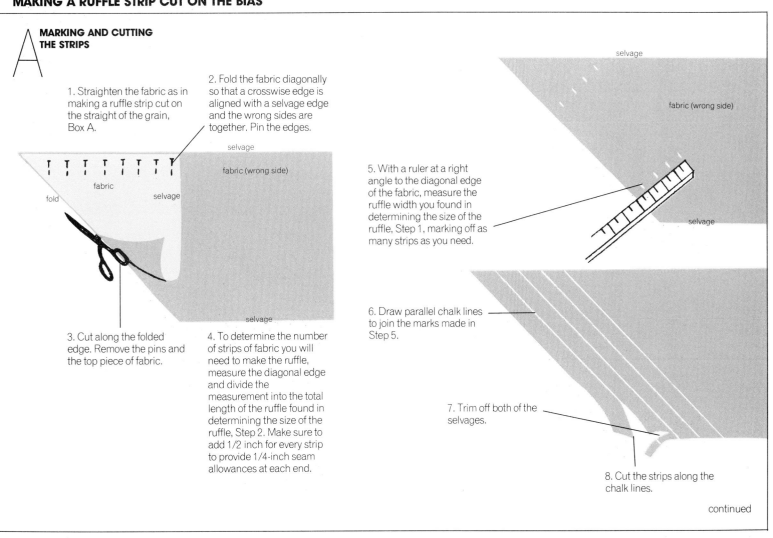

A. MARKING AND CUTTING THE STRIPS

1. Straighten the fabric as in making a ruffle strip cut on the straight of the grain, Box A.

2. Fold the fabric diagonally so that a crosswise edge is aligned with a selvage edge and the wrong sides are together. Pin the edges.

fabric

fold

fabric (wrong side)

selvage

selvage

selvage

selvage

selvage

fabric (wrong side)

3. Cut along the folded edge. Remove the pins and the top piece of fabric.

4. To determine the number of strips of fabric you will need to make the ruffle, measure the diagonal edge and divide the measurement into the total length of the ruffle found in determining the size of the ruffle, Step 2. Make sure to add 1/2 inch for every strip to provide 1/4-inch seam allowances at each end.

5. With a ruler at a right angle to the diagonal edge of the fabric, measure the ruffle width you found in determining the size of the ruffle, Step 1, marking off as many strips as you need.

6. Draw parallel chalk lines to join the marks made in Step 5.

7. Trim off both of the selvages.

8. Cut the strips along the chalk lines.

continued

B | JOINING THE FABRIC STRIPS

9. If the ruffle is to be made from one strip of fabric, skip to Step 16.

10. If the ruffle requires more than one strip of fabric, mark 1/4-inch seam allowances with chalk on both ends of each strip.

11. Place two strips together, wrong sides out, so that the strips form a V-shape. Align the seam lines and pin.

12. Baste just outside the seam line and remove the pins.

13. Machine stitch and remove the basting.

14. Repeat Steps 10-13 until you have one long ruffle strip.

15. Press open the seams.

16A. If the ruffle is to be attached to a garment edge that has an opening (on the hem of an apron, for example) cut off one end of the strip at a right angle to the long edges. Measure the strip to the length you found in determining the size of the ruffle, Step 2, making sure to add 1 inch for 1/2-inch hems at each end, and cut at a right angle to the long edges.

16B. If the ruffle is to be attached to a garment edge that has no opening (on the hems of many skirts, for example) measure the strip to the length you found in determining the size of the ruffle, Step 2, adding 1/2 inch for 1/4-inch seam allowances at each end. Cut away the excess material, making sure the cut is parallel to the end of the strip. Join the two ends to make a continuous circular strip by repeating Steps 11-13. Press open the seam.

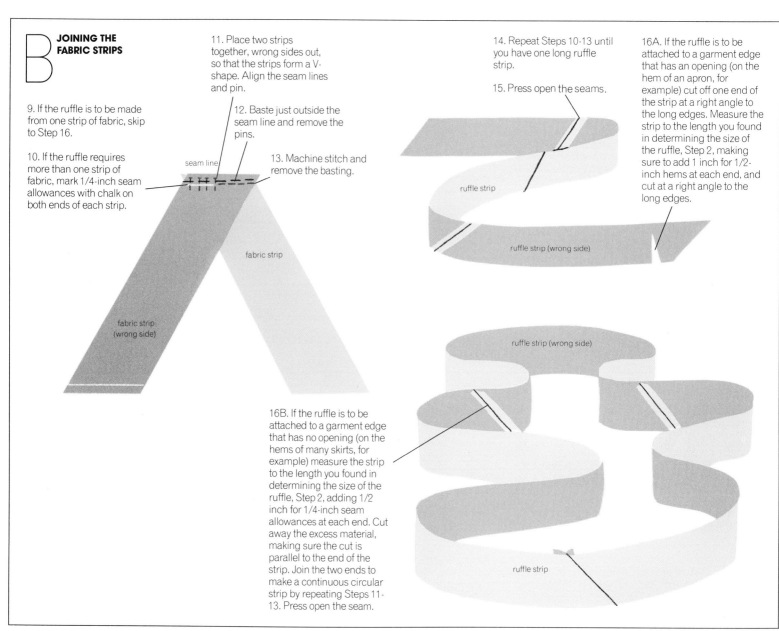

FINISHING THE IN-SEAM RUFFLE STRIP

A | HEMMING THE RUFFLE STRIP

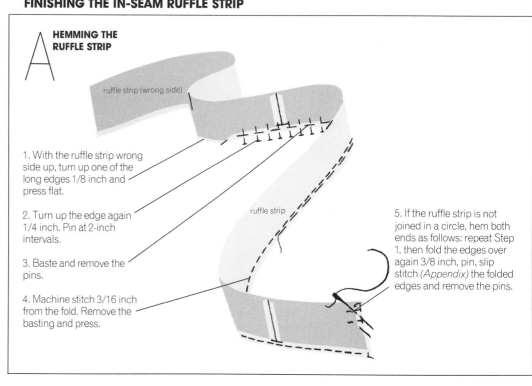

1. With the ruffle strip wrong side up, turn up one of the long edges 1/8 inch and press flat.

2. Turn up the edge again 1/4 inch. Pin at 2-inch intervals.

3. Baste and remove the pins.

4. Machine stitch 3/16 inch from the fold. Remove the basting and press.

5. If the ruffle strip is not joined in a circle, hem both ends as follows: repeat Step 1, then fold the edges over again 3/8 inch, pin, slip stitch (Appendix) the folded edges and remove the pins.

B GATHERING THE RUFFLE

6. Replace the regular thread on the bobbin of your sewing machine with heavy-duty thread or buttonhole twist.

7. Turn the ruffle strip wrong side down and run a line of machine basting (6 stitches to the inch) 5/8 inch from the unhemmed edge. Leave about 4 inches of loose thread at each end of the stitching.

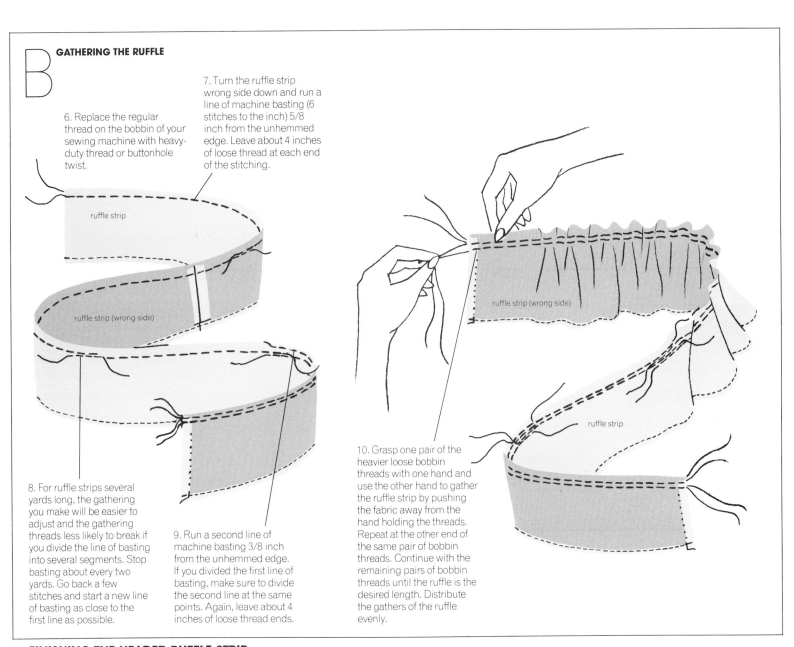

ruffle strip

ruffle strip (wrong side)

ruffle strip (wrong side)

ruffle strip

8. For ruffle strips several yards long, the gathering you make will be easier to adjust and the gathering threads less likely to break if you divide the line of basting into several segments. Stop basting about every two yards. Go back a few stitches and start a new line of basting as close to the first line as possible.

9. Run a second line of machine basting 3/8 inch from the unhemmed edge. If you divided the first line of basting, make sure to divide the second line at the same points. Again, leave about 4 inches of loose thread ends.

10. Grasp one pair of the heavier loose bobbin threads with one hand and use the other hand to gather the ruffle strip by pushing the fabric away from the hand holding the threads. Repeat at the other end of the same pair of bobbin threads. Continue with the remaining pairs of bobbin threads until the ruffle is the desired length. Distribute the gathers of the ruffle evenly.

FINISHING THE HEADED RUFFLE STRIP

A HEMMING THE RUFFLE STRIP

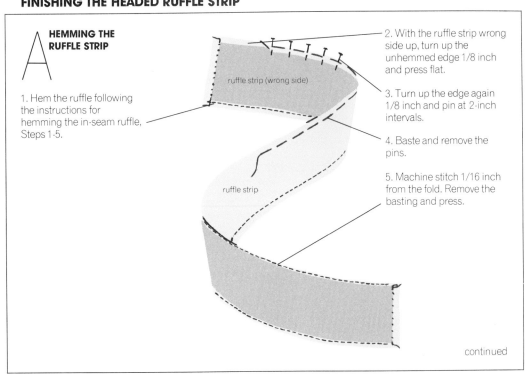

ruffle strip (wrong side)

ruffle strip

1. Hem the ruffle following the instructions for hemming the in-seam ruffle, Steps 1-5.

2. With the ruffle strip wrong side up, turn up the unhemmed edge 1/8 inch and press flat.

3. Turn up the edge again 1/8 inch and pin at 2-inch intervals.

4. Baste and remove the pins.

5. Machine stitch 1/16 inch from the fold. Remove the basting and press.

continued

GATHERING THE RUFFLE

B

6. Replace the regular thread on the bobbin of your sewing machine with heavy-duty thread or buttonhole twist.

7. Turn the ruffle strip wrong side down and run a line of machine basting—6 stitches to the inch—3/8 inch from the edge of the hem made in Steps 2-5. Leave about 4 inches of loose thread at each end of the stitching.

8. For ruffle strips several yards long, the gathering you make will be easier to adjust and the gathering threads less likely to break if you divide the line of basting into several segments. Stop basting about every two yards. Go back a few stitches and start a new line of basting as close to the first line as possible.

9. Grasp the heavier loose bobbin thread at the end of the strip with one hand and use the other hand to gather the ruffle strip by pushing the fabric away from the hand holding the thread. Repeat at the other end of the same bobbin thread. Continue with the remaining loose bobbin threads until the ruffle is the desired length. Distribute the gathers of the ruffle evenly.

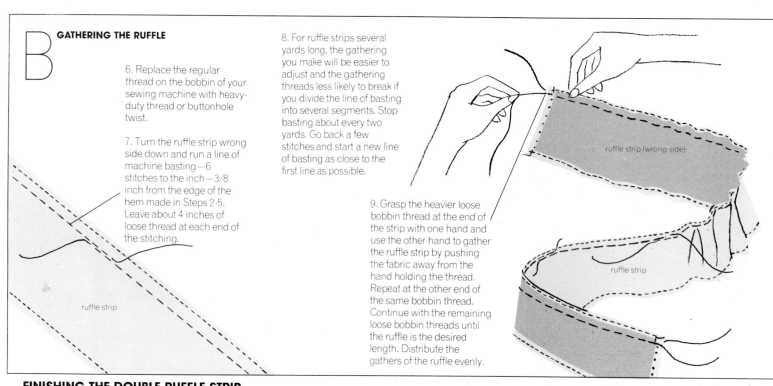

FINISHING THE DOUBLE RUFFLE STRIP

A HEMMING THE RUFFLE STRIP

1. With the ruffle strip wrong side up, turn up both long edges 1/8 inch and press flat.

2. Turn up the edges again 1/8 inch. Pin at 2-inch intervals.

3. Baste and remove the pins.

4. Machine stitch 1/16 inch from the turned edges. Remove the basting and press.

5. If the ruffle strip is not joined in a circle, hem both ends as follows: repeat Step 1, then fold the edges over again 3/8 inch, pin, slip stitch (*Appendix*) the folded edges and remove the pins.

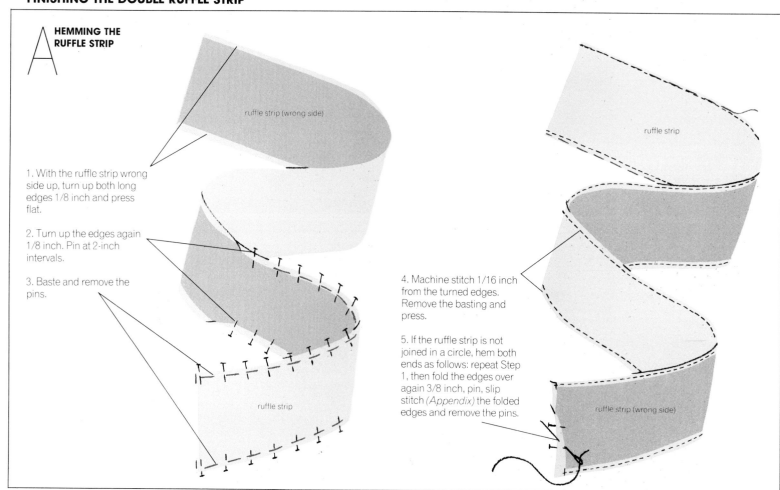

B GATHERING THE RUFFLE

6. Replace the regular thread on the bobbin of your sewing machine with heavy-duty thread or buttonhole twist.

7. Turn the ruffle strip wrong side down and run a line of machine basting (6 stitches to the inch) down the center of the ruffle strip. Leave about 4 inches of loose thread at each end of the stitching.

8. For ruffle strips several yards long, the gathering you make will be easier to adjust and the gathering threads less likely to break if you divide the line of basting into several segments. Stop basting about every two yards. Go back a few stitches and start a new line of basting as close to the first line as possible.

9. Grasp the heavier loose bobbin thread at the end of the strip with one hand and use the other hand to gather the ruffle strip by pushing the fabric away from the hand holding the thread. Repeat with the other end of the same bobbin thread. Continue with the remaining loose bobbin threads until the ruffle is the desired length. Distribute the gathers of the ruffle evenly.

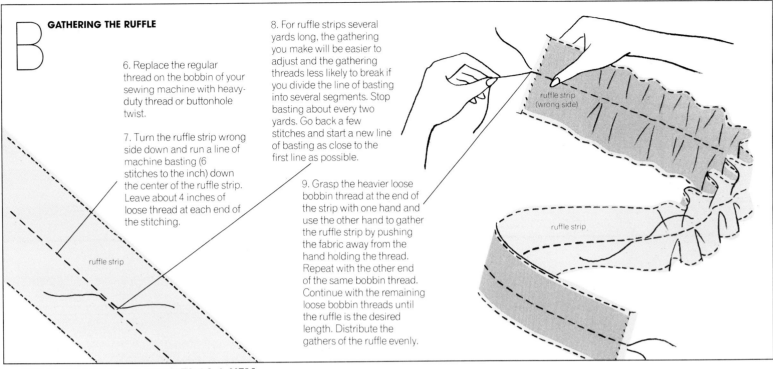

ruffle strip

ruffle strip (wrong side)

ruffle strip

ATTACHING IN-SEAM RUFFLES AS A HEM

A STITCHING THE RUFFLE TO THE GARMENT

1. Measure the desired length of the garment (a skirt in this example) without the ruffle. Add 5/8 inch for the seam allowance, and trim away any excess at the hem edge.

2. Place the ruffle, wrong side out, on the right side of the garment (the side that will be visible when the garment is completed). Align the gathered edge of the ruffle with the hem edge.

3. Pin the ruffle to the garment at 2-inch intervals, adjusting the gathers evenly.

4. Baste between the two lines of machine basting on the ruffle. Remove the pins.

5. Machine stitch the ruffle to the garment just inside the machine basting farthest from the edge. As you sew, pull the gathers straight to keep them small and even. Remove the basting made in Step 4.

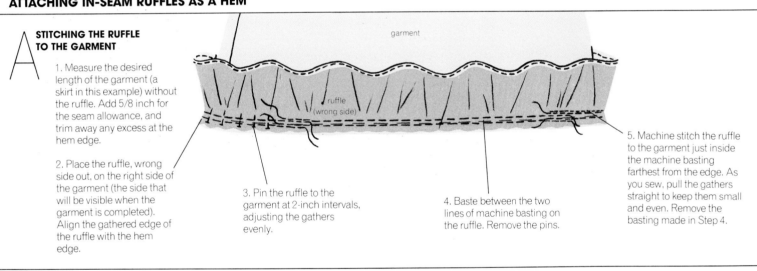

garment

ruffle (wrong side)

B FINISHING THE RUFFLE

6. Turn the garment wrong side out. Turn the ruffle away from the garment.

7. Trim off the long loose ends of the gathering threads.

8. Trim the garment seam allowance to 3/8 inch.

9. Turn the garment right side out. Press the seam flat, making sure to keep the hemline seam allowances underneath turned toward the garment, using the tip of the iron to avoid pressing the gathers of the ruffle.

10. If any gathering threads are visible, make sure to remove them with a seam ripper, as shown.

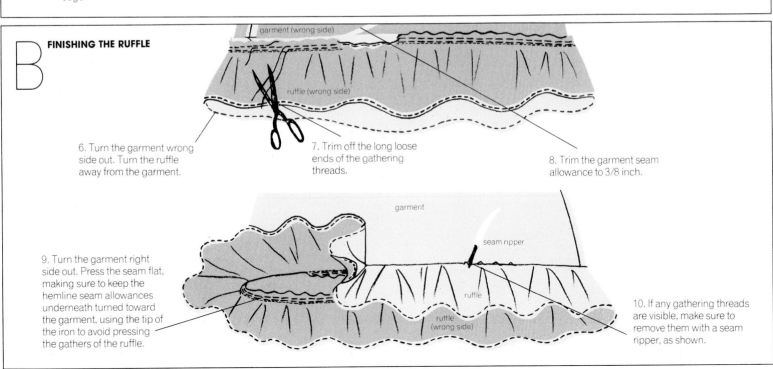

garment (wrong side)

ruffle (wrong side)

garment

seam ripper

ruffle

ruffle (wrong side)

ATTACHING THE IN-SEAM RUFFLE WITH A BIAS STRIP

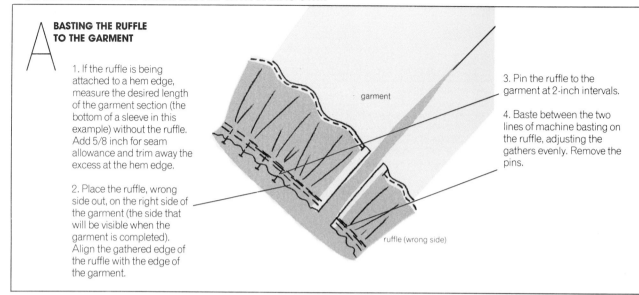

A **BASTING THE RUFFLE TO THE GARMENT**

1. If the ruffle is being attached to a hem edge, measure the desired length of the garment section (the bottom of a sleeve in this example) without the ruffle. Add 5/8 inch for seam allowance and trim away the excess at the hem edge.

2. Place the ruffle, wrong side out, on the right side of the garment (the side that will be visible when the garment is completed). Align the gathered edge of the ruffle with the edge of the garment.

3. Pin the ruffle to the garment at 2-inch intervals.

4. Baste between the two lines of machine basting on the ruffle, adjusting the gathers evenly. Remove the pins.

garment

ruffle (wrong side)

B **ATTACHING THE BIAS STRIP**

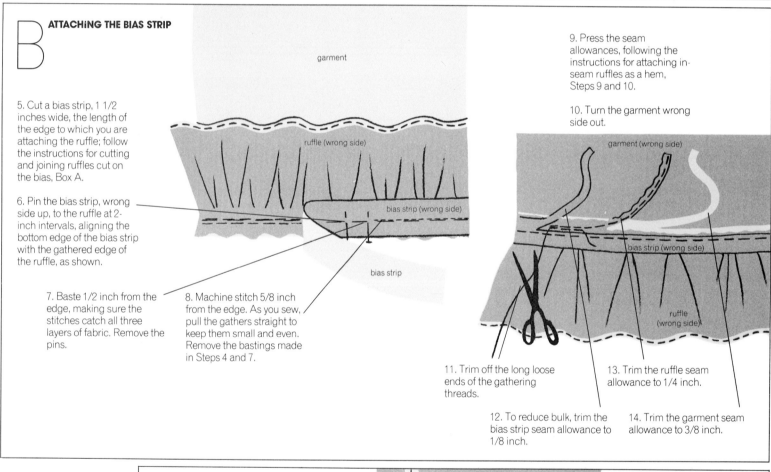

5. Cut a bias strip, 1 1/2 inches wide, the length of the edge to which you are attaching the ruffle; follow the instructions for cutting and joining ruffles cut on the bias, Box A.

6. Pin the bias strip, wrong side up, to the ruffle at 2-inch intervals, aligning the bottom edge of the bias strip with the gathered edge of the ruffle, as shown.

7. Baste 1/2 inch from the edge, making sure the stitches catch all three layers of fabric. Remove the pins.

8. Machine stitch 5/8 inch from the edge. As you sew, pull the gathers straight to keep them small and even. Remove the bastings made in Steps 4 and 7.

9. Press the seam allowances, following the instructions for attaching in-seam ruffles as a hem, Steps 9 and 10.

10. Turn the garment wrong side out.

11. Trim off the long loose ends of the gathering threads.

12. To reduce bulk, trim the bias strip seam allowance to 1/8 inch.

13. Trim the ruffle seam allowance to 1/4 inch.

14. Trim the garment seam allowance to 3/8 inch.

garment

ruffle (wrong side)

bias strip (wrong side)

bias strip

garment (wrong side)

bias strip (wrong side)

ruffle (wrong side)

C **FINISHING THE RUFFLE**

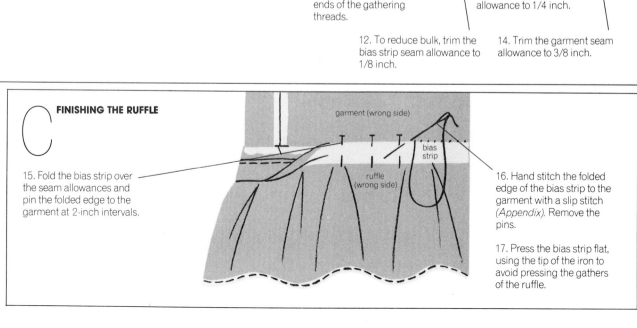

15. Fold the bias strip over the seam allowances and pin the folded edge to the garment at 2-inch intervals.

16. Hand stitch the folded edge of the bias strip to the garment with a slip stitch *(Appendix)*. Remove the pins.

17. Press the bias strip flat, using the tip of the iron to avoid pressing the gathers of the ruffle.

garment (wrong side)

bias strip

ruffle (wrong side)

ATTACHING THE IN-SEAM RUFFLE WITH A FACING

A BASTING THE RUFFLE TO THE GARMENT

1. Place the garment (a blouse front in this example) wrong side down. Place the ruffle, wrong side out, over the garment. Align the gathered edge of the ruffle with the edge of the seam allowance of the garment where it will be attached.

2. Pin the ruffle to the garment at 2-inch intervals, adjusting the gathers evenly.

3. If the ruffle will turn around the outside of a corner in the finished garment, adjust the gathers as you pin so that the ruffle is fuller at the corner as shown. (If the ruffle will turn around the inside of a corner, adjust the gathers as you pin so that the ruffle is less full at the corner.)

4. If the ruffle tapers into a seam, cut the end of the ruffle diagonally and align the cut end with the edge of the seam allowance of the garment as you pin.

5. Baste between the two lines of machine basting on the ruffle. Remove the pins.

ruffle (wrong side)

garment

B ATTACHING THE FACING

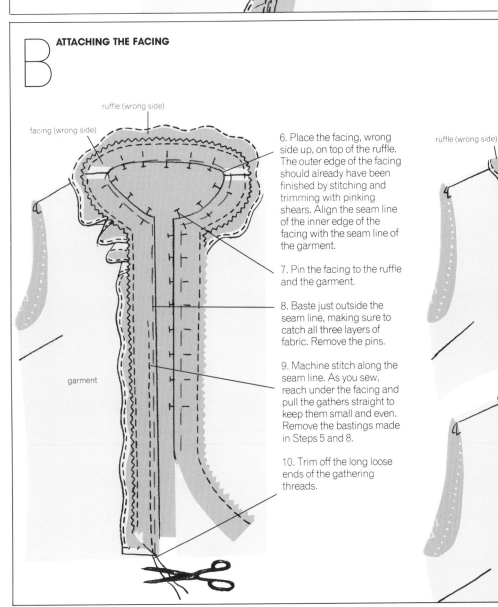

facing (wrong side)

ruffle (wrong side)

garment

6. Place the facing, wrong side up, on top of the ruffle. The outer edge of the facing should already have been finished by stitching and trimming with pinking shears. Align the seam line of the inner edge of the facing with the seam line of the garment.

7. Pin the facing to the ruffle and the garment.

8. Baste just outside the seam line, making sure to catch all three layers of fabric. Remove the pins.

9. Machine stitch along the seam line. As you sew, reach under the facing and pull the gathers straight to keep them small and even. Remove the bastings made in Steps 5 and 8.

10. Trim off the long loose ends of the gathering threads.

11. To reduce bulk, trim the facing seam allowance to 1/8 inch.

12. Trim the ruffle seam allowance to 1/4 inch.

13. Trim the garment seam allowance to 3/8 inch.

14. Trim any corners diagonally.

ruffle (wrong side)

facing (wrong side)

facing

ruffle (wrong side)

15. Turn the facing over the trimmed seam allowances and press the seam flat, using the tip of the iron to avoid pressing the gathers of the ruffle.

16. Make a line of machine stitching—called understitching—on the facing as close to the seam as possible, catching the trimmed seam allowances beneath the facing.

continued

C FINISHING THE RUFFLE

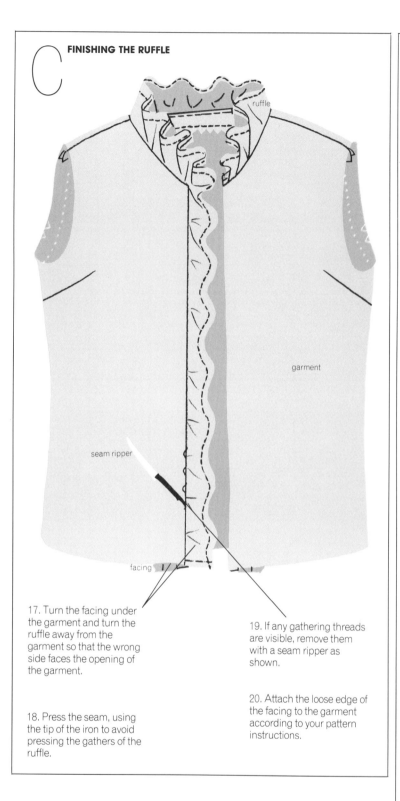

seam ripper

ruffle

garment

facing

17. Turn the facing under the garment and turn the ruffle away from the garment so that the wrong side faces the opening of the garment.

18. Press the seam, using the tip of the iron to avoid pressing the gathers of the ruffle.

19. If any gathering threads are visible, remove them with a seam ripper as shown.

20. Attach the loose edge of the facing to the garment according to your pattern instructions.

A STITCHING THE RUFFLE TO THE GARMENT

1. Complete the two garment pieces (a bodice and a sleeve in this example) according to your pattern instructions, up to the point when you would normally join them.

2. Using the garment piece from which you want the ruffle to extend (the bodice in this example), place the ruffle, wrong side up, on the right side of the garment piece (the side that will be visible when the garment is completed). Align the gathered edge of the ruffle with the edge of the seam allowance of the garment piece.

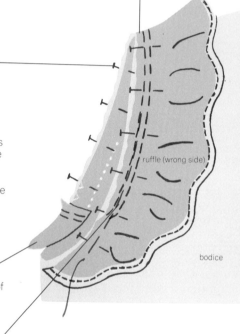

ruffle (wrong side)

bodice

3. Pin the ruffle to the garment piece at 2-inch intervals, adjusting the gathers evenly.

4. If the ruffle will turn around the outside of a corner in the finished garment, adjust the gathers as you pin so that the ruffle is fuller at the corner. If the ruffle will turn around the inside of a corner, adjust the gathers as you pin so that the ruffle is less full at the corner.

5. If the ruffle tapers into a seam, cut the end of the ruffle diagonally and align the cut end with the edge of the seam allowance of the garment as you pin.

6. Baste between the two lines of machine basting on the ruffle. Remove the pins.

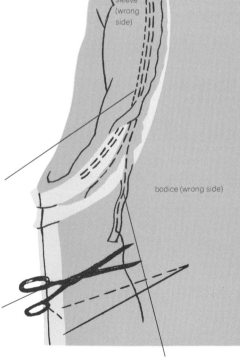

sleeve (wrong side)

bodice (wrong side)

7. Attach the adjoining garment piece (the sleeve in this example) according to your pattern instructions. When you machine stitch the seam, make sure to reach under the top garment piece and pull the gathers straight to keep them small and even.

8. With the garment wrong side out, trim off the long loose ends of the gathering threads.

9. Trim the ruffle seam allowance to 1/4 inch.

FINISHING THE RUFFLE

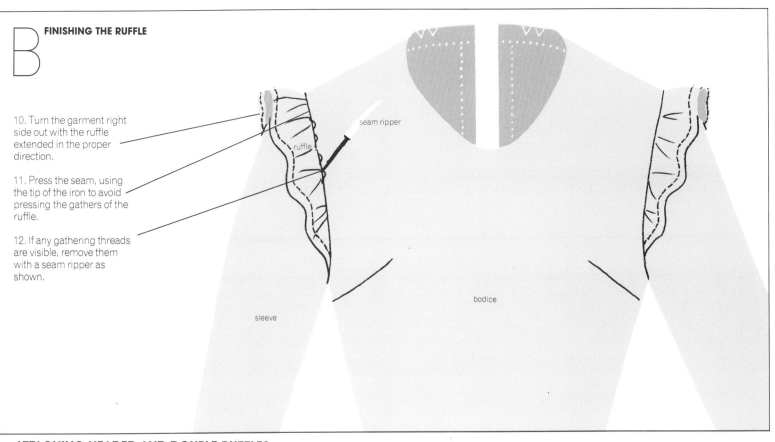

10. Turn the garment right side out with the ruffle extended in the proper direction.

11. Press the seam, using the tip of the iron to avoid pressing the gathers of the ruffle.

12. If any gathering threads are visible, remove them with a seam ripper as shown.

seam ripper

ruffle

sleeve

bodice

ATTACHING HEADED AND DOUBLE RUFFLES

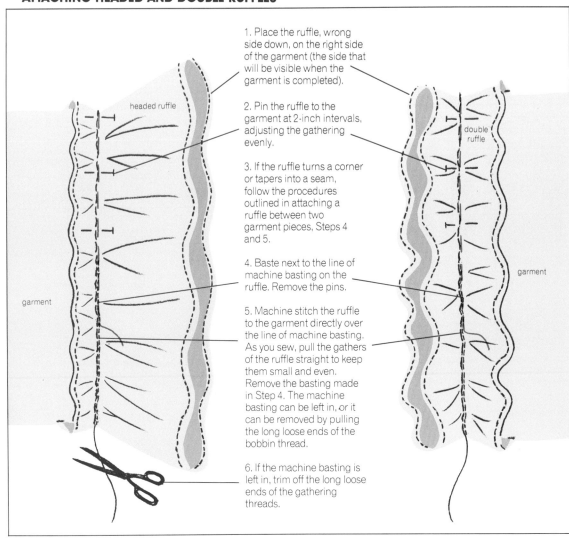

1. Place the ruffle, wrong side down, on the right side of the garment (the side that will be visible when the garment is completed).

2. Pin the ruffle to the garment at 2-inch intervals, adjusting the gathering evenly.

3. If the ruffle turns a corner or tapers into a seam, follow the procedures outlined in attaching a ruffle between two garment pieces, Steps 4 and 5.

4. Baste next to the line of machine basting on the ruffle. Remove the pins.

5. Machine stitch the ruffle to the garment directly over the line of machine basting. As you sew, pull the gathers of the ruffle straight to keep them small and even. Remove the basting made in Step 4. The machine basting can be left in, or it can be removed by pulling the long loose ends of the bobbin thread.

6. If the machine basting is left in, trim off the long loose ends of the gathering threads.

headed ruffle

double ruffle

garment

garment

TRIM WITH ONE DECORATIVE EDGE

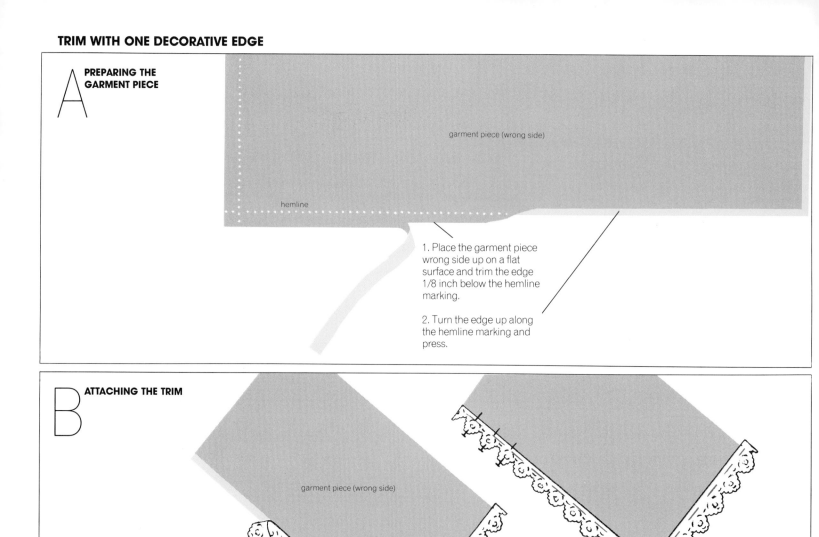

A PREPARING THE GARMENT PIECE

garment piece (wrong side)

hemline

1. Place the garment piece wrong side up on a flat surface and trim the edge 1/8 inch below the hemline marking.

2. Turn the edge up along the hemline marking and press.

B ATTACHING THE TRIM

garment piece (wrong side)

3. Place the trim wrong side up on the garment piece, aligning the nondecorative edge of the trim with the turned-up edge of the hem. Pin at 3-inch intervals until you reach a corner.

4. At the corners, pin the trim so that the outer decorative edge lies flat and the inner, nondecorative edge bunches up as shown.

5. Baste the trim to the garment piece through all three layers—the trim, the turned up hem and the garment itself—until you reach a corner. Skip over the bunched-up trim and continue basting along the next edge. Remove the pins.

6. Clip diagonally across the bunched-up trim to the corner—cutting up to but not into the decorative edge. Cut away the excess trim along the clip until the two sides meet diagonally without overlapping.

C FINISHING THE TRIM

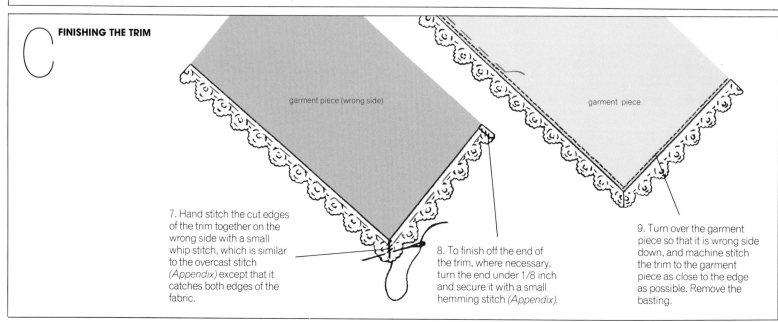

garment piece (wrong side)

garment piece

7. Hand stitch the cut edges of the trim together on the wrong side with a small whip stitch, which is similar to the overcast stitch (Appendix) except that it catches both edges of the fabric.

8. To finish off the end of the trim, where necessary, turn the end under 1/8 inch and secure it with a small hemming stitch (Appendix).

9. Turn over the garment piece so that it is wrong side down, and machine stitch the trim to the garment piece as close to the edge as possible. Remove the basting.

TRIM WITH TWO DECORATIVE EDGES

A PREPARING THE GARMENT PIECE

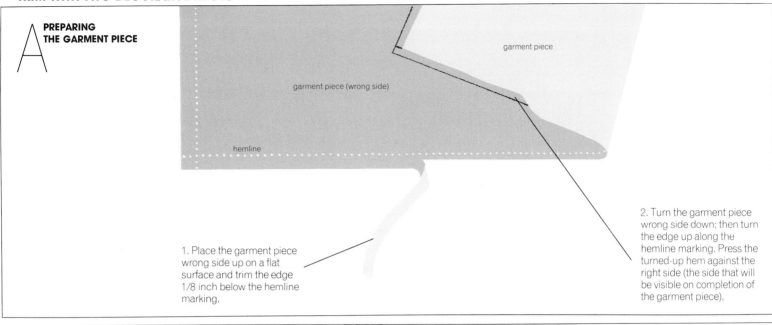

garment piece (wrong side)

garment piece

hemline

1. Place the garment piece wrong side up on a flat surface and trim the edge 1/8 inch below the hemline marking.

2. Turn the garment piece wrong side down; then turn the edge up along the hemline marking. Press the turned-up hem against the right side (the side that will be visible on completion of the garment piece).

B ATTACHING THE TRIM

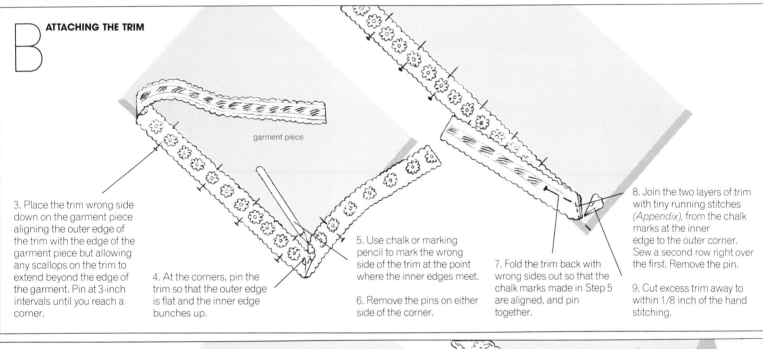

garment piece

3. Place the trim wrong side down on the garment piece aligning the outer edge of the trim with the edge of the garment piece but allowing any scallops on the trim to extend beyond the edge of the garment. Pin at 3-inch intervals until you reach a corner.

4. At the corners, pin the trim so that the outer edge is flat and the inner edge bunches up.

5. Use chalk or marking pencil to mark the wrong side of the trim at the point where the inner edges meet.

6. Remove the pins on either side of the corner.

7. Fold the trim back with wrong sides out so that the chalk marks made in Step 5 are aligned, and pin together.

8. Join the two layers of trim with tiny running stitches (Appendix), from the chalk marks at the inner edge to the outer corner. Sew a second row right over the first. Remove the pin.

9. Cut excess trim away to within 1/8 inch of the hand stitching.

C FINISHING THE EDGING

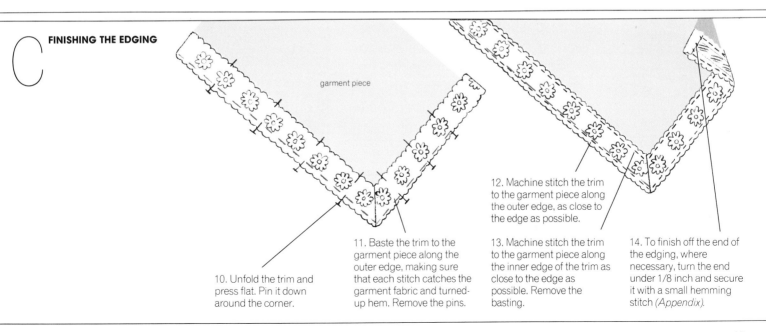

garment piece

10. Unfold the trim and press flat. Pin it down around the corner.

11. Baste the trim to the garment piece along the outer edge, making sure that each stitch catches the garment fabric and turned-up hem. Remove the pins.

12. Machine stitch the trim to the garment piece along the outer edge, as close to the edge as possible.

13. Machine stitch the trim to the garment piece along the inner edge of the trim as close to the edge as possible. Remove the basting.

14. To finish off the end of the edging, where necessary, turn the end under 1/8 inch and secure it with a small hemming stitch (Appendix).

Smocking in a honeycomb design

As decorative as it looks, the pleating technique called smocking also serves the very practical function of controlling fullness without limiting movement. The diamond-shaped, or honeycomb, design shown here is the easiest smocking stitch. Traditionally used on bodices *(examples at right)*, it can also be worked into aprons, patch pockets, dirndls and linens. The smocking is created by pulling horizontal rows of stitches taut to form vertical rows of gathers, or smocking pleats. The stitching is done with six-strand embroidery or pearl cotton on a grid of evenly spaced dots. In making up a pattern, it is best to work on a rectangular or square piece at least twice the desired width of the finished piece.

Because they feature uniformly spaced checks or dots, gingham and dotted swiss are particularly suitable for smocking; the designs themselves serve as the grid. To form a grid on plain fabrics or other patterned ones, use hot-iron transfers, or draw your own dots using an L-square and a pencil, as shown overleaf. As you work, pull the fabric lengthwise to straighten the pleats.

Honeycomb smocking, a popular decorative detail in Victorian times, was revived in the 1970s to embellish contemporary styles.

HONEYCOMB SMOCKING

A PREPARING THE FABRIC

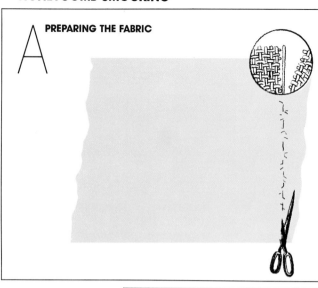

1. If you are smocking part of a garment without a pattern, first be sure the crosswise and lengthwise threads of your fabric are at right angles to each other. Snip the fabric, snag a crosswise thread with a pin and pull the thread gently until it shows as a puckered line. Trim along this line. If the piece of fabric has no selvage edge, repeat along a lengthwise edge.

2. Using an L square, align the other two edges of the rectangle with the two straightened edges and trim.

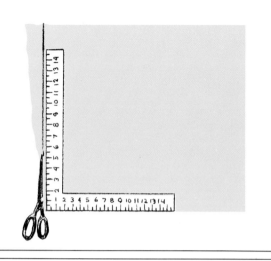

B MAKING THE GRID PATTERN

3. Place the fabric wrong side down on a flat surface.

4. Set the L square at the top left corner of the fabric about 1 inch in from either edge. Lightly mark a row of equally spaced pencil dots 1/4 to 1 inch apart, depending on the pattern effect you want; mark the dots along both outside edges of the L square.

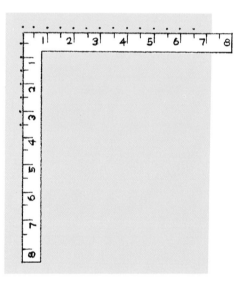

5. Move the L square down so that the top corner is aligned with the second dot down and mark off another horizontal row of dots.

6. Carefully continue marking evenly spaced rows of dots until the grid pattern covers the piece of fabric to be smocked.

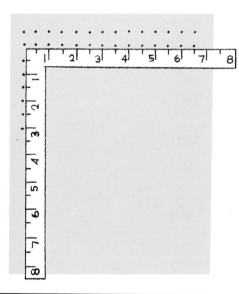

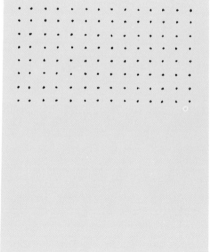

C MAKING THE FIRST SMOCKING PLEAT

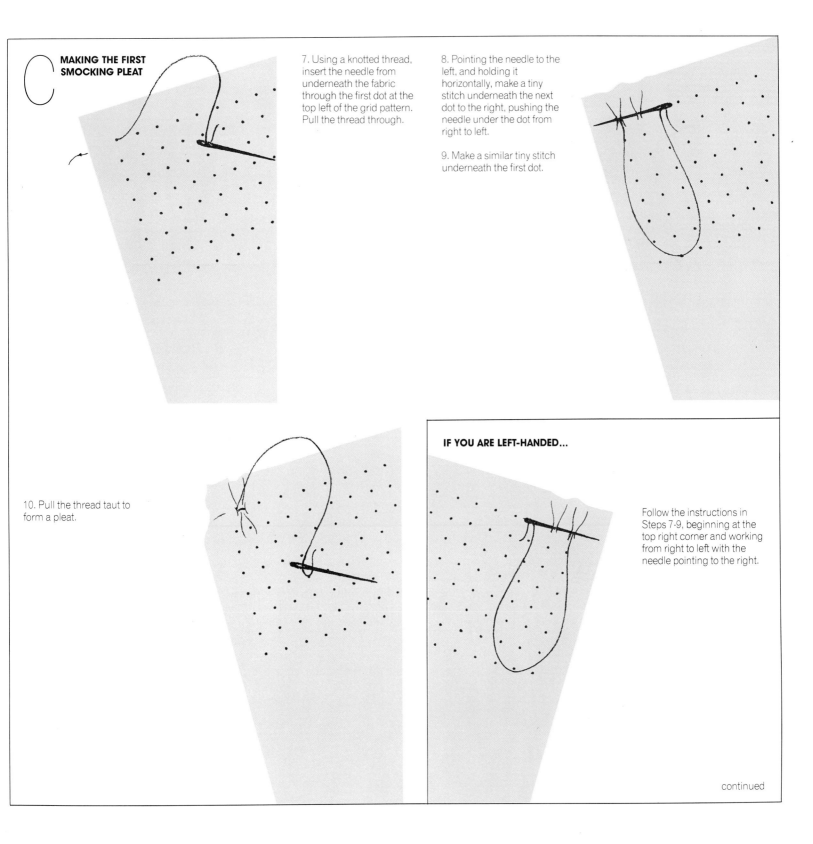

7. Using a knotted thread, insert the needle from underneath the fabric through the first dot at the top left of the grid pattern. Pull the thread through.

8. Pointing the needle to the left, and holding it horizontally, make a tiny stitch underneath the next dot to the right, pushing the needle under the dot from right to left.

9. Make a similar tiny stitch underneath the first dot.

10. Pull the thread taut to form a pleat.

IF YOU ARE LEFT-HANDED...

Follow the instructions in Steps 7-9, beginning at the top right corner and working from right to left with the needle pointing to the right.

continued

D FORMING THE FIRST ROW OF SMOCKING PLEATS

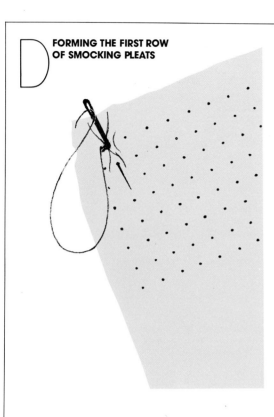

11. Pointing the needle down, insert it through the fabric as close as possible to the stitch holding the first smocking pleat made in Box C as shown, and bring it out through the dot directly below the right-hand side of the pleat—the second dot from the edge.

12. Make a tiny stitch underneath the next dot to the right, as shown.

13. Make a similar tiny stitch underneath the dot to its left —the one through which the needle emerged in Step 11. Pull the thread taut.

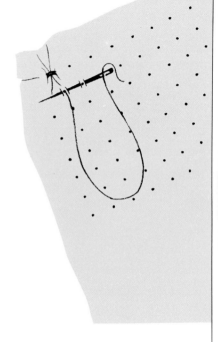

14. Pointing the needle up, insert it through the fabric as close as possible to the stitch holding the smocking pleat made in Step 13 as shown, and bring it out through the dot above—that is, the third dot in the first row. Pull the thread taut.

15. Repeat Steps 8-14 across the row, making sure that the last stitch in each row is made according to the instructions in Step 8.

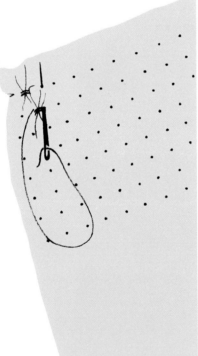

IF YOU ARE LEFT-HANDED...

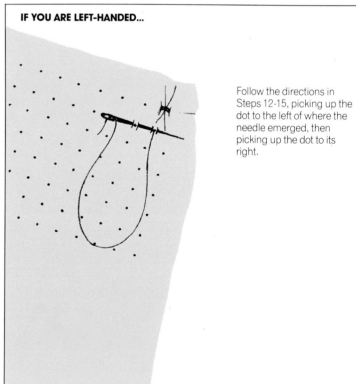

Follow the directions in Steps 12-15, picking up the dot to the left of where the needle emerged, then picking up the dot to its right.

E | FORMING THE SECOND ROW OF SMOCKING PLEATS

16. At the end of the first row of work (using the first two rows of dots), turn the work around so the pleats are nearest you. Pointing the needle down, insert it through the fabric as close as possible to the last smocking stitch holding the pleat at the left (at the right if you are left-handed).

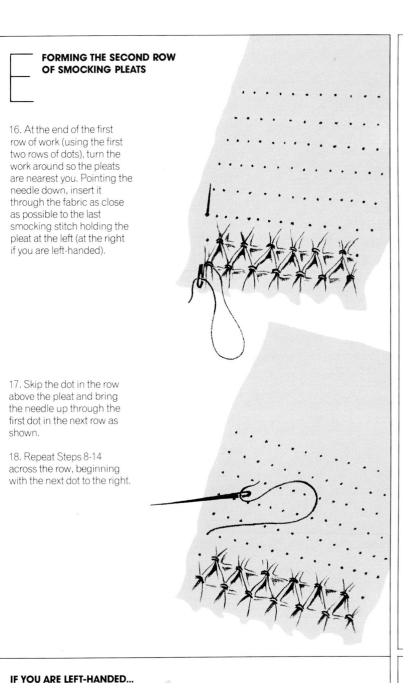

17. Skip the dot in the row above the pleat and bring the needle up through the first dot in the next row as shown.

18. Repeat Steps 8-14 across the row, beginning with the next dot to the right.

F | FINISHING THE SMOCKING PATTERN

19. At the end of the second row of work (using the next two rows of dots), turn the fabric around again. Insert the needle through the fabric underneath the last smocking pleat and bring it up through the outermost dot on the next row.

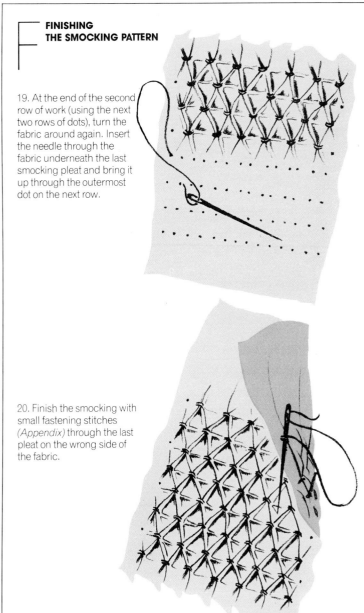

20. Finish the smocking with small fastening stitches *(Appendix)* through the last pleat on the wrong side of the fabric.

IF YOU ARE LEFT-HANDED...

Follow the directions in Steps 16-18, working from right to left and pointing the needle to the right.

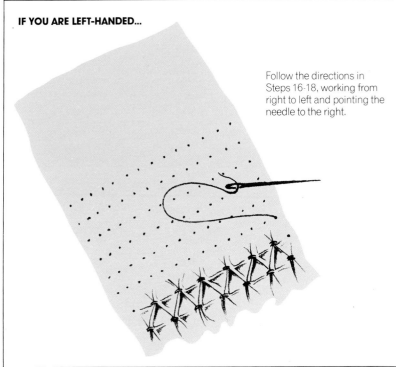

G | SETTING THE SMOCKING PLEATS

21. Pin the finished smocking to the pad of an ironing board. Holding the iron about 1/2 inch above the fabric, steam it for 20 seconds. Do not touch the pleats directly with the iron.

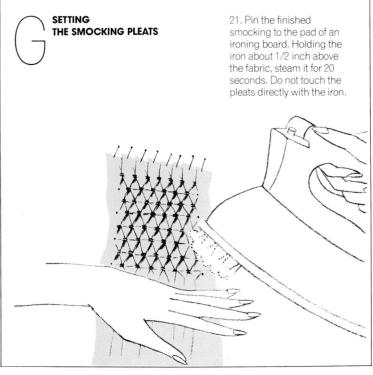

The flattery of demure necklines

Whether primly covered or artfully bared, the traditional necklines described on the following pages flatter anyone who wears them. The low-cut sweetheart neckline *(right)* lies gracefully over the bosom; the high ruffled collar *(pages 65-67)* demurely frames the face.

The elegantly named jabot is a tier of ruffles, fastened at the base of a standing collar to cascade prettily across the front of a bodice. And the shawl collar—made by cutting each collar and its lapel in one piece —forms an elegant curve that circles the neck and continues down the front of the garment.

The sweetheart neckline and high ruffled collar take shape best in a tightly woven fabric—like calico or fine crepe. The ruffles of a jabot may be made of either light- or medium-weight fabric. The arc of a shawl collar, on the other hand, dictates fabric that has some body, such as shantung or mediumweight flannel.

Like all necklines, the loveliness of each of these depends on perfect fit —and often entails adjusting the pattern before the fabric is cut out, as shown overleaf.

A modern sweetheart neckline, elegant and uncluttered, recalls the fastidiously arranged bare neckline in an 1848 illustration.

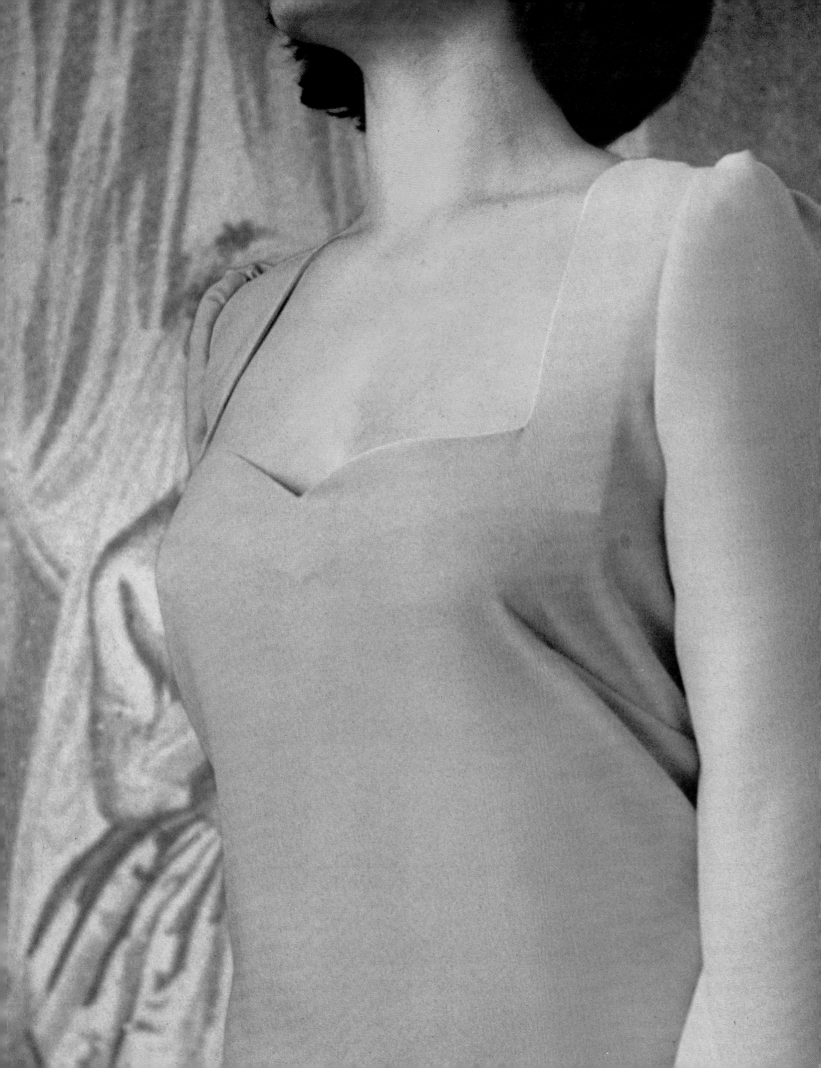

**IF A LOW-CUT
NECKLINE GAPES...**

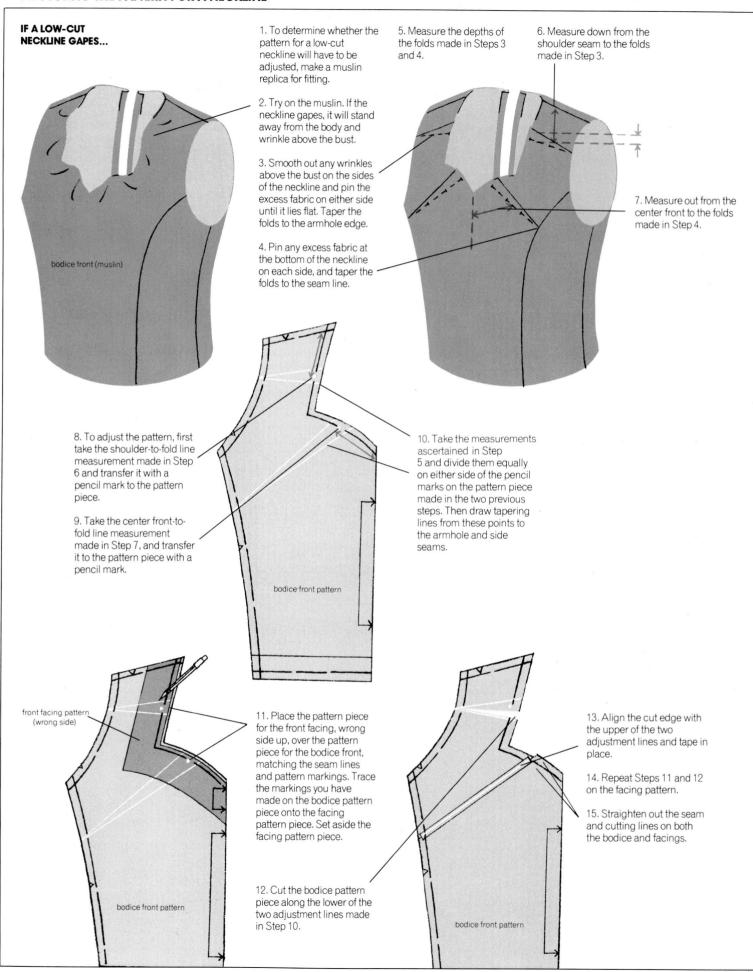

bodice front (muslin)

1. To determine whether the pattern for a low-cut neckline will have to be adjusted, make a muslin replica for fitting.

2. Try on the muslin. If the neckline gapes, it will stand away from the body and wrinkle above the bust.

3. Smooth out any wrinkles above the bust on the sides of the neckline and pin the excess fabric on either side until it lies flat. Taper the folds to the armhole edge.

4. Pin any excess fabric at the bottom of the neckline on each side, and taper the folds to the seam line.

5. Measure the depths of the folds made in Steps 3 and 4.

6. Measure down from the shoulder seam to the folds made in Step 3.

7. Measure out from the center front to the folds made in Step 4.

8. To adjust the pattern, first take the shoulder-to-fold line measurement made in Step 6 and transfer it with a pencil mark to the pattern piece.

9. Take the center front-to-fold line measurement made in Step 7, and transfer it to the pattern piece with a pencil mark.

10. Take the measurements ascertained in Step 5 and divide them equally on either side of the pencil marks on the pattern piece made in the two previous steps. Then draw tapering lines from these points to the armhole and side seams.

bodice front pattern

front facing pattern (wrong side)

bodice front pattern

11. Place the pattern piece for the front facing, wrong side up, over the pattern piece for the bodice front, matching the seam lines and pattern markings. Trace the markings you have made on the bodice pattern piece onto the facing pattern piece. Set aside the facing pattern piece.

12. Cut the bodice pattern piece along the lower of the two adjustment lines made in Step 10.

13. Align the cut edge with the upper of the two adjustment lines and tape in place.

14. Repeat Steps 11 and 12 on the facing pattern.

15. Straighten out the seam and cutting lines on both the bodice and facings.

bodice front pattern

IF A V NECKLINE GAPES...

1. To determine whether the pattern for a V neckline will have to be adjusted, first make it from muslin for fitting.

2. Try on the muslin. As with the low-cut neckline, if the V line gapes, it will stand away from the body and wrinkle above the bust.

3. Smooth out the wrinkles and pin the excess fabric on both sides of the neckline until the neckline lies flat. Taper the folds to the armhole edges.

4. Measure down from the shoulder seam to the line of the fold.

5. Measure the depth of the fold at the neckline.

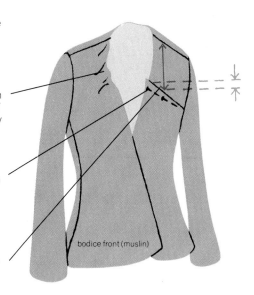

bodice front (muslin)

6. To adjust the pattern, first take the shoulder-to-fold line measurements made in Step 4, and transfer them to the pattern piece with a pencil mark.

7. Now take the measurement for the depth of the folds made in Step 5 and divide it equally on either side of the pencil marks created on the pattern piece in the previous step. Then draw lines tapering from these dots to the armhole seam.

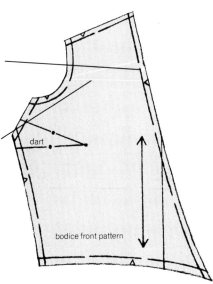

dart

bodice front pattern

8. Place the pattern piece for the front facing, wrong side up, over the pattern piece for the bodice, matching seam lines and pattern markings. Trace the markings you have made on the bodice pattern piece onto the facing pattern piece. Set aside the facing pattern.

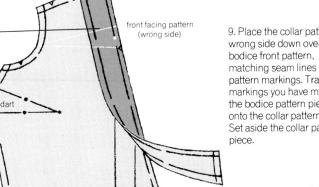

front facing pattern (wrong side)

dart

bodice front pattern

9. Place the collar pattern wrong side down over the bodice front pattern, matching seam lines and pattern markings. Trace the markings you have made on the bodice pattern piece onto the collar pattern piece. Set aside the collar pattern piece.

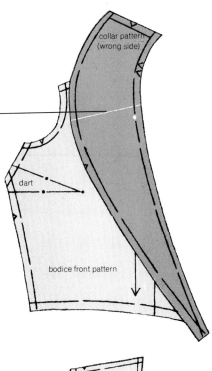

collar pattern (wrong side)

dart

bodice front pattern

10. Cut the bodice pattern piece along the lower of the two adjustment lines made in Step 7.

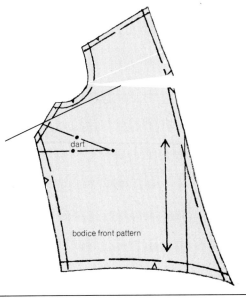

dart

bodice front pattern

11. Align the cut edge with the upper of the two adjustment lines and tape in place.

12. Repeat Steps 10 and 11 on the facing and collar.

13. Smooth out the seam and cutting lines on the bodice, facing and collar.

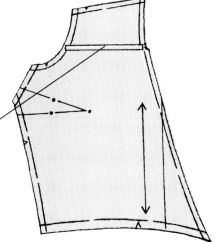

A ATTACHING THE INTERFACING TO THE BODICE

1. Machine stitch around the neckline of the front and back sections of the bodice just outside the seam-line markings to prevent the neckline from pulling out of shape as you work.

2. Place the bodice front wrong side up on a flat surface and place the interfacing for the front of the neckline over it, matching the pattern markings. If the pattern does not include a separate pattern piece for the interfacing, use the pattern piece for the facing to cut one out.

3. Pin the interfacing to the bodice front. Baste just outside the seam line and remove the pins.

4. Trim the interfacing around the neckline and shoulder edges close to the basting line made in Step 3.

5. Trim 3/8 inch from the bottom edge of the interfacing so that the facing, when attached, will conceal it.

6. Pin, baste and trim the interfacings for the back section of the neckline following the instructions in Steps 2-5.

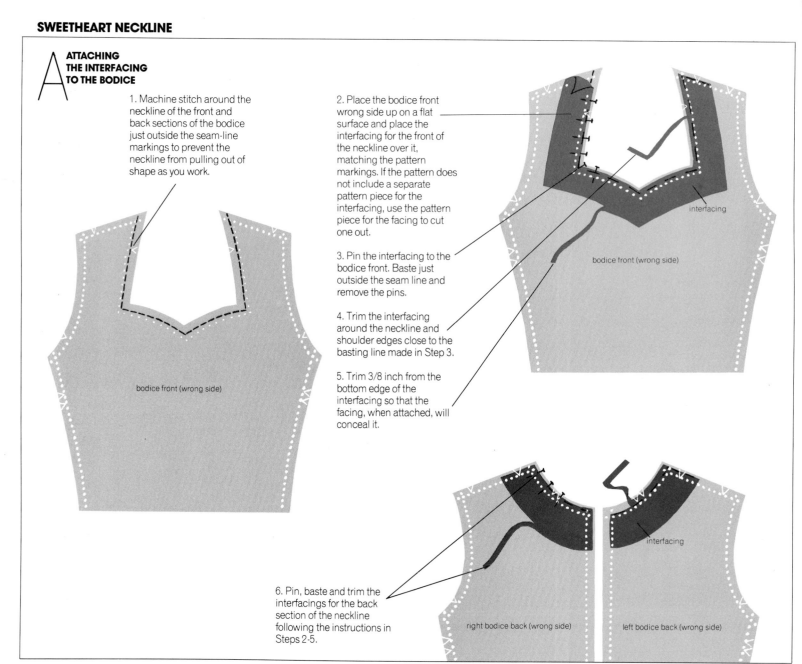

bodice front (wrong side)

interfacing

bodice front (wrong side)

right bodice back (wrong side)

interfacing

left bodice back (wrong side)

B ASSEMBLING THE BODICE

7. Pin and baste the bodice pieces together. Remove the pins and adjust for fit. Stitch and press any darts indicated by the pattern. Stitch the shoulder and side seams. Remove the bastings, and press the seams open.

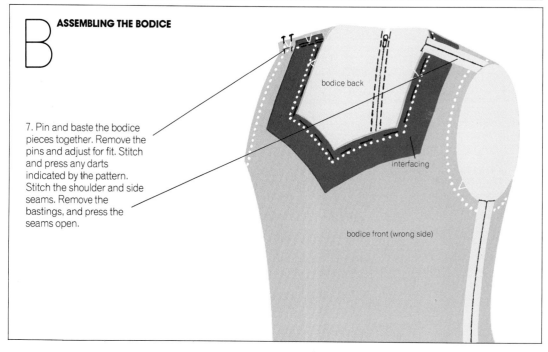

bodice back

interfacing

bodice front (wrong side)

C PREPARING THE FACING

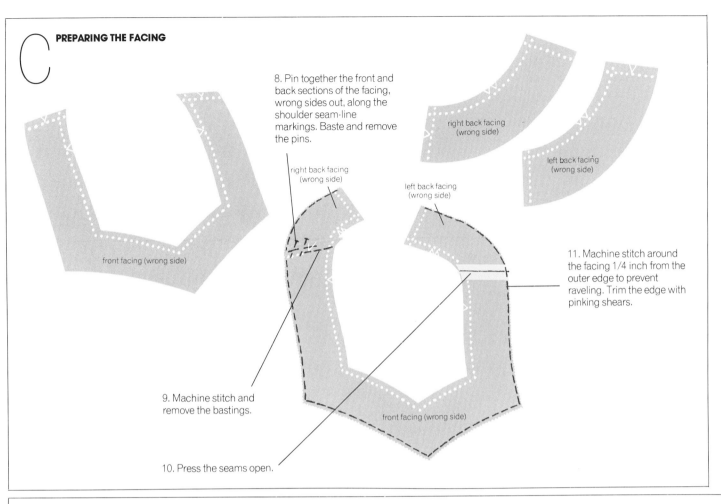

8. Pin together the front and back sections of the facing, wrong sides out, along the shoulder seam-line markings. Baste and remove the pins.

right back facing (wrong side)

left back facing (wrong side)

right back facing (wrong side)

left back facing (wrong side)

front facing (wrong side)

11. Machine stitch around the facing 1/4 inch from the outer edge to prevent raveling. Trim the edge with pinking shears.

9. Machine stitch and remove the bastings.

front facing (wrong side)

10. Press the seams open.

D ATTACHING THE FACING TO THE GARMENT

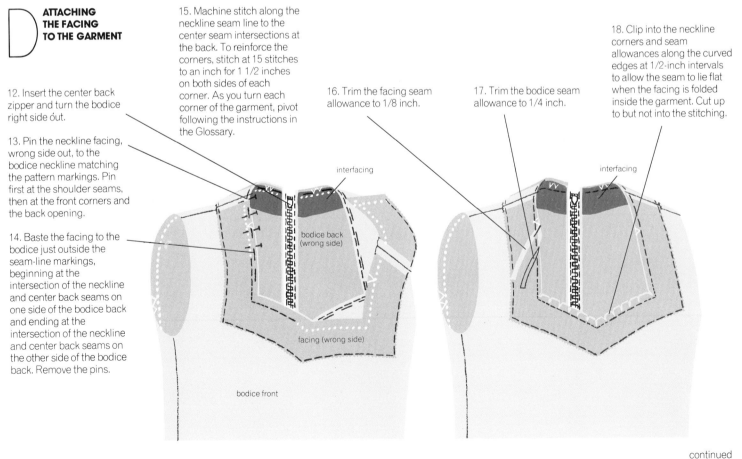

12. Insert the center back zipper and turn the bodice right side out.

13. Pin the neckline facing, wrong side out, to the bodice neckline matching the pattern markings. Pin first at the shoulder seams, then at the front corners and the back opening.

14. Baste the facing to the bodice just outside the seam-line markings, beginning at the intersection of the neckline and center back seams on one side of the bodice back and ending at the intersection of the neckline and center back seams on the other side of the bodice back. Remove the pins.

15. Machine stitch along the neckline seam line to the center seam intersections at the back. To reinforce the corners, stitch at 15 stitches to an inch for 1 1/2 inches on both sides of each corner. As you turn each corner of the garment, pivot following the instructions in the Glossary.

16. Trim the facing seam allowance to 1/8 inch.

17. Trim the bodice seam allowance to 1/4 inch.

18. Clip into the neckline corners and seam allowances along the curved edges at 1/2-inch intervals to allow the seam to lie flat when the facing is folded inside the garment. Cut up to but not into the stitching.

interfacing

bodice back (wrong side)

facing (wrong side)

bodice front

interfacing

continued

FINISHING THE FACING

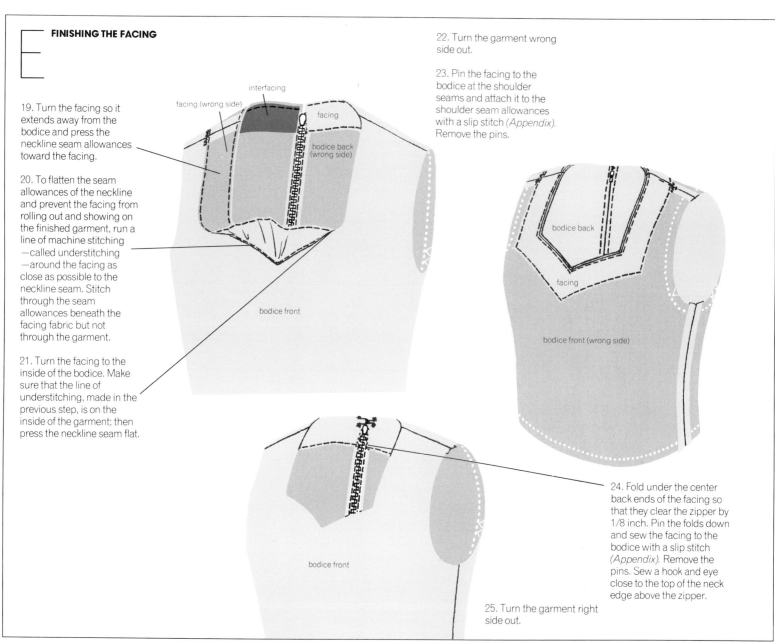

19. Turn the facing so it extends away from the bodice and press the neckline seam allowances toward the facing.

20. To flatten the seam allowances of the neckline and prevent the facing from rolling out and showing on the finished garment, run a line of machine stitching —called understitching —around the facing as close as possible to the neckline seam. Stitch through the seam allowances beneath the facing fabric but not through the garment.

21. Turn the facing to the inside of the bodice. Make sure that the line of understitching, made in the previous step, is on the inside of the garment; then press the neckline seam flat.

22. Turn the garment wrong side out.

23. Pin the facing to the bodice at the shoulder seams and attach it to the shoulder seam allowances with a slip stitch (Appendix). Remove the pins.

24. Fold under the center back ends of the facing so that they clear the zipper by 1/8 inch. Pin the folds down and sew the facing to the bodice with a slip stitch (Appendix). Remove the pins. Sew a hook and eye close to the top of the neck edge above the zipper.

25. Turn the garment right side out.

SHAWL COLLAR

A PREPARING THE GARMENT

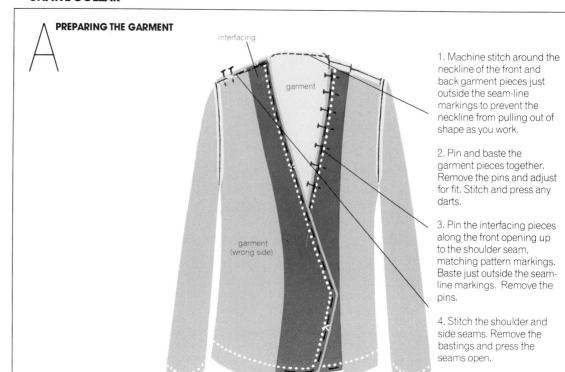

1. Machine stitch around the neckline of the front and back garment pieces just outside the seam-line markings to prevent the neckline from pulling out of shape as you work.

2. Pin and baste the garment pieces together. Remove the pins and adjust for fit. Stitch and press any darts.

3. Pin the interfacing pieces along the front opening up to the shoulder seam, matching pattern markings. Baste just outside the seam-line markings. Remove the pins.

4. Stitch the shoulder and side seams. Remove the bastings and press the seams open.

B PREPARING THE UNDERCOLLAR

5. Assemble the pieces you will need to interface the undercollar: the two undercollar sections, to be joined together, and their matching interfacing sections. If the pattern does not provide separate pattern pieces for the interfacings, use the undercollar pattern pieces to cut them out.

6. Pin and baste the interfacing sections to their corresponding undercollar sections, matching the pattern markings. Remove the pins.

7. Pin the interfaced sections of the undercollar together along the center seam line, interfaced sides out, matching the pattern markings.

8. Baste the center seam, remove the pins, and machine stitch. Remove the basting.

9. Trim the center seam allowance of the interfacing to 1/8 inch. Press the seam open.

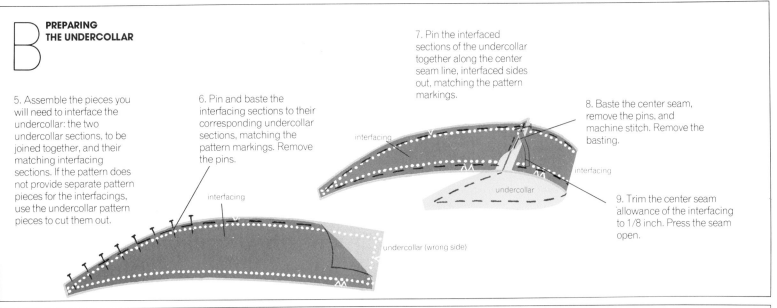

interfacing

undercollar (wrong side)

interfacing

undercollar

C ATTACHING THE UNDERCOLLAR TO THE GARMENT

10. Turn the garment right side out and place the undercollar along the neckline and front opening, interfacing side up, matching the pattern markings.

11. Pin the undercollar to the neckline first at the center back and at each end; then pin along the seam line at 1-inch intervals. Baste just outside the seam line and remove the pins.

12. Machine stitch the undercollar to the garment from one end of the neckline to the other along the seam line. Remove the basting along the stitched edge.

13. Trim the undercollar seam allowance to 1/4 inch.

14. Trim the garment seam allowance to 1/4 inch.

15. Trim the interfacing seam allowances of the undercollar and the garment to 1/8 inch.

16. Clip the seam allowance of the garment around the curved edge of the neck at 2-inch intervals, cutting up to but not into the stitching.

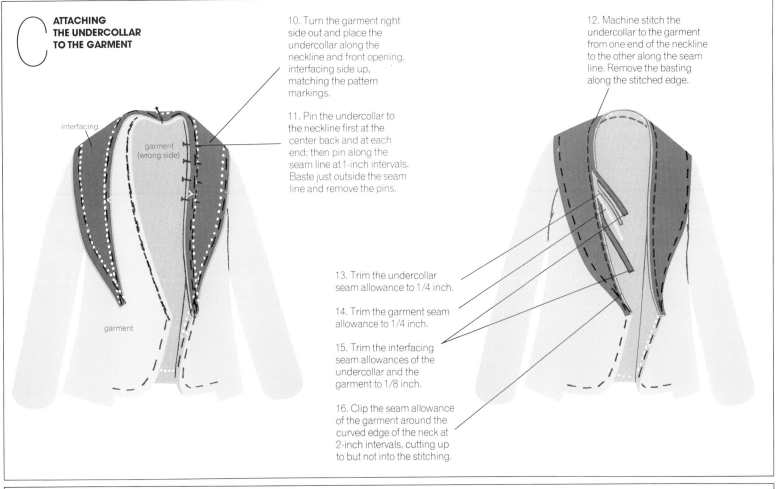

interfacing

garment (wrong side)

garment

D PREPARING THE COLLAR FACING

17. Pin the neck and side facing pieces together at the shoulder seams, wrong sides out, matching the pattern markings.

18. Baste, then remove the pins and machine stitch.

19. Remove the bastings, and press the shoulder seams open.

20. To prevent the collar facing from stretching as you work, machine stitch —at 12 stitches to an inch —along the inner edge of the facing just outside the seam-line marking.

21. Turn up the outer edge of the facing 1/4 inch; press, and machine stitch 1/8 inch from the fold.

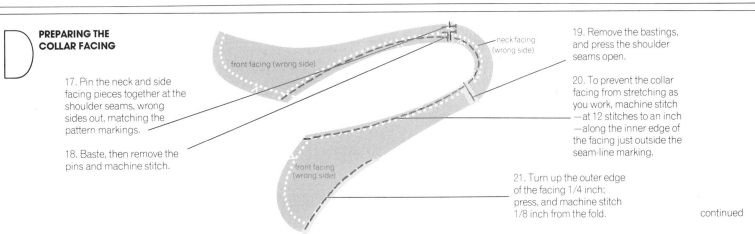

front facing (wrong side)

neck facing (wrong side)

front facing (wrong side)

continued

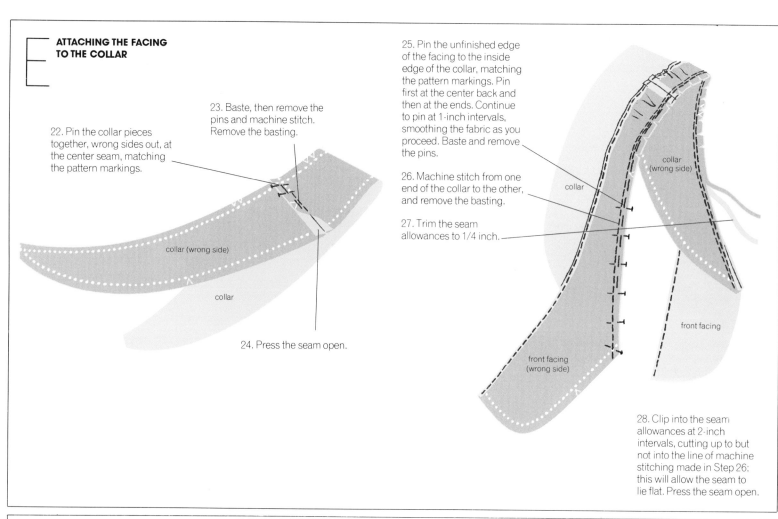

ATTACHING THE FACING TO THE COLLAR

22. Pin the collar pieces together, wrong sides out, at the center seam, matching the pattern markings.

23. Baste, then remove the pins and machine stitch. Remove the basting.

24. Press the seam open.

collar (wrong side)

collar

25. Pin the unfinished edge of the facing to the inside edge of the collar, matching the pattern markings. Pin first at the center back and then at the ends. Continue to pin at 1-inch intervals, smoothing the fabric as you proceed. Baste and remove the pins.

26. Machine stitch from one end of the collar to the other, and remove the basting.

27. Trim the seam allowances to 1/4 inch.

collar (wrong side)

collar

front facing

front facing (wrong side)

28. Clip into the seam allowances at 2-inch intervals, cutting up to but not into the line of machine stitching made in Step 26; this will allow the seam to lie flat. Press the seam open.

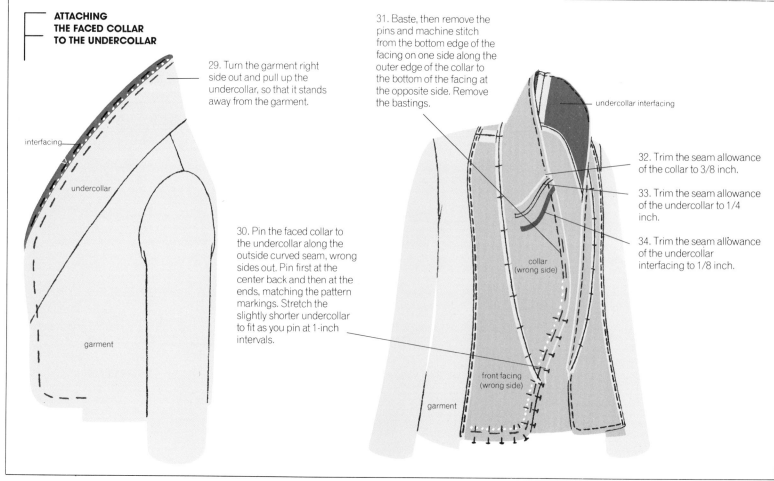

ATTACHING THE FACED COLLAR TO THE UNDERCOLLAR

29. Turn the garment right side out and pull up the undercollar, so that it stands away from the garment.

interfacing

undercollar

garment

30. Pin the faced collar to the undercollar along the outside curved seam, wrong sides out. Pin first at the center back and then at the ends, matching the pattern markings. Stretch the slightly shorter undercollar to fit as you pin at 1-inch intervals.

31. Baste, then remove the pins and machine stitch from the bottom edge of the facing on one side along the outer edge of the collar to the bottom of the facing at the opposite side. Remove the bastings.

undercollar interfacing

32. Trim the seam allowance of the collar to 3/8 inch.

33. Trim the seam allowance of the undercollar to 1/4 inch.

34. Trim the seam allowance of the undercollar interfacing to 1/8 inch.

collar (wrong side)

front facing (wrong side)

garment

G FINISHING THE COLLAR

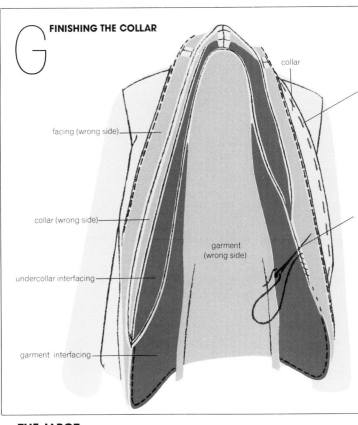

collar

facing (wrong side)

collar (wrong side)

garment (wrong side)

undercollar interfacing

garment interfacing

35. Turn the collar out. Roll the outside of the collar seam between your fingers to bring the stitching out to the edge and turn the seam slightly onto the undercollar side. Baste the folded edge of the collar and press it flat.

36. Align the seam of the collar and facing with the seam of the undercollar and garment. Join them together loosely with a hemming stitch (Appendix).

37. Join the facing to the garment at the shoulder seams with a slip stitch (Appendix).

38. Turn the garment right side out and remove the basting around the outer edge of the collar. Finish the garment according to the pattern instructions.

garment

THE JABOT

A PREPARING THE GARMENT

1. Machine stitch around the neckline of the front and back sections of the bodice just outside the seam-line markings, to prevent the neckline from pulling out of shape as you work.

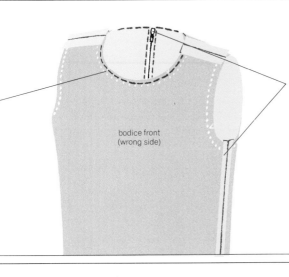

bodice front (wrong side)

2. Pin and baste the bodice pieces together. Remove the pins and adjust for fit. Stitch and press any darts indicated by the pattern. Stitch and press the shoulder and side seams. Remove the bastings and press the seams open. Insert the zipper.

B CUTTING OUT THE RUFFLES

3. To make the two semicircles required for a jabot, spread out the fabric in a single layer, wrong side up, and pin it to a piece of cardboard to prevent it from slipping as you work.

4. Using a piece of string with a pin attached at one end to hold it to the working surface and a pencil at the other, measure out and mark a semicircle with a radius of 9 inches.

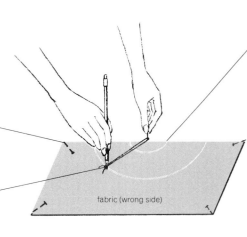

fabric (wrong side)

5. Without moving the pinned end of the string, measure out and mark another semicircle with a radius of 3 inches.

6. On another part of the fabric, measure out and mark an outer semicircle with a radius of 7 inches and an inner semicircle with a radius of 3 inches, as in Steps 4 and 5.

7. Remove the fabric from the cardboard and cut out both semicircles.

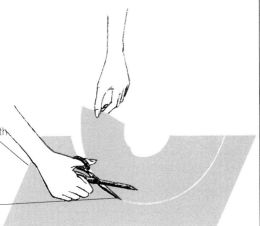

continued

C MAKING THE RUFFLES

8. Place one semicircle on top of the other to check the alignment of the inner circles. If they are not exactly the same, trim them to match.

9. Hem the semicircles and gather them into ruffles, following the instructions for finishing the in-seam ruffle strip on pages 36-37, until the gathered edge of each measures 2 inches.

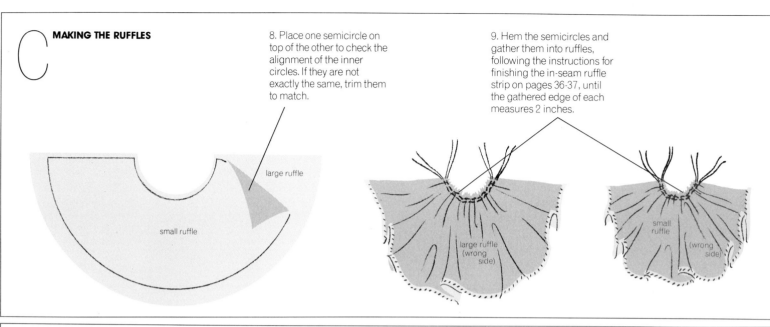

D ATTACHING THE RUFFLES TO THE BODICE

10. Clip the neckline seam allowance of the bodice at 1/2-inch intervals, cutting up to but not into the line of machine stitching made in Step 1.

11. Pin the gathered edge of the larger ruffle, wrong side down, to the bodice, adjusting the gathers evenly. Baste just outside the neckline seam line. Remove the pins.

12. Pin the gathered edge of the smaller ruffle evenly over the larger ruffle. Baste and remove the pins.

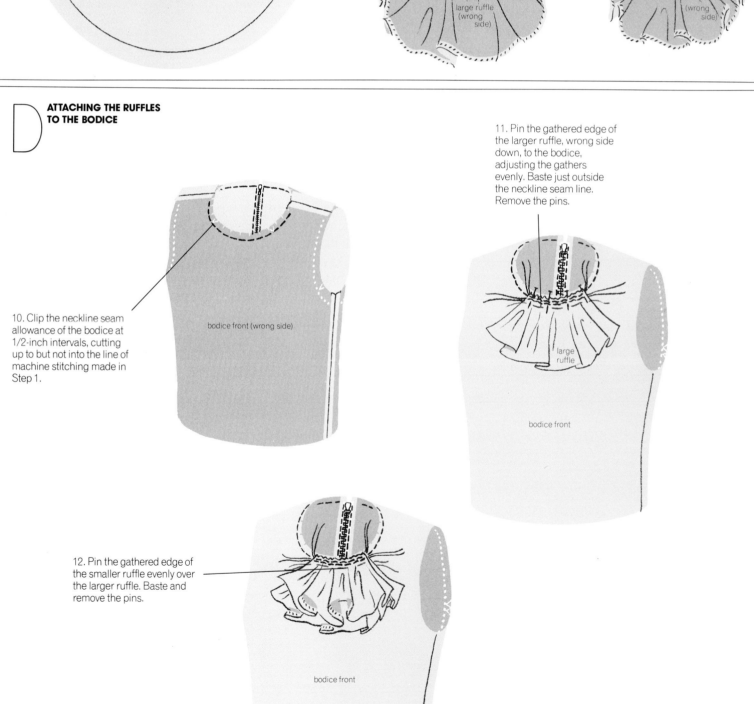

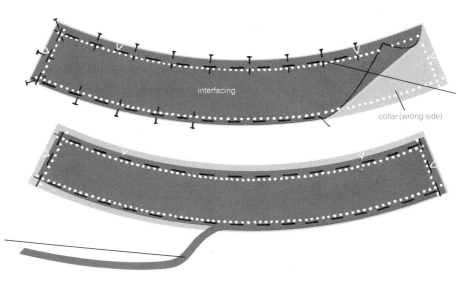

13. Assemble the pieces you will need to interface the collar: the collar itself, the underpart of the collar (called the undercollar) and the interfacing that will be stitched between the two to provide stiffening. If the pattern does not include a separate piece for the interfacing, use the pattern piece for the undercollar to cut it out.

14. Pin the interfacing to the wrong side of the collar, matching the pattern markings. Baste just outside the seam line and remove the pins.

15. Trim the interfacing seam allowance outside the basting to 1/8 inch.

16. Place the undercollar wrong side up on a flat surface and fold up the bottom edge along the pattern markings for the seam line. Press the fold and trim the seam allowance to 1/4 inch.

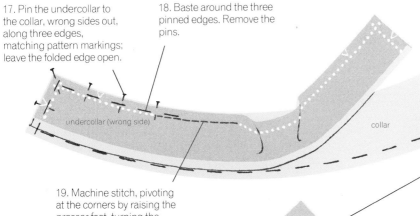

17. Pin the undercollar to the collar, wrong sides out, along three edges, matching pattern markings; leave the folded edge open.

18. Baste around the three pinned edges. Remove the pins.

19. Machine stitch, pivoting at the corners by raising the presser foot, turning the fabric, lowering the presser foot and continuing to stitch. Remove the bastings along the stitched edges.

20. Trim the seam allowances of the collar to 1/4 inch.

21. Trim the seam allowances of the undercollar to 1/8 inch.

22. Trim the upper corners, diagonally, cutting up to but not into the stitching.

23. Clip the seam allowances along the upper edge at 1/2-inch intervals cutting up to but not into the stitching.

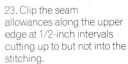

24. Turn the assembled collar right side out, gently pushing out the corners with the closed points of a blunt scissors. Pull the points out farther with a pin from the outside.

continued

G ATTACHING THE COLLAR BAND TO THE BODICE

25. Turn the bodice wrong side out.

26. Pin the collar to the neckline of the bodice as shown, leaving the undercollar free. Baste and remove the pins.

27. Machine stitch all around the neckline along the seam-line markings. As you sew, pull the gathers of the ruffle straight to keep them small and even. Remove the basting.

28. Trim the bodice seam allowance to 3/8 inch.

29. Trim the ruffle seam allowances to 1/4 inch.

30. Trim the collar seam allowance to 1/8 inch.

31. Press the seam allowances toward the collar, using the tip of the iron to avoid pressing the gathers of the ruffle.

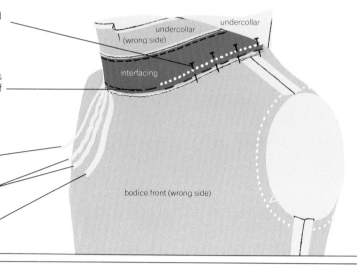

H FINISHING THE COLLAR

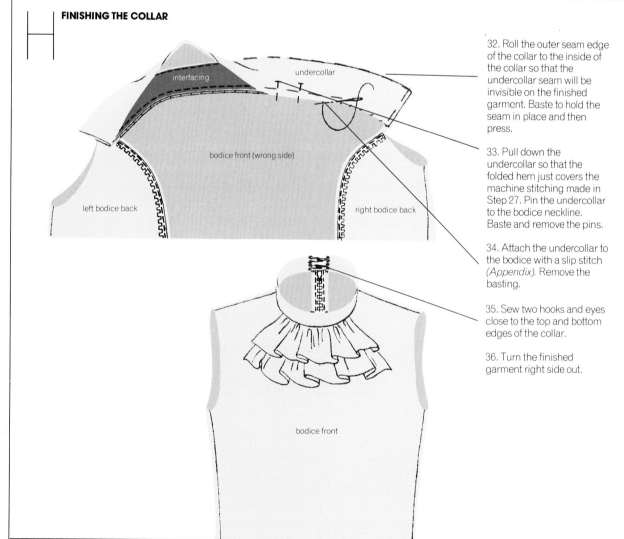

32. Roll the outer seam edge of the collar to the inside of the collar so that the undercollar seam will be invisible on the finished garment. Baste to hold the seam in place and then press.

33. Pull down the undercollar so that the folded hem just covers the machine stitching made in Step 27. Pin the undercollar to the bodice neckline. Baste and remove the pins.

34. Attach the undercollar to the bodice with a slip stitch (*Appendix*). Remove the basting.

35. Sew two hooks and eyes close to the top and bottom edges of the collar.

36. Turn the finished garment right side out.

THE HIGH RUFFLED COLLAR

A PREPARING THE GARMENT

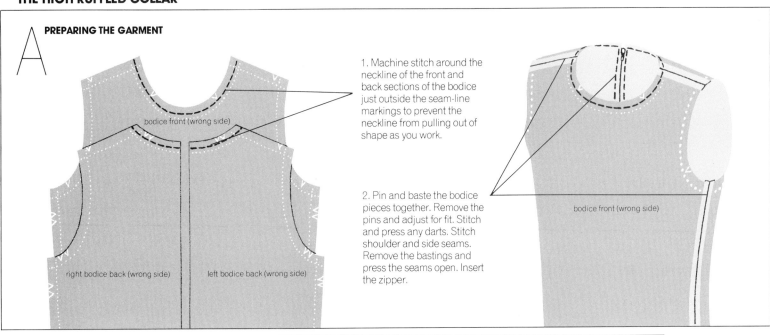

bodice front (wrong side)

right bodice back (wrong side)

left bodice back (wrong side)

bodice front (wrong side)

1. Machine stitch around the neckline of the front and back sections of the bodice just outside the seam-line markings to prevent the neckline from pulling out of shape as you work.

2. Pin and baste the bodice pieces together. Remove the pins and adjust for fit. Stitch and press any darts. Stitch shoulder and side seams. Remove the bastings and press the seams open. Insert the zipper.

B PREPARING THE RUFFLES

3. Assemble the pieces you will need to make the ruffles: if your pattern has provided ruffles of two lengths, the longer piece is for the lower ruffle, to be attached to the bodice neckline below the collar. The shorter piece is for the upper ruffle, to be attached to the top of the collar. Both ruffles are made the same way.

4. Make the ruffles following the instructions for finishing the in-seam ruffle strip on pages 36-37.

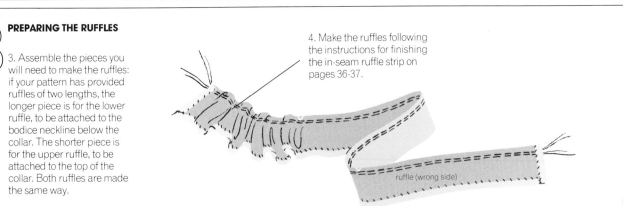

ruffle (wrong side)

C ATTACHING THE LOWER RUFFLE TO THE BODICE

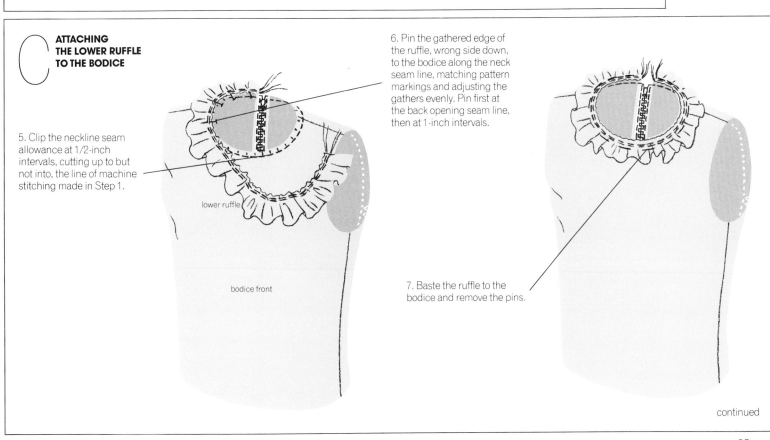

5. Clip the neckline seam allowance at 1/2-inch intervals, cutting up to but not into, the line of machine stitching made in Step 1.

lower ruffle

bodice front

6. Pin the gathered edge of the ruffle, wrong side down, to the bodice along the neck seam line, matching pattern markings and adjusting the gathers evenly. Pin first at the back opening seam line, then at 1-inch intervals.

7. Baste the ruffle to the bodice and remove the pins.

continued

D ATTACHING THE INTERFACING TO THE COLLAR

8. Assemble the pieces you will need to make the collar: the actual collar, the under part of the collar (called the undercollar), the interfacing that will be stitched between the two to provide stiffening, and the upper ruffle. If the pattern does not include a separate pattern piece for the interfacing, use the pattern piece for the undercollar to cut it out.

9. Pin the interfacing to the wrong side of the collar, matching the pattern markings. Baste just outside the seam line and remove the pins.

10. Trim the interfacing just outside the line of basting all around the collar.

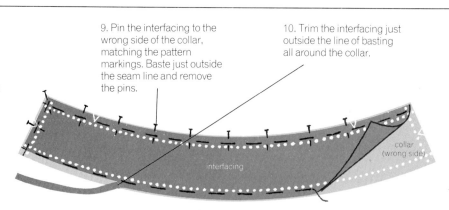

E ATTACHING THE UPPER RUFFLE TO THE COLLAR

11. Turn the collar wrong side down.

12. Place the upper ruffle, wrong side up, over it, with the gathered edge along the top seam line of the collar and the hemmed edges of the ruffle aligned with the seam lines at the ends of the collar. Pin the hemmed ends and the center of the ruffle first.

13. Then pin the rest of the ruffle to the collar at 1-inch intervals, adjusting the gathers evenly. Baste just outside the seam line and remove the pins.

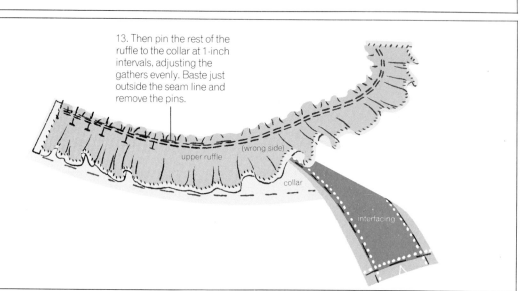

F ATTACHING THE UNDERCOLLAR TO THE COLLAR

14. Place the undercollar on a flat surface, wrong side up, and turn up the bottom edge along the pattern markings for the seam line. Press the fold and trim the seam allowance to 1/4 inch.

15. Place the undercollar, wrong side up, over the basted collar and ruffle, with the ruffle in the middle. Pin the top and side edges together, matching the pattern markings. Baste around the pinned edges just outside the seam line. Remove the pins.

16. Machine stitch the undercollar to the collar and ruffle along the seam lines of the basted sides. As you sew, pull the gathers of the ruffle straight to keep them small and even. Pivot at the corners by raising the presser foot, turning the fabric, lowering the presser foot and continuing to stitch. Remove all the hand bastings along the machine stitched edges.

17. Trim the seam allowances of the ruffle to 1/8 inch.

18. Trim the seam allowances of the collar and undercollar to 1/4 inch.

19. Trim off the upper corners diagonally, cutting up to but not into the stitching.

20. Clip the trimmed seam allowances along the upper edge at 1/2-inch intervals, cutting up to but not into the stitching.

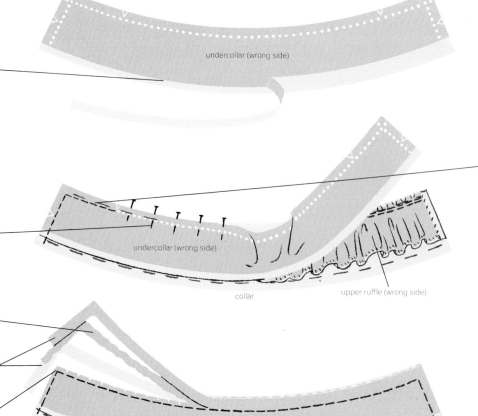

G FINISHING THE COLLAR

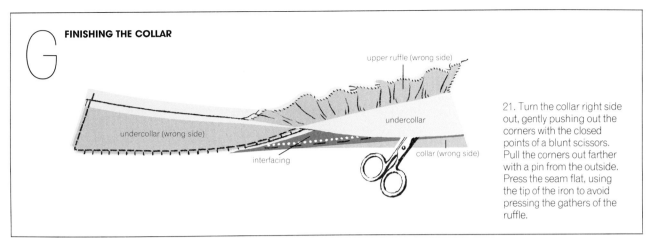

upper ruffle (wrong side)

undercollar (wrong side)

undercollar

interfacing

collar (wrong side)

21. Turn the collar right side out, gently pushing out the corners with the closed points of a blunt scissors. Pull the corners out farther with a pin from the outside. Press the seam flat, using the tip of the iron to avoid pressing the gathers of the ruffle.

H ATTACHING THE COLLAR TO THE BODICE

22. Turn the bodice wrong side out.

23. Pin the collar to the neckline of the bodice as shown, leaving the undercollar free. Baste and remove the pins.

24. Machine stitch all around the neckline along the seam-line markings. As you sew, pull the gathers of the ruffle straight to keep them small and even. Remove the basting.

25. Trim the bodice seam allowance to 3/8 inch.

26. Trim the lower ruffle seam allowance to 1/4 inch.

27. Trim the collar seam allowance to 1/8 inch.

28. Press the seam allowances toward the collar, using the tip of the iron to avoid pressing the gathers of the ruffle.

29. Turn the undercollar down so that the folded edge just covers the machine stitching made in Step 24. Pin the undercollar to the bodice neckline. Baste and remove the pins.

30. Attach the undercollar to the bodice with a slip stitch *(Appendix).* Remove the basting.

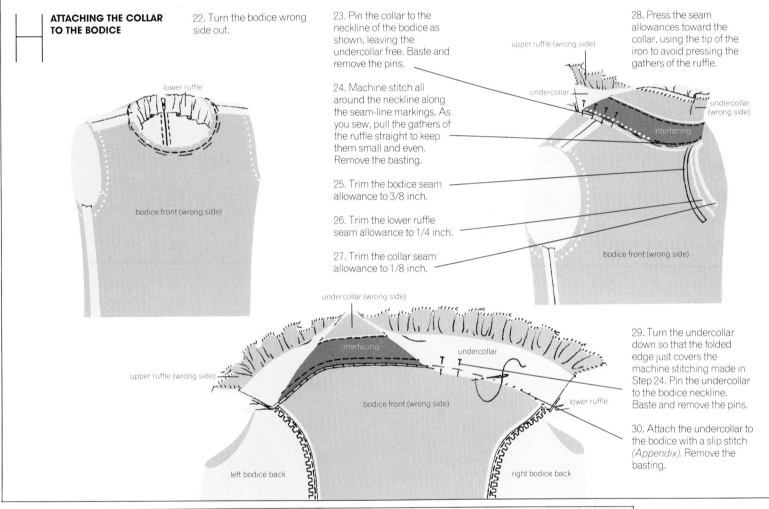

lower ruffle

bodice front (wrong side)

upper ruffle (wrong side)

undercollar

undercollar (wrong side)

interfacing

bodice front (wrong side)

undercollar (wrong side)

interfacing

undercollar

bodice front (wrong side)

lower ruffle

left bodice back

right bodice back

FINISHING THE COLLAR

31. Sew two hooks and eyes close to the top and bottom edges of the collar.

32. Turn the finished garment right side out.

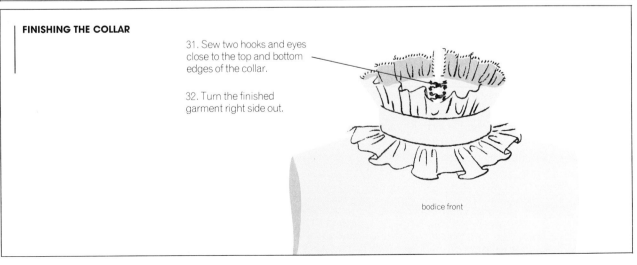

bodice front

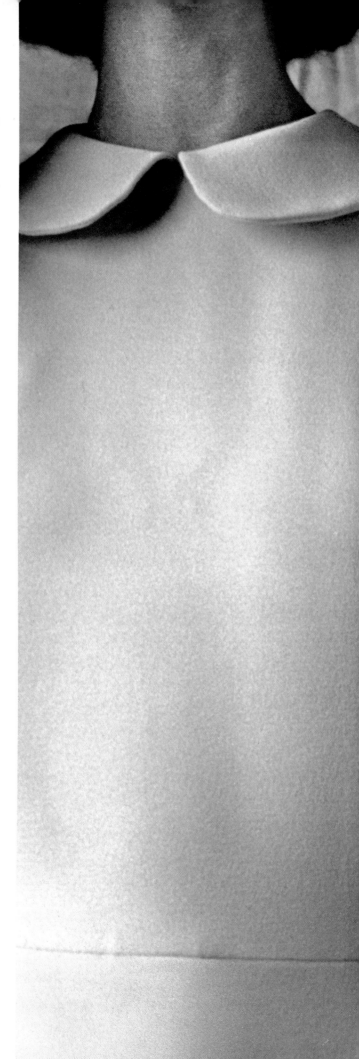

Engaging puffery for a sleeve

Now, as in Victorian days, puffy sleeves transform the most everyday styles into elegant dresses and blouses. On the simple puffed sleeve shown at right, the fabric rises briefly from the shoulder to be caught in a band halfway to the elbow. The leg-of-mutton sleeve *(page 76)* balloons at the shoulder, then gradually tapers into a wrist-length sheath. The bishop sleeve *(page 81)* fits smoothly at the shoulder, then billows out above the wrist.

Wherever the sleeve swells, the fabric must be gathered with care —and by machine (hand stitches will not be as tight or as even). This means making sure that the gathers are created by pulling the bobbin thread—not the thread on the needle side of the fabric, which will lock and perhaps break. It also means frequent distribution of the extra fullness to get the ripples even. Any of the three sleeves may need additional special adjustments, which are best accomplished (as described overleaf) before the final sleeve is cut from the garment fabric.

The modern puffed sleeve, a slimmer version of the bouffant sleeves of 1895 *(background)*, is every bit as becoming as was its predecessor.

ADJUSTING THE PATTERN FOR A SLEEVE

IF THE TOP OF THE SLEEVE IS TOO FULL...

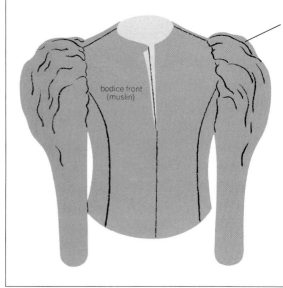

1. To determine whether the pattern for a full sleeve will have to be adjusted at the top, first make a fitting muslin.

2. If the puff at the shoulder is too extreme, it will extend too far up and out, and you will need to adjust the pattern piece.

3. To determine how to adjust the pattern piece, first draw a new gathering line 1 inch inside the original at the top curve of the sleeve cap on the muslin. Taper the new line to 1/2 inch at the pattern markings, indicating the outside limits of the gathering line, and run it back into the original seam line at the underarm.

4. Rebaste the muslin and try it on again to check the fit.

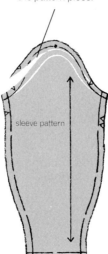

5. Transfer the new gathering line to the paper pattern, and draw a new cutting line 5/8 inch outside the new gathering line. Trim the pattern piece.

IF THE BOTTOM OF A FULL SLEEVE IS TOO WIDE...

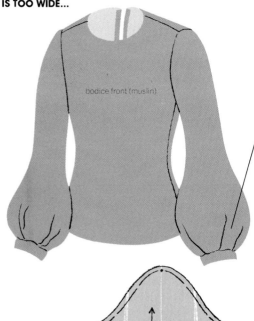

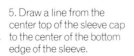

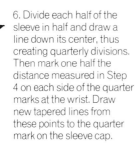

1. To determine whether the pattern for a full sleeve will have to be adjusted at the cuff, first make it from muslin for fitting.

2. Try the muslin on. If the sleeve is too wide, it will hang loosely over the cuff.

3. Remove the wristband and pin the excess fabric equally in two places, at either side of the sleeve.

4. Measure the depth of each fold made in Step 3.

5. Draw a line from the center top of the sleeve cap to the center of the bottom edge of the sleeve.

6. Divide each half of the sleeve in half and draw a line down its center, thus creating quarterly divisions. Then mark one half the distance measured in Step 4 on each side of the quarter marks at the wrist. Draw new tapered lines from these points to the quarter mark on the sleeve cap.

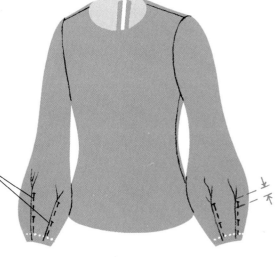

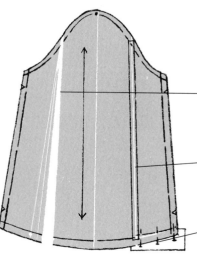

7. Working first on one side of the sleeve, then on the other, cut along the two inside lines drawn in Step 6, cutting up to but not through the edge of the sleeve cap.

8. Place the slashed line directly over the other drawn line and tape it in place.

9. Pin a paper extension to the pattern piece, and redraw the bottom curve of the sleeve to make a smooth cutting line.

IF THE TOP OF A SET-IN SLEEVE IS LOOSE...

1. To determine whether the pattern for a set-in sleeve will have to be adjusted at the top, first make a fitting muslin.

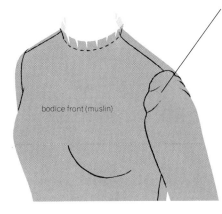

bodice front (muslin)

2. Try the muslin on. If the top is loose, it will roll up above the shoulder seam of the muslin to create a puffed effect. Wrinkles will appear across the top along the armhole seam.

3. Open the seam at the top of the sleeve at least 4 inches on either side of the shoulder seam.

4. Smooth the sleeve top up to the shoulder seam, then fold under the fabric at the center edge of the sleeve top. Pin the fold at the shoulder seam line.

5. Fold under the seam allowance of the sleeve top in front and back and pin it to the armhole, tapering into the original seam line midway down the armhole. Take off the muslin.

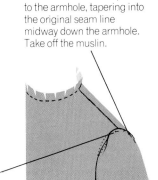

6. Turn the muslin wrong side out and measure the distance between the new sleeve top seam line and the original sleeve top seam line as shown.

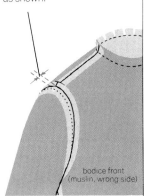

bodice front (muslin, wrong side)

7. To transfer these corrections to the pattern, measure 3 inches down the sleeve pattern from the center top point of the original seam line and draw a line at a right angle to the grain-line marking.

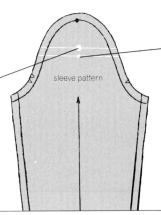

sleeve pattern

8. Measure from the line made in Step 7 to a point below the line, equal to the distance measured in Step 6. Draw a line through the point parallel to the line made in Step 7.

9. Fold the pattern so that the two parallel lines meet. Pin this tuck flat. Then pin a piece of paper under the tuck.

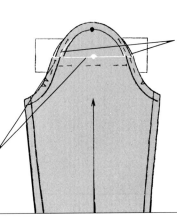

10. Draw new seam lines on each side of the sleeve from the bottom of the tuck to taper into the original seam line along the top of the sleeve an inch or so above the tuck. Draw new cutting lines on the paper extension 5/8 inch outside the new seam lines and parallel to them. Trim away the excess paper.

IF THE TOP OF A SET-IN SLEEVE IS TIGHT...

1. To determine whether the pattern for a set-in sleeve will have to be adjusted at the top, first make a fitting muslin.

2. Try on the muslin. If the top is tight, the sleeve top will feel snug around the upper arm and wrinkles will radiate from the armhole on both the sleeve top and the shoulder.

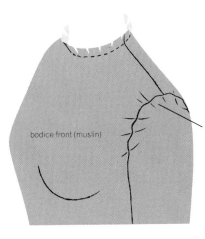

bodice front (muslin)

3. Open the seam at the top of the sleeve, at least 4 inches on either side of the shoulder seam.

4. Smooth the sleeve top up to the shoulder and fold under enough of the sleeve top seam allowance so that it meets the armhole seam line.

5. Pin the folded edge to the armhole of the bodice at the shoulder seam line. Take off the muslin.

6. At the shoulder seam line, measure the distance from the edge of the fold made in Step 4 to the original armhole seam line as shown.

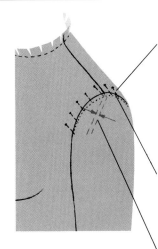

7. To transfer these corrections to the pattern, measure 3 inches down on the sleeve pattern from the center top point, and draw a line at a right angle to the grain-line marking.

8. Cut off the sleeve top along the line made in Step 7.

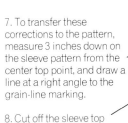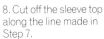
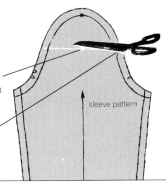

sleeve pattern

9. Slide a piece of shelf paper under the cut pattern and spread the pattern pieces until the distance between their edges is equal to the measurement made in Step 6. Make sure the edges of the pattern pieces are parallel, then pin them to the shelf paper.

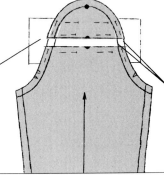

10. On both sides of the sleeve draw new seam lines on the paper extension joining the original seam lines. Draw new cutting lines 5/8 inch outside the new seam lines. Trim away excess paper.

THE PUFFED SLEEVE

A PREPARING THE SLEEVE

1. Make two parallel rows of machine basting (6 stitches to the inch) around the curved upper edge, or cap, of the sleeve between the pattern markings (usually notches) indicating where the fullness of the sleeve will be gathered. Sew one line of machine basting just outside the seam line, the other 1/4 inch outside the first. Leave 4-inch-long loose threads at each end of the bastings.

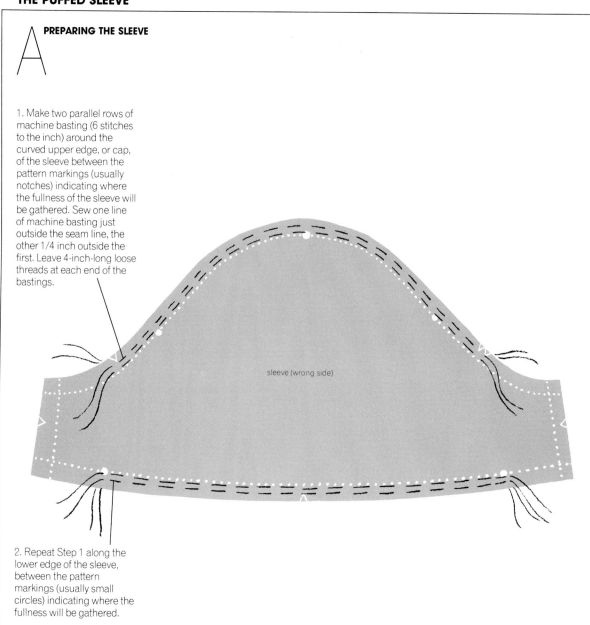

sleeve (wrong side)

2. Repeat Step 1 along the lower edge of the sleeve, between the pattern markings (usually small circles) indicating where the fullness will be gathered.

B PREPARING THE SLEEVE BAND

3. Place the sleeve band on a flat surface, wrong side up, with the notched edge at the top. Fold over the unnotched edge of the band along the seam-line marking and press.

4. Trim the folded edge to 1/4 inch.

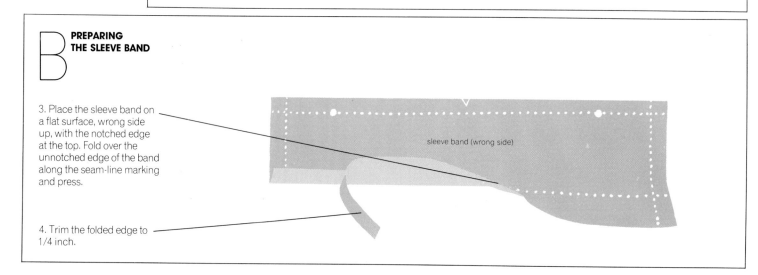

sleeve band (wrong side)

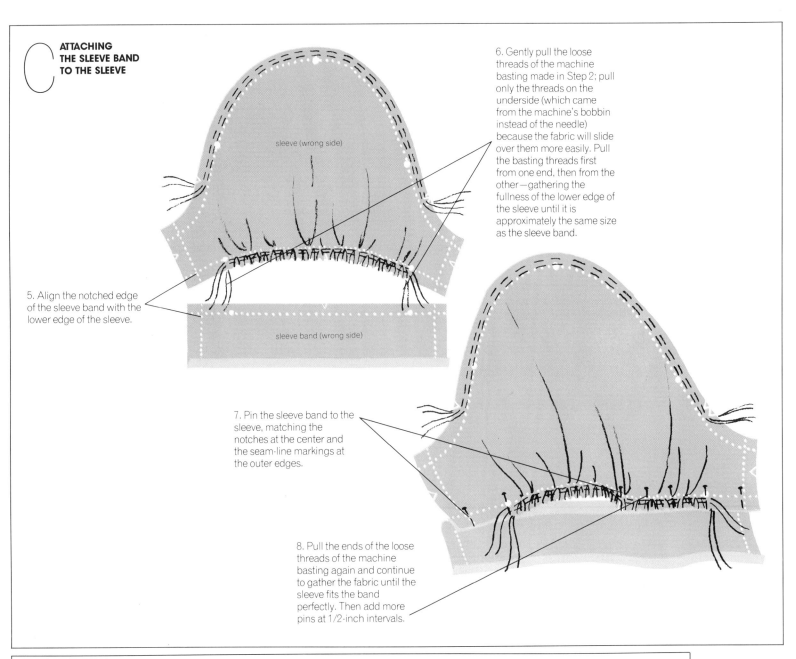

C ATTACHING THE SLEEVE BAND TO THE SLEEVE

5. Align the notched edge of the sleeve band with the lower edge of the sleeve.

6. Gently pull the loose threads of the machine basting made in Step 2; pull only the threads on the underside (which came from the machine's bobbin instead of the needle) because the fabric will slide over them more easily. Pull the basting threads first from one end, then from the other—gathering the fullness of the lower edge of the sleeve until it is approximately the same size as the sleeve band.

7. Pin the sleeve band to the sleeve, matching the notches at the center and the seam-line markings at the outer edges.

8. Pull the ends of the loose threads of the machine basting again and continue to gather the fabric until the sleeve fits the band perfectly. Then add more pins at 1/2-inch intervals.

D STITCHING THE SLEEVE BAND TO THE SLEEVE

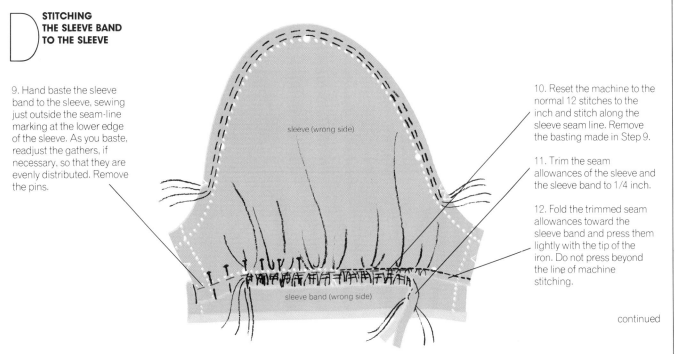

9. Hand baste the sleeve band to the sleeve, sewing just outside the seam-line marking at the lower edge of the sleeve. As you baste, readjust the gathers, if necessary, so that they are evenly distributed. Remove the pins.

10. Reset the machine to the normal 12 stitches to the inch and stitch along the sleeve seam line. Remove the basting made in Step 9.

11. Trim the seam allowances of the sleeve and the sleeve band to 1/4 inch.

12. Fold the trimmed seam allowances toward the sleeve band and press them lightly with the tip of the iron. Do not press beyond the line of machine stitching.

continued

E | JOINING THE UNDERARM SEAM

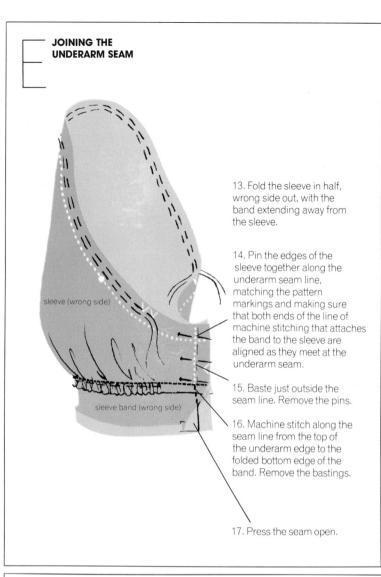

sleeve (wrong side)

sleeve band (wrong side)

13. Fold the sleeve in half, wrong side out, with the band extending away from the sleeve.

14. Pin the edges of the sleeve together along the underarm seam line, matching the pattern markings and making sure that both ends of the line of machine stitching that attaches the band to the sleeve are aligned as they meet at the underarm seam.

15. Baste just outside the seam line. Remove the pins.

16. Machine stitch along the seam line from the top of the underarm edge to the folded bottom edge of the band. Remove the bastings.

17. Press the seam open.

F | FINISHING THE SLEEVE BAND

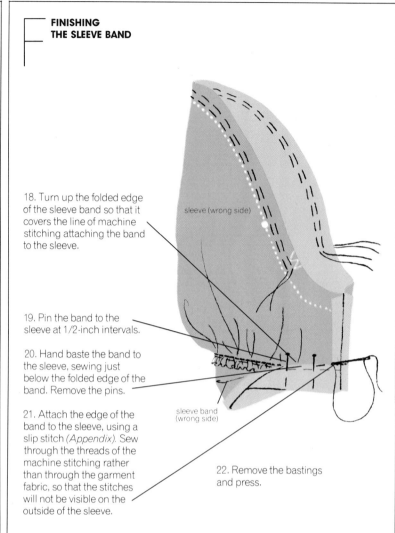

sleeve (wrong side)

sleeve band (wrong side)

18. Turn up the folded edge of the sleeve band so that it covers the line of machine stitching attaching the band to the sleeve.

19. Pin the band to the sleeve at 1/2-inch intervals.

20. Hand baste the band to the sleeve, sewing just below the folded edge of the band. Remove the pins.

21. Attach the edge of the band to the sleeve, using a slip stitch (Appendix). Sew through the threads of the machine stitching rather than through the garment fabric, so that the stitches will not be visible on the outside of the sleeve.

22. Remove the bastings and press.

G | FITTING THE SLEEVE TO THE GARMENT

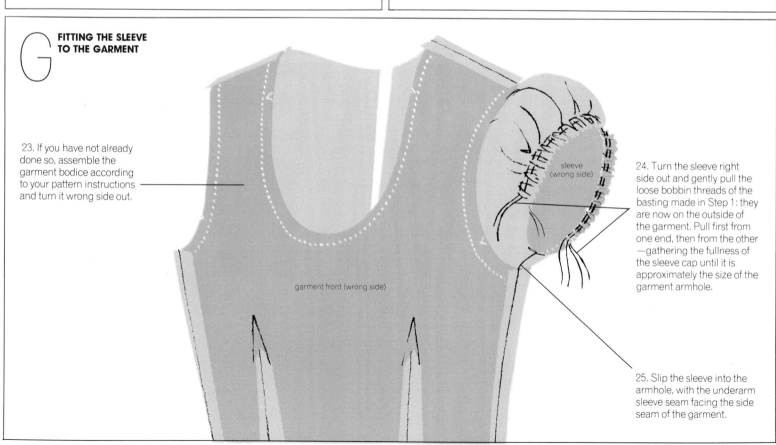

garment front (wrong side)

sleeve (wrong side)

23. If you have not already done so, assemble the garment bodice according to your pattern instructions and turn it wrong side out.

24. Turn the sleeve right side out and gently pull the loose bobbin threads of the basting made in Step 1: they are now on the outside of the garment. Pull first from one end, then from the other —gathering the fullness of the sleeve cap until it is approximately the size of the garment armhole.

25. Slip the sleeve into the armhole, with the underarm sleeve seam facing the side seam of the garment.

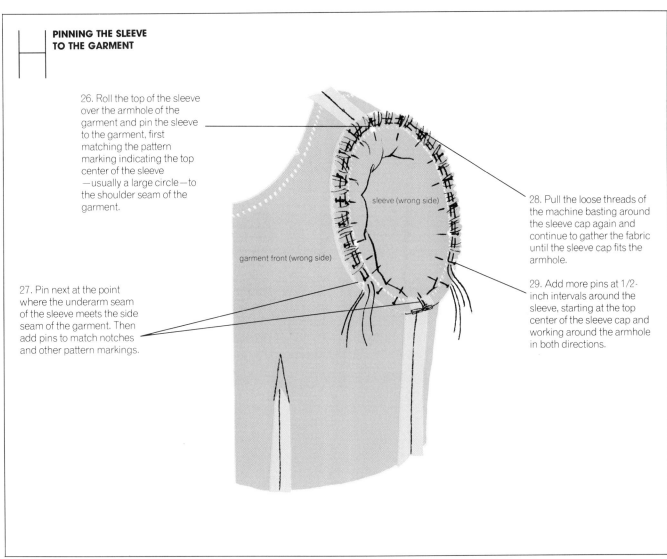

26. Roll the top of the sleeve over the armhole of the garment and pin the sleeve to the garment, first matching the pattern marking indicating the top center of the sleeve —usually a large circle—to the shoulder seam of the garment.

27. Pin next at the point where the underarm seam of the sleeve meets the side seam of the garment. Then add pins to match notches and other pattern markings.

28. Pull the loose threads of the machine basting around the sleeve cap again and continue to gather the fabric until the sleeve cap fits the armhole.

29. Add more pins at 1/2-inch intervals around the sleeve, starting at the top center of the sleeve cap and working around the armhole in both directions.

sleeve (wrong side)

garment front (wrong side)

STITCHING THE SLEEVE TO THE GARMENT

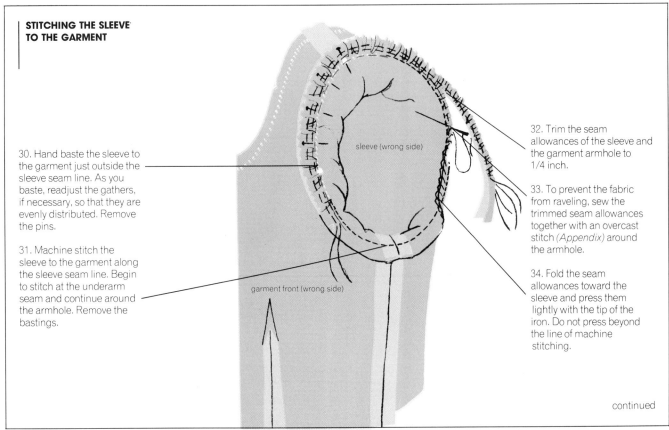

30. Hand baste the sleeve to the garment just outside the sleeve seam line. As you baste, readjust the gathers, if necessary, so that they are evenly distributed. Remove the pins.

31. Machine stitch the sleeve to the garment along the sleeve seam line. Begin to stitch at the underarm seam and continue around the armhole. Remove the bastings.

32. Trim the seam allowances of the sleeve and the garment armhole to 1/4 inch.

33. To prevent the fabric from raveling, sew the trimmed seam allowances together with an overcast stitch (Appendix) around the armhole.

34. Fold the seam allowances toward the sleeve and press them lightly with the tip of the iron. Do not press beyond the line of machine stitching.

sleeve (wrong side)

garment front (wrong side)

continued

J FINISHING THE SLEEVES

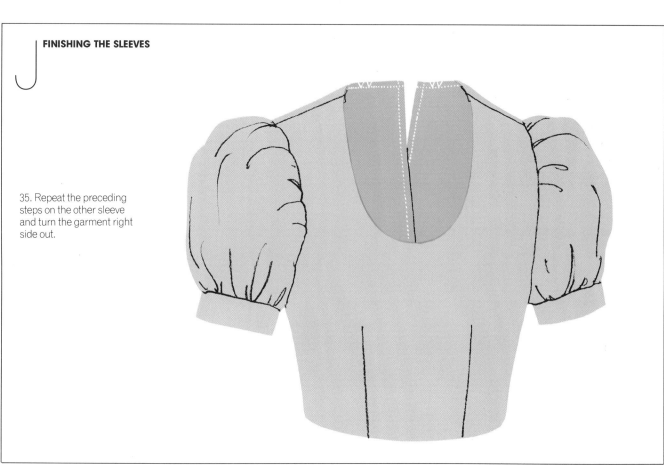

35. Repeat the preceding steps on the other sleeve and turn the garment right side out.

THE LEG-OF-MUTTON SLEEVE

A PREPARING THE SLEEVE

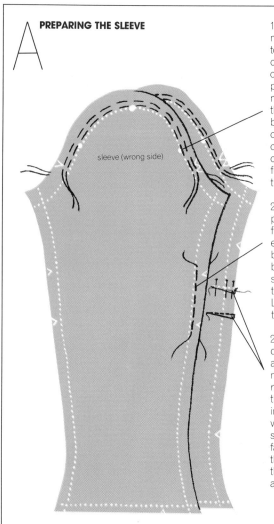

sleeve (wrong side)

1. Make two parallel rows of machine basting (6 stitches to the inch) around the curved upper edge, or cap, of the sleeve between the pattern markings (usually notches) indicating where the fullness of the sleeve will be gathered. Sew one line of machine basting just outside the seam line, the other 1/4 inch outside the first. Leave 4-inch-long loose threads at each end.

2A. If your pattern calls for pulling in, or easing, the fullness of the sleeve at the elbow, machine baste between the notches on the back of the sleeve (they are slightly farther apart than the notches on the front). Leave 4-inch-long loose threads at each end.

2B. If your pattern calls for darts to control the fullness at the elbow, pin, baste and machine stitch them, resetting your machine to the normal 12 stitches to the inch. Begin stitching at the widest end. Sew a few stitches off the edge of the fabric at the tip end. Cut the threads and hand knot them. Remove the bastings and press the darts down.

B JOINING THE UNDERARM SEAM

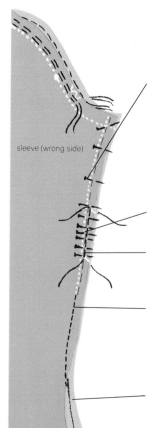

sleeve (wrong side)

3. Fold the sleeve in half, wrong side out.

4. Pin the edges of the sleeve together along the underarm seam lines at 1-inch intervals, matching the pattern markings. If the sleeve is to be pulled in, leave the section between the notches unpinned.

5. For the sleeve that is to be eased in at the elbow, gently pull the loose threads of the machine basting made in Step 2A—first from one end, then from the other—until the sleeve edges are the same length between the notches. Then add more pins.

6. Baste just outside the seam line. Remove the pins.

7. Reset the machine to the normal 12 stitches to the inch. Machine stitch along the underarm seam line. Remove the basting.

8. Press the underarm seam open. Instead of an ironing board use a seam roll, holding it inside the garment as the iron presses the wrong side.

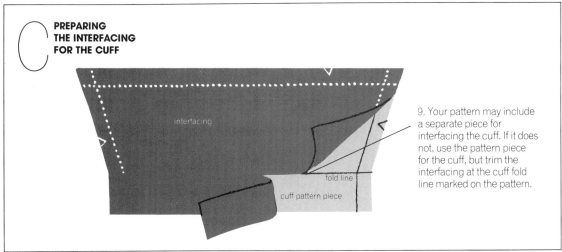

C PREPARING THE INTERFACING FOR THE CUFF

9. Your pattern may include a separate piece for interfacing the cuff. If it does not, use the pattern piece for the cuff, but trim the interfacing at the cuff fold line marked on the pattern.

interfacing

fold line

cuff pattern piece

D ATTACHING THE INTERFACING TO THE CUFF

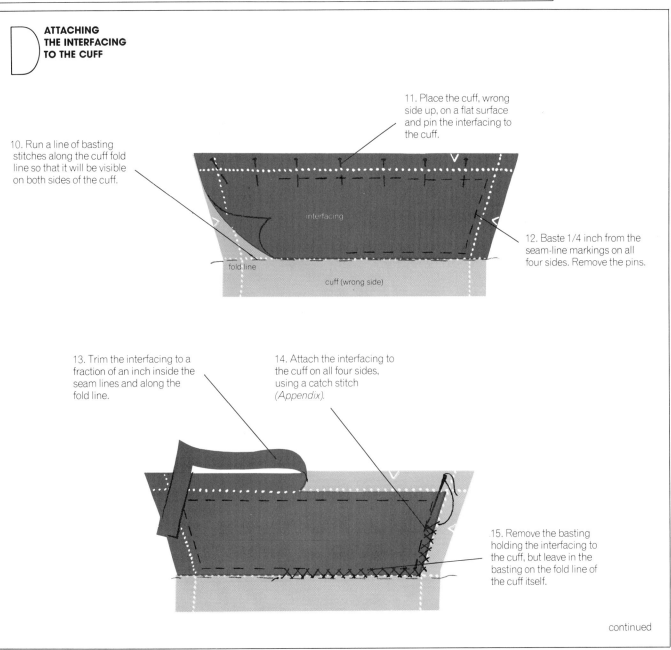

10. Run a line of basting stitches along the cuff fold line so that it will be visible on both sides of the cuff.

11. Place the cuff, wrong side up, on a flat surface and pin the interfacing to the cuff.

12. Baste 1/4 inch from the seam-line markings on all four sides. Remove the pins.

interfacing

fold line

cuff (wrong side)

13. Trim the interfacing to a fraction of an inch inside the seam lines and along the fold line.

14. Attach the interfacing to the cuff on all four sides, using a catch stitch (Appendix).

15. Remove the basting holding the interfacing to the cuff, but leave in the basting on the fold line of the cuff itself.

continued

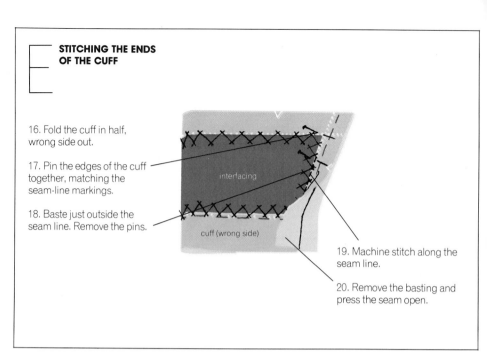

16. Fold the cuff in half, wrong side out.

17. Pin the edges of the cuff together, matching the seam-line markings.

18. Baste just outside the seam line. Remove the pins.

interfacing

cuff (wrong side)

19. Machine stitch along the seam line.

20. Remove the basting and press the seam open.

ATTACHING THE CUFF TO THE SLEEVE

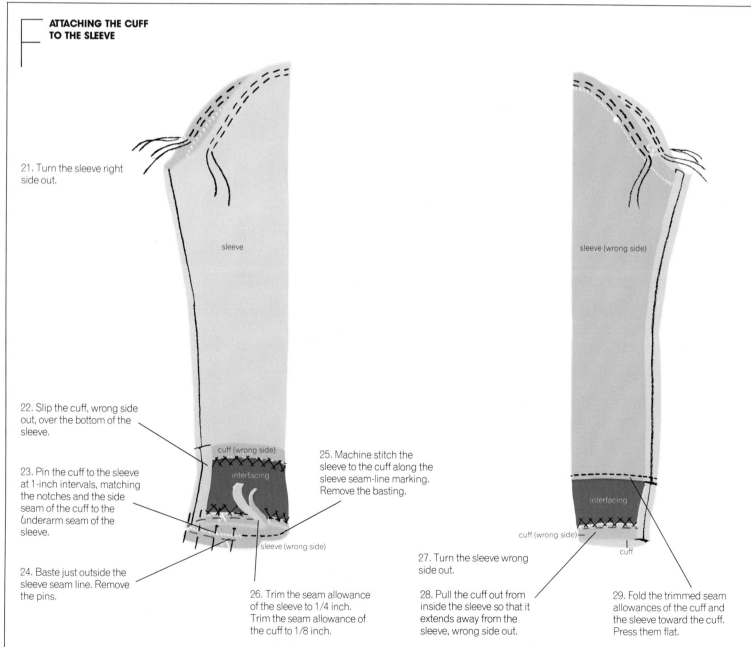

21. Turn the sleeve right side out.

sleeve

sleeve (wrong side)

22. Slip the cuff, wrong side out, over the bottom of the sleeve.

cuff (wrong side)

interfacing

23. Pin the cuff to the sleeve at 1-inch intervals, matching the notches and the side seam of the cuff to the underarm seam of the sleeve.

sleeve (wrong side)

24. Baste just outside the sleeve seam line. Remove the pins.

25. Machine stitch the sleeve to the cuff along the sleeve seam-line marking. Remove the basting.

26. Trim the seam allowance of the sleeve to 1/4 inch. Trim the seam allowance of the cuff to 1/8 inch.

interfacing

cuff (wrong side)

cuff

27. Turn the sleeve wrong side out.

28. Pull the cuff out from inside the sleeve so that it extends away from the sleeve, wrong side out.

29. Fold the trimmed seam allowances of the cuff and the sleeve toward the cuff. Press them flat.

G HEMMING THE CUFF

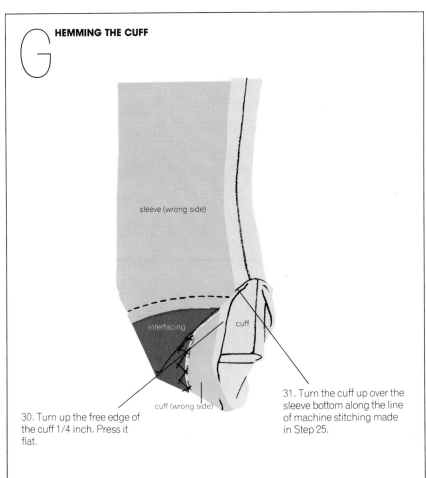

30. Turn up the free edge of the cuff 1/4 inch. Press it flat.

31. Turn the cuff up over the sleeve bottom along the line of machine stitching made in Step 25.

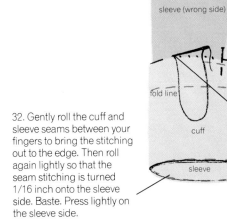

32. Gently roll the cuff and sleeve seams between your fingers to bring the stitching out to the edge. Then roll again lightly so that the seam stitching is turned 1/16 inch onto the sleeve side. Baste. Press lightly on the sleeve side.

33. Pin the upper edge of the cuff to the sleeve, matching the side seam of the cuff to the underarm seam of the sleeve.

34. Baste 1/8 inch below the folded edge of the cuff. Remove the pins.

35. Attach the cuff to the sleeve, using a slip stitch (*Appendix*). Remove the basting.

H FINISHING THE CUFF

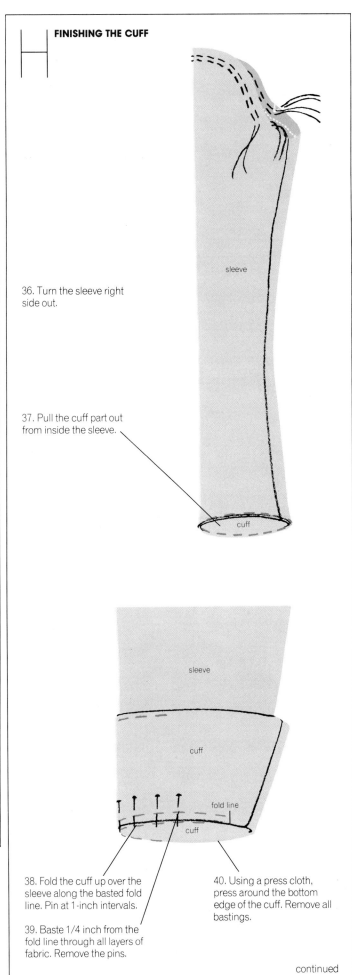

36. Turn the sleeve right side out.

37. Pull the cuff part out from inside the sleeve.

38. Fold the cuff up over the sleeve along the basted fold line. Pin at 1-inch intervals.

39. Baste 1/4 inch from the fold line through all layers of fabric. Remove the pins.

40. Using a press cloth, press around the bottom edge of the cuff. Remove all bastings.

continued

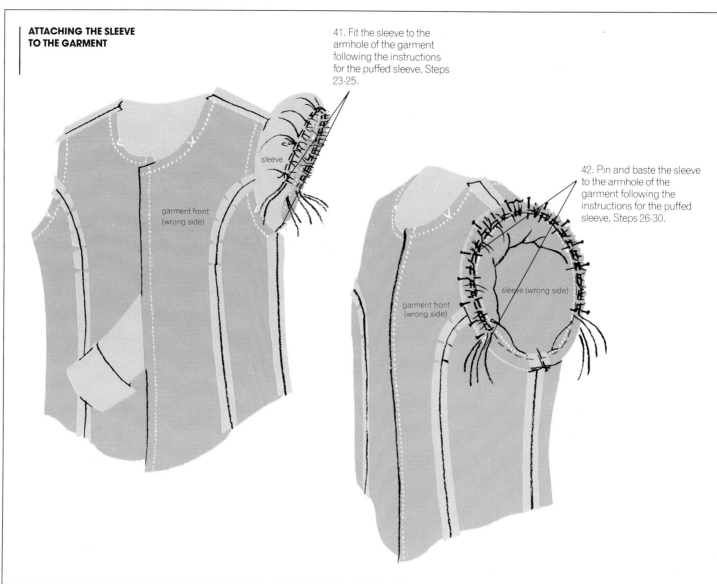

ATTACHING THE SLEEVE TO THE GARMENT

41. Fit the sleeve to the armhole of the garment following the instructions for the puffed sleeve, Steps 23-25.

sleeve

garment front (wrong side)

42. Pin and baste the sleeve to the armhole of the garment following the instructions for the puffed sleeve, Steps 26-30.

sleeve (wrong side)

garment front (wrong side)

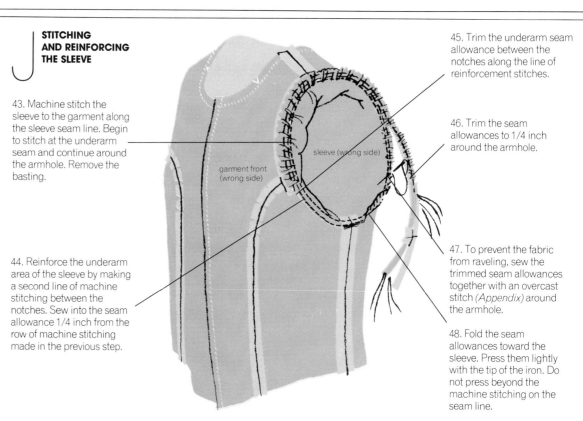

STITCHING AND REINFORCING THE SLEEVE

43. Machine stitch the sleeve to the garment along the sleeve seam line. Begin to stitch at the underarm seam and continue around the armhole. Remove the basting.

44. Reinforce the underarm area of the sleeve by making a second line of machine stitching between the notches. Sew into the seam allowance 1/4 inch from the row of machine stitching made in the previous step.

45. Trim the underarm seam allowance between the notches along the line of reinforcement stitches.

46. Trim the seam allowances to 1/4 inch around the armhole.

47. To prevent the fabric from raveling, sew the trimmed seam allowances together with an overcast stitch *(Appendix)* around the armhole.

48. Fold the seam allowances toward the sleeve. Press them lightly with the tip of the iron. Do not press beyond the machine stitching on the seam line.

garment front (wrong side)

sleeve (wrong side)

K FINISHING THE SLEEVES

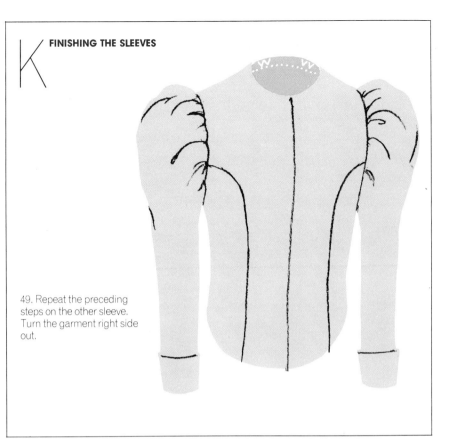

49. Repeat the preceding steps on the other sleeve. Turn the garment right side out.

THE BISHOP SLEEVE

A PREPARING THE SLEEVE AND THE CUFF OPENING

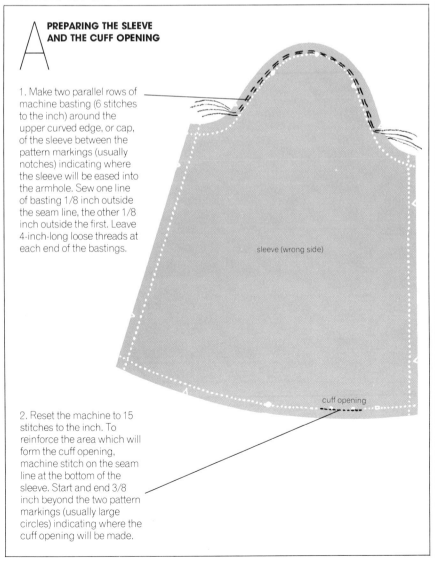

1. Make two parallel rows of machine basting (6 stitches to the inch) around the upper curved edge, or cap, of the sleeve between the pattern markings (usually notches) indicating where the sleeve will be eased into the armhole. Sew one line of basting 1/8 inch outside the seam line, the other 1/8 inch outside the first. Leave 4-inch-long loose threads at each end of the bastings.

sleeve (wrong side)

cuff opening

2. Reset the machine to 15 stitches to the inch. To reinforce the area which will form the cuff opening, machine stitch on the seam line at the bottom of the sleeve. Start and end 3/8 inch beyond the two pattern markings (usually large circles) indicating where the cuff opening will be made.

B MAKING THE CUFF OPENING

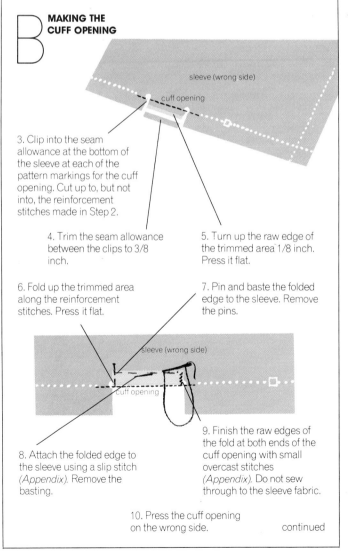

sleeve (wrong side)

cuff opening

3. Clip into the seam allowance at the bottom of the sleeve at each of the pattern markings for the cuff opening. Cut up to, but not into, the reinforcement stitches made in Step 2.

4. Trim the seam allowance between the clips to 3/8 inch.

5. Turn up the raw edge of the trimmed area 1/8 inch. Press it flat.

6. Fold up the trimmed area along the reinforcement stitches. Press it flat.

7. Pin and baste the folded edge to the sleeve. Remove the pins.

sleeve (wrong side)

cuff opening

8. Attach the folded edge to the sleeve using a slip stitch (Appendix). Remove the basting.

9. Finish the raw edges of the fold at both ends of the cuff opening with small overcast stitches (Appendix). Do not sew through to the sleeve fabric.

10. Press the cuff opening on the wrong side.

continued

C JOINING THE UNDERARM SEAM

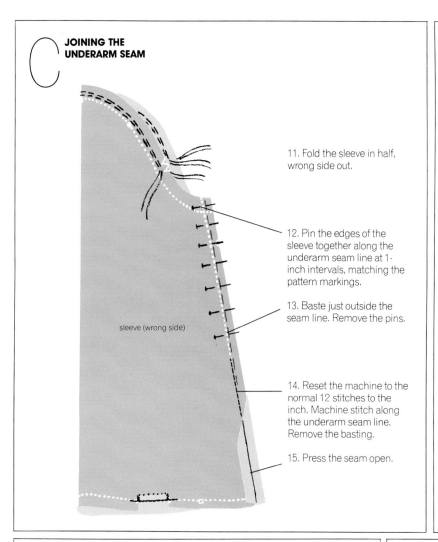

11. Fold the sleeve in half, wrong side out.

12. Pin the edges of the sleeve together along the underarm seam line at 1-inch intervals, matching the pattern markings.

13. Baste just outside the seam line. Remove the pins.

sleeve (wrong side)

14. Reset the machine to the normal 12 stitches to the inch. Machine stitch along the underarm seam line. Remove the basting.

15. Press the seam open.

D GATHERING THE BOTTOM OF THE SLEEVE

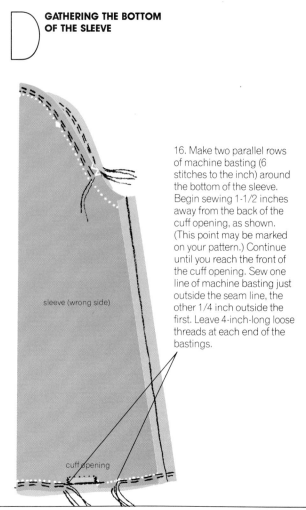

16. Make two parallel rows of machine basting (6 stitches to the inch) around the bottom of the sleeve. Begin sewing 1-1/2 inches away from the back of the cuff opening, as shown. (This point may be marked on your pattern.) Continue until you reach the front of the cuff opening. Sew one line of machine basting just outside the seam line, the other 1/4 inch outside the first. Leave 4-inch-long loose threads at each end of the bastings.

sleeve (wrong side)

cuff opening

E PREPARING THE CUFF

17. Lay the cuff, wrong side up, on a flat surface. Run a line of basting stitches along the fold line at the center of the cuff.

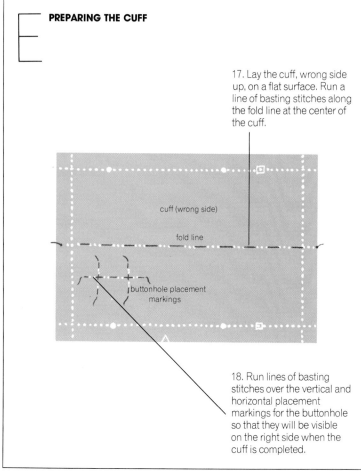

cuff (wrong side)

fold line

buttonhole placement markings

18. Run lines of basting stitches over the vertical and horizontal placement markings for the buttonhole so that they will be visible on the right side when the cuff is completed.

F PREPARING THE INTERFACING FOR THE CUFF

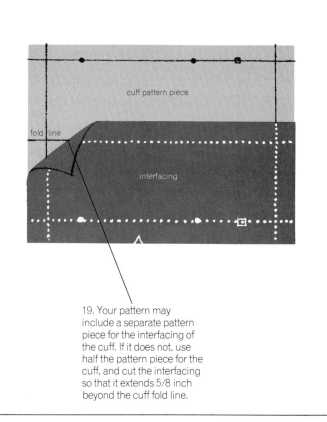

cuff pattern piece

fold line

interfacing

19. Your pattern may include a separate pattern piece for the interfacing of the cuff. If it does not, use half the pattern piece for the cuff, and cut the interfacing so that it extends 5/8 inch beyond the cuff fold line.

ATTACHING THE INTERFACING TO THE CUFF

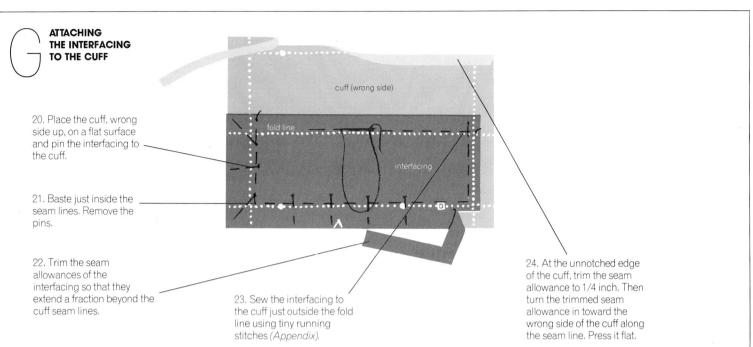

20. Place the cuff, wrong side up, on a flat surface and pin the interfacing to the cuff.

21. Baste just inside the seam lines. Remove the pins.

22. Trim the seam allowances of the interfacing so that they extend a fraction beyond the cuff seam lines.

23. Sew the interfacing to the cuff just outside the fold line using tiny running stitches (*Appendix*).

24. At the unnotched edge of the cuff, trim the seam allowance to 1/4 inch. Then turn the trimmed seam allowance in toward the wrong side of the cuff along the seam line. Press it flat.

H
COMPLETING THE CUFF

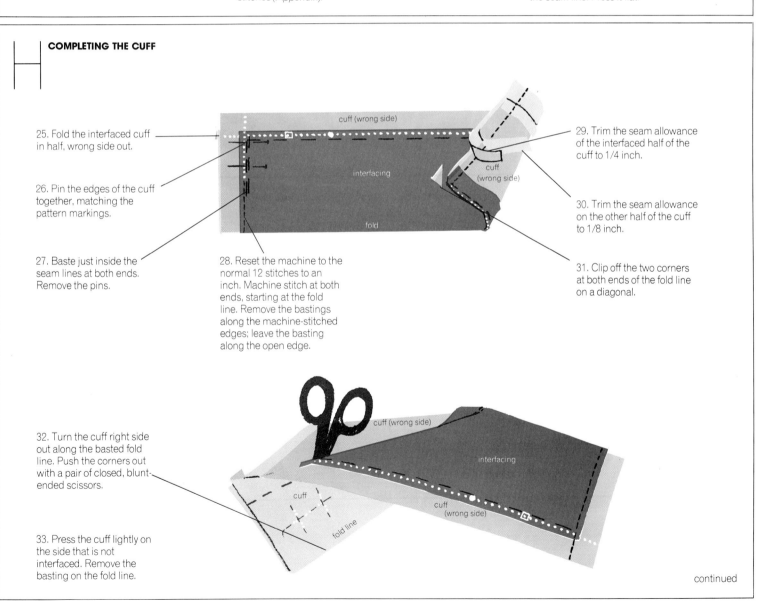

25. Fold the interfaced cuff in half, wrong side out.

26. Pin the edges of the cuff together, matching the pattern markings.

27. Baste just inside the seam lines at both ends. Remove the pins.

28. Reset the machine to the normal 12 stitches to an inch. Machine stitch at both ends, starting at the fold line. Remove the bastings along the machine-stitched edges; leave the basting along the open edge.

29. Trim the seam allowance of the interfaced half of the cuff to 1/4 inch.

30. Trim the seam allowance on the other half of the cuff to 1/8 inch.

31. Clip off the two corners at both ends of the fold line on a diagonal.

32. Turn the cuff right side out along the basted fold line. Push the corners out with a pair of closed, blunt-ended scissors.

33. Press the cuff lightly on the side that is not interfaced. Remove the basting on the fold line.

continued

ATTACHING THE CUFF TO THE SLEEVE

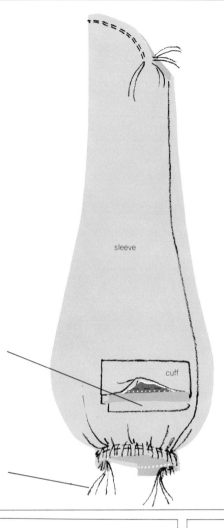

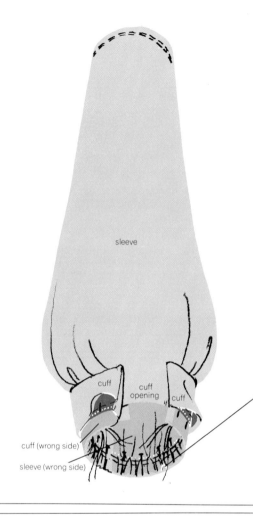

34. Turn the sleeve right side out.

35. Align the cuff with the bottom of the sleeve, keeping the open edge facing toward the bottom of the sleeve.

36. Gently pull the loose bobbin threads of the machine basting along the bottom of the sleeve; they are now on the outside of the sleeve. Pull first from one end, then from the other, until the bottom of the sleeve is approximately the same size as the cuff.

37. Pin the edge of the interfaced side of the cuff to the sleeve along the sleeve seam line, matching the pattern markings. Make sure the ends of the cuff are aligned with the edges of the cuff opening at the bottom of the sleeve.

J STITCHING THE CUFF TO THE SLEEVE

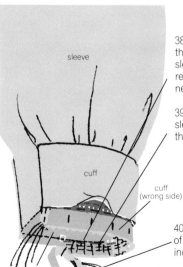

38. Hand baste the cuff to the sleeve, just outside the sleeve seam line, readjusting the gathers, if necessary. Remove the pins.

39. Machine stitch along the sleeve seam line. Remove the bastings.

40. Trim the seam allowance of the sleeve edge to 3/8 inch.

41. Trim the cuff edge to 1/4 inch.

K FINISHING THE CUFF

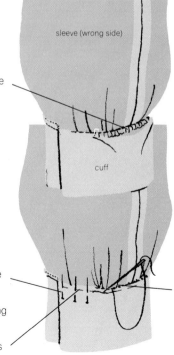

42. Turn the sleeve wrong side out and pull the cuff out.

43. Press the seam allowances trimmed in Steps 40 and 41 toward the cuff.

44. Pin the free edge of the cuff to the sleeve so that it just covers the line of machine stitching attaching the cuff to the sleeve.

45. Baste through all layers of fabric. Remove the pins.

46. Attach the cuff to the sleeve, using a slip stitch (Appendix). Sew through the threads of machine stitching attaching the cuff to the sleeve, rather than through the garment fabric, so that your stitches will not be visible on the outside of the sleeve. Remove the basting.

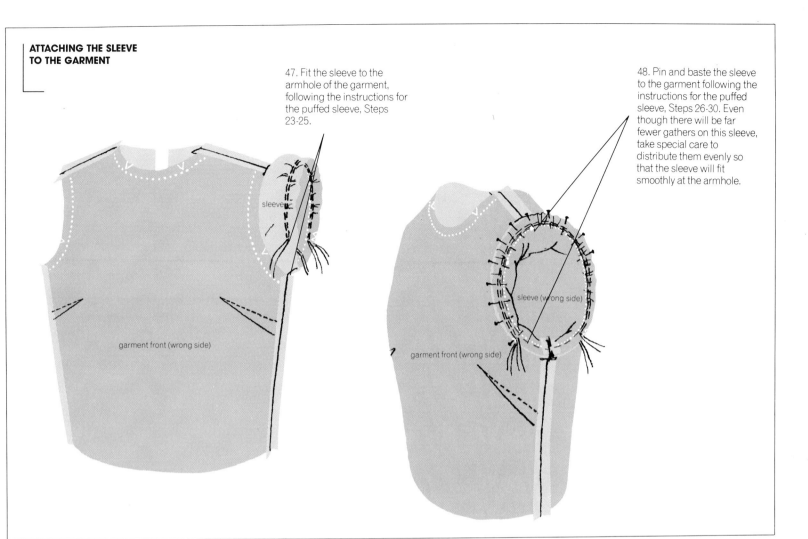

47. Fit the sleeve to the armhole of the garment, following the instructions for the puffed sleeve, Steps 23-25.

48. Pin and baste the sleeve to the garment following the instructions for the puffed sleeve, Steps 26-30. Even though there will be far fewer gathers on this sleeve, take special care to distribute them evenly so that the sleeve will fit smoothly at the armhole.

M | STITCHING AND REINFORCING THE SLEEVE

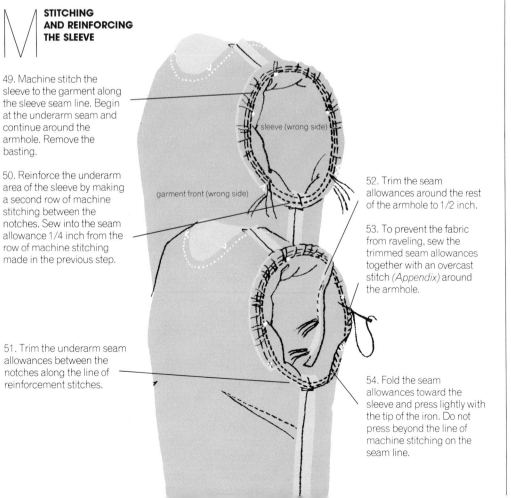

49. Machine stitch the sleeve to the garment along the sleeve seam line. Begin at the underarm seam and continue around the armhole. Remove the basting.

50. Reinforce the underarm area of the sleeve by making a second row of machine stitching between the notches. Sew into the seam allowance 1/4 inch from the row of machine stitching made in the previous step.

51. Trim the underarm seam allowances between the notches along the line of reinforcement stitches.

52. Trim the seam allowances around the rest of the armhole to 1/2 inch.

53. To prevent the fabric from raveling, sew the trimmed seam allowances together with an overcast stitch (Appendix) around the armhole.

54. Fold the seam allowances toward the sleeve and press lightly with the tip of the iron. Do not press beyond the line of machine stitching on the seam line.

N | FINISHING THE SLEEVES

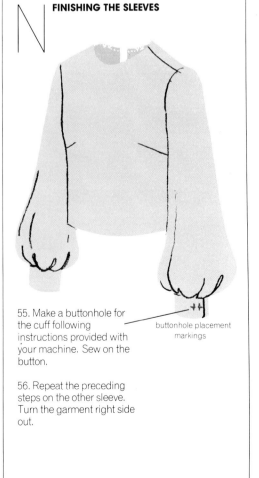

55. Make a buttonhole for the cuff following instructions provided with your machine. Sew on the button.

56. Repeat the preceding steps on the other sleeve. Turn the garment right side out.

buttonhole placement markings

The perky peplum

Though bustles went out of style with gaslights, the peplums they inspired remain as an attractive—and more subtle—legacy. The peplum of today is a kind of overskirt, a short flounce flowing from the waist over the hips, and designed to accentuate the silhouette of the dress. The peplum may be made in one piece or in two, as shown at right. In either case it should be faced if it is not lined, even where the pattern does not specify facing. A facing will give any fabric that is used for the peplum enough form and body to hang evenly and drape gracefully.

Because peplums are meant to flatter the figure, they can be lengthened or shortened as taste would dictate—just so long as they do not extend below the bottom line of the hips. As a general rule, peplums may be made of almost any firmly woven dress or suit fabric. But to ensure a perfect finished product, the length of the peplum should be as carefully coordinated with your fabric as it is with your figure: The longer the peplum, the lighter must be the fabric chosen. For short peplums, heavier fabrics look best.

The modern peplum, like the old-fashioned bustle from which it was adapted, makes a waistline look smaller and hips appear wider.

A PREPARING THE GARMENT

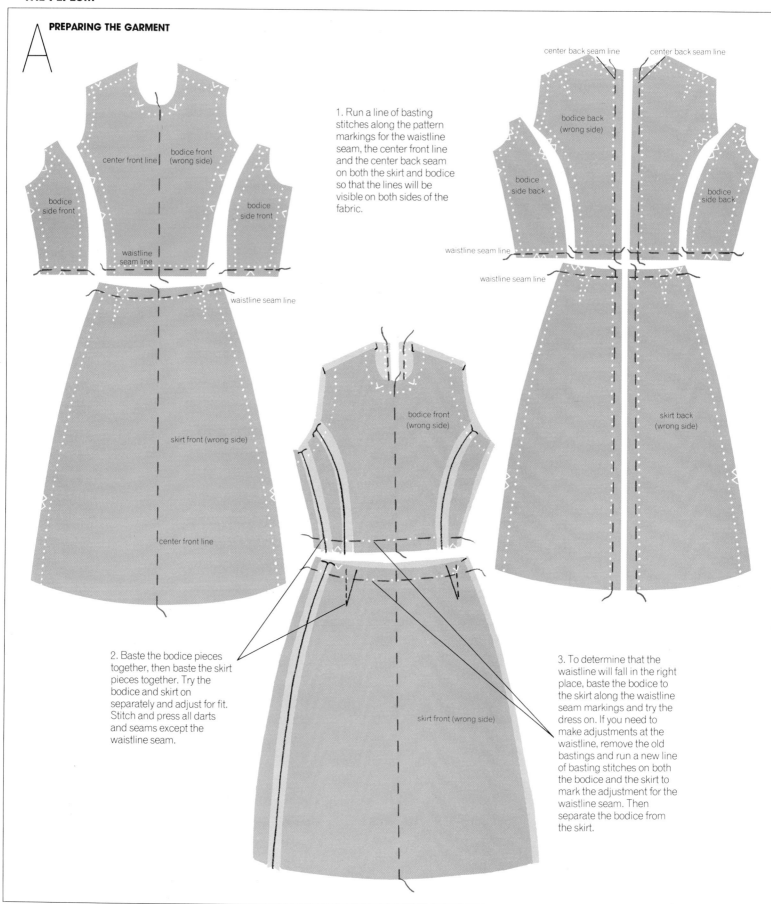

1. Run a line of basting stitches along the pattern markings for the waistline seam, the center front line and the center back seam on both the skirt and bodice so that the lines will be visible on both sides of the fabric.

center back seam line   center back seam line

bodice back (wrong side)

bodice side back

bodice side back

waistline seam line

waistline seam line

skirt back (wrong side)

center front line   bodice front (wrong side)

bodice side front

bodice side front

waistline seam line

waistline seam line

skirt front (wrong side)

center front line

bodice front (wrong side)

skirt front (wrong side)

2. Baste the bodice pieces together, then baste the skirt pieces together. Try the bodice and skirt on separately and adjust for fit. Stitch and press all darts and seams except the waistline seam.

3. To determine that the waistline will fall in the right place, baste the bodice to the skirt along the waistline seam markings and try the dress on. If you need to make adjustments at the waistline, remove the old bastings and run a new line of basting stitches on both the bodice and the skirt to mark the adjustment for the waistline seam. Then separate the bodice from the skirt.

B PREPARING THE PEPLUM AND THE PEPLUM FACING

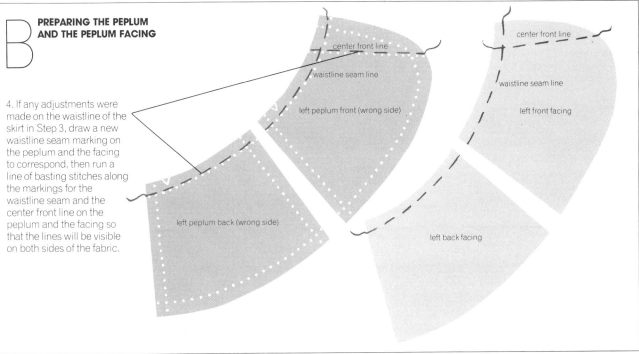

4. If any adjustments were made on the waistline of the skirt in Step 3, draw a new waistline seam marking on the peplum and the facing to correspond, then run a line of basting stitches along the markings for the waistline seam and the center front line on the peplum and the facing so that the lines will be visible on both sides of the fabric.

center front line

waistline seam line

left peplum front (wrong side)

left peplum back (wrong side)

center front line

waistline seam line

left front facing

left back facing

C FACING THE PEPLUM

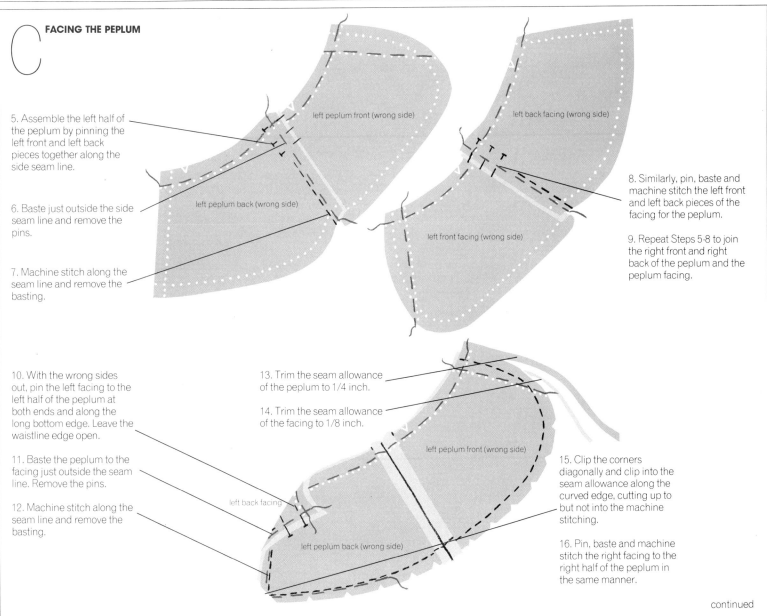

5. Assemble the left half of the peplum by pinning the left front and left back pieces together along the side seam line.

6. Baste just outside the side seam line and remove the pins.

7. Machine stitch along the seam line and remove the basting.

left peplum front (wrong side)

left peplum back (wrong side)

left back facing (wrong side)

left front facing (wrong side)

8. Similarly, pin, baste and machine stitch the left front and left back pieces of the facing for the peplum.

9. Repeat Steps 5-8 to join the right front and right back of the peplum and the peplum facing.

10. With the wrong sides out, pin the left facing to the left half of the peplum at both ends and along the long bottom edge. Leave the waistline edge open.

11. Baste the peplum to the facing just outside the seam line. Remove the pins.

12. Machine stitch along the seam line and remove the basting.

13. Trim the seam allowance of the peplum to 1/4 inch.

14. Trim the seam allowance of the facing to 1/8 inch.

left peplum front (wrong side)

left back facing

left peplum back (wrong side)

15. Clip the corners diagonally and clip into the seam allowance along the curved edge, cutting up to but not into the machine stitching.

16. Pin, baste and machine stitch the right facing to the right half of the peplum in the same manner.

continued

D FINISHING THE PEPLUM

17. Turn the peplum pieces right side out; push out the corners with the closed end of a blunt pair of scissors.

18. Roll the lower edge of the peplum between your fingers so that the seam joining the peplum to the facing will be turned slightly toward the underside. Baste and press.

19. Baste the open waistline edges of both pieces together just outside the seam-line markings.

20. Run a line of machine stitching just outside the basting to hold the waist seam line in shape. Remove the basting.

21. Place the two peplum sections on a flat surface, faced sides down. Pin the two sections together so that the right half overlaps the left half and the basted markings indicating the center front lines made in Step 4 are aligned.

22. Baste and remove the pins.

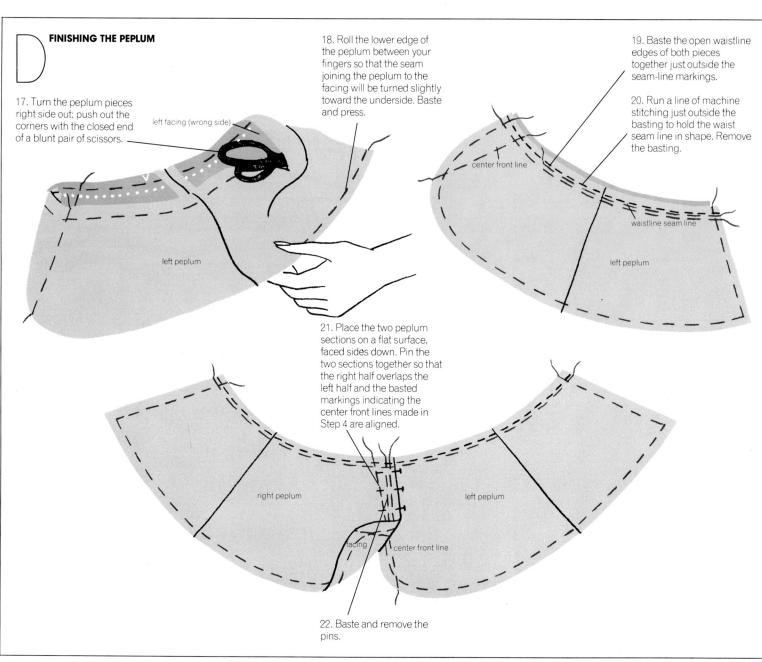

E ATTACHING THE PEPLUM TO THE SKIRT

23. Turn the skirt of the dress right side out.

24. Pin the peplum, faced side down, to the skirt. Pin first at the center front lines, then at the side seams.

25. Align the back edges of the peplum with the seam-line markings for the center back seam and pin. Then insert pins around the waist at 1-inch intervals.

26. Baste the peplum to the skirt just outside the waistline seam line and remove the pins.

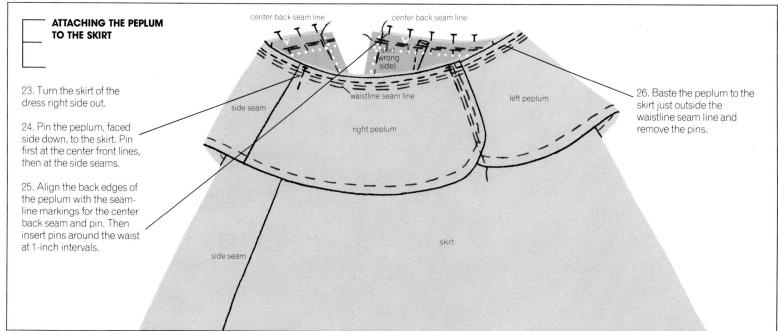

F ATTACHING THE BODICE TO THE SKIRT AND PEPLUM

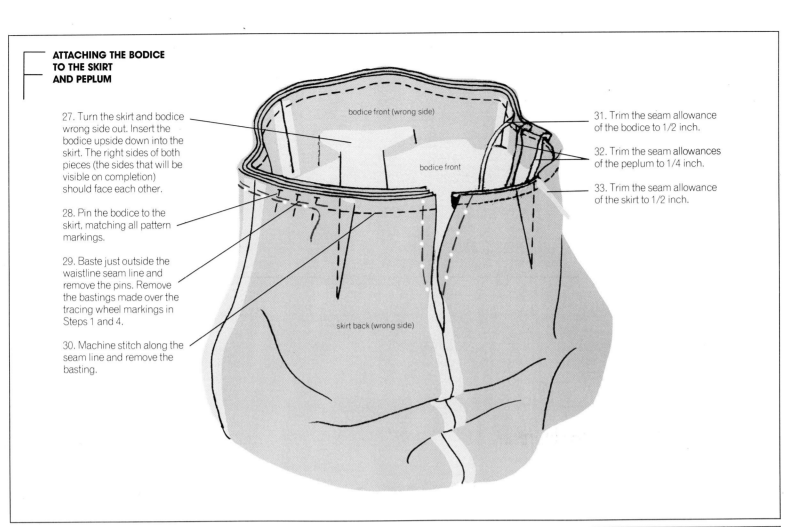

27. Turn the skirt and bodice wrong side out. Insert the bodice upside down into the skirt. The right sides of both pieces (the sides that will be visible on completion) should face each other.

28. Pin the bodice to the skirt, matching all pattern markings.

29. Baste just outside the waistline seam line and remove the pins. Remove the bastings made over the tracing wheel markings in Steps 1 and 4.

30. Machine stitch along the seam line and remove the basting.

31. Trim the seam allowance of the bodice to 1/2 inch.

32. Trim the seam allowances of the peplum to 1/4 inch.

33. Trim the seam allowance of the skirt to 1/2 inch.

bodice front (wrong side)

bodice front

skirt back (wrong side)

G FINISHING THE DRESS

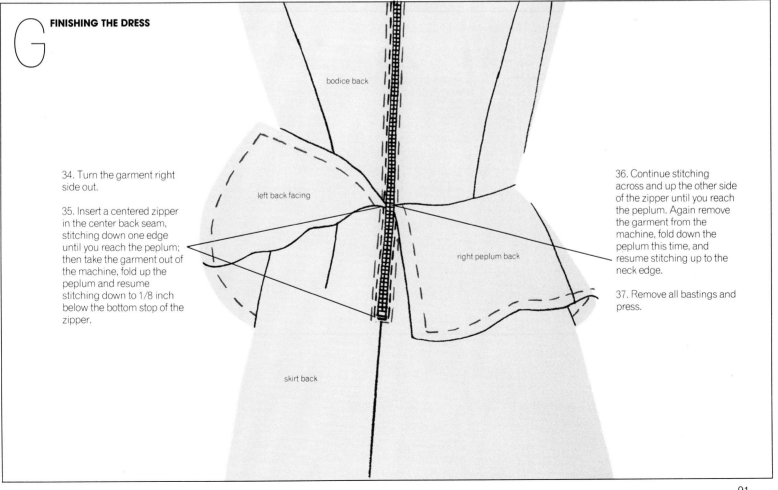

34. Turn the garment right side out.

35. Insert a centered zipper in the center back seam, stitching down one edge until you reach the peplum; then take the garment out of the machine, fold up the peplum and resume stitching down to 1/8 inch below the bottom stop of the zipper.

36. Continue stitching across and up the other side of the zipper until you reach the peplum. Again remove the garment from the machine, fold down the peplum this time, and resume stitching up to the neck edge.

37. Remove all bastings and press.

bodice back

left back facing

right peplum back

skirt back

3
FABRICS BY PATCHWORK

A mong the highlights of the year for earlier generations of Americans were the lively events known as quilting bees, the traditional occasions when women, often accompanied by their families, gathered from miles around to make quilted bed covers out of patchwork designs. The patterns they created and the techniques they used —not to mention the fun, good food and gossip that went along with such affairs

REVIVING A COLORFUL PIONEER ART

—have become the basis for a widespread revival of a distinctively American art form, fabrics made of quilted patchwork.

Some quilting in the 18th and 19th centuries, as today, was pieced—made up of small bits of cloth stitched together into squares called blocks, which were in turn sewn together into larger designs. Others were appliquéd—made by sewing cutout strips and swatches of fabric directly on larger backgrounds of cloth. In both cases the result was the thrifty, and often highly imaginative, creation of new fabrics out of the scraps of old. At their best the fabrics were veritable mosaics of ingenuity and affection, fashioned out of everything from fragments of grandpa's favorite waistcoat to salvaged bits of a bed coverlet beyond repair. The industrious ladies who produced the quilts generally worked at home alone, using their few idle daytime moments or their long winter evenings creating the components for the elaborate tops. But when they were ready to put their creations together, they often welcomed help and companionship in the quilting—sewing the pieces together into the decorative top, stitched through to an undercloth, usually of plain material, with a warm filler of fluffy cotton or wool batting in between.

Making a quilt was far from a frivolous pursuit: the winters in the hills and on the prairies were often bitter cold and the houses drafty, and an ample supply of bed covers was needed to keep everyone warm. Yet at the same time the pioneer women took artistic pride in their work, and though some popular patterns with names like Log Cabin, The Drunkard's Path or Goose Tracks appeared over and over again, no two quilts were ever precisely the same. Often the scraps of materials available suggested ideas for designs, which ranged from semirealistic scenes (a minority) to abstract geometric patterns, adapted and embellished into individual expressions that frequently rivaled the boldest canvases of what we call modern art.

No season lacked its quilting bees, but perhaps the best ones were those that came when the last flake of snow had melted, the birds had returned and the new leaves were puffing out the trees. The anticipation of such an occasion, and the preparations for it, could be as prodigious as the event itself. At least one main feast was assembled, each of the quilters supplying her quota of homemade pies, cakes, jams, cookies, breads or meats. The household that was to host the bee was scrubbed and scoured. Among the families of the guests, shoes were polished, hair was slicked, horses curried, buggies oiled.

When the appointed day arrived, the families came in buckboards, wagons, on horseback or, if they were near enough, on foot. With little time wasted on any more preliminaries, the ladies set up the elevated rectangular contraptions known as quilting frames and began working—in the front parlor, on the porch or, in fine weather, under shade trees outside. Seated around a quilt, they sewed, talked and sometimes sang. The men and boys stayed awhile to watch and offer comments, then drifted away to their own pursuits, swapping stories or perhaps helping the host fix a silo or work the fields. Children tumbled about everywhere like jellybeans; often smaller ones were assigned to stand under the quilt, catching the needles as they came through the layers, pulling them through and then poking them back.

Generally, it took only an afternoon of stitching for six or eight women to complete an ordinary or utility quilt. Special quilts required more quilters or more time. Of these, the most elaborate was the bride's quilt. Custom required that a young woman have 12 quilts ready by the time of her betrothal; the bride's quilt, which made a baker's dozen, was more splendid than the others and usually of an ornate design. Other special quilts included the Presentation, or Album, quilt, a handsome gift for a minister, mayor or other distinguished member of the community; the Freedom quilt, presented to a young man on his twenty-first birthday from his mother, sisters and female friends; and the Friendship Medley quilt, usually prepared for a girl by her friends and presented at a surprise party.

When the quilts were finished, it was time to put the quilting frames away and settle down for the festivities. The men and boys drifted back to wash up and the supper was brought out, often to a long table set up underneath the trees. The meal might be as grand as a Thanksgiving dinner, for the women had worked as hard preparing their food as they had on their quilts.

After the feast, the dancing and the games began, and the guests made up for the long, work-filled months of winter loneliness that had separated them. Girls were courted, business deals arranged, gossip exchanged, recipes discussed. Wrote Harriet Beecher Stowe in her novel *The Minister's Wooing:* "One might have learned in that instructive assembly how best to keep moths out of blankets—how to make fritters of India corn undistinguishable from oysters—how to bring up babies by hand . . . how to take out grease from a brocade . . . and how to put down the Democratic party." Finally, unless the bee was to be resumed

on the following day, the evening drew to a close in time for families to return to distant homes—and to plan for the next such event.

Although quilting bees are no longer big family functions, the custom has by no means disappeared from the American scene, and in fact quilting is enjoying a healthy comeback in a variety of ways. Church, social and senior-citizen groups set up old-fashioned quilting frames, put on a pot of tea and go happily to work. In less affluent regions, quilting has spurred a number of flourishing cottage industries that provide people with a new livelihood. Perhaps the best known of these is the Mountain Artisans, started in 1968 as part of the antipoverty program in the Appalachian hills; another is a Western group called Dakota Handcrafts, composed primarily of Sioux Indian women who sell their Indian-motif quilts through department stores. Many other women have taken to quilting simply as a fresh artistic challenge. Judy Raffael, a young California artist, has organized at least one highly successful quilting bee: she asked a group of friends to design and make their own quilt blocks at home, then invited them and their families for a weekend of work and play. After three days of busy bedlam, complete with children, pets and quantities of homemade food, they emerged with four handsome quilts, which artist Raffael exhibited on a triumphant cross-country tour.

Ms. Raffael's efforts, and the work of others like her, reflect how highly quilting has come to be regarded as an original artistic expression as well as a useful craft. And rightly so, for to examine the best quilts of yesteryear is to discover unexpected precursors of contemporary art. Some of the boldly colorful designs bear startling resemblances to the large-scale, hard-edge canvases of today. Others are nothing less than Op Art, their patched designs pulsating with color and eye-fooling effects. It is perhaps less surprising that New York's prestigious Whitney Museum not long ago mounted an exhibit devoted solely to patchwork quilts, mainly of the 19th Century, and that the show was a critical success.

Perhaps the most significant result of the patchwork revival, however, has been its adaptation to a wide range of uses beyond the walls of art galleries or the warm covers of a bed. Amateur sewers are still creating their own private kaleidoscopes of color, emulating their ancestors by making unique, one-of-a-kind fabrics out of saved-up scraps. But they are also using the fabrics thus produced in new ways: on pillow covers, as decorative wall hangings, tablecloths, slipcovers, and beyond that, for all sorts of clothing and accessories—jackets, skirts, shawls, cummerbunds, hats and even parasols. One enthusiastic lady, having tried everything from a lampshade to a dog blanket, finally topped these efforts with her ultimate achievement: she sat down and made a personal, pleasing and eminently comfortable quilt for her own bed.

A 19th Century quilting bee was much more than a sewing session, as indicated by this typically lively scene, painted by an unknown artist in a primitive style. The quilters bend industriously over their frame while assorted mates, friends and children dispense refreshments and indulge in long-awaited camaraderie. Amid all the conviviality, one couple, at right, seizes an opportunity for some surreptitious handholding.

A bright fancy of patchwork patterns

Few fabrics lend a more traditional—or more original—touch to contemporary apparel than quilted material created from patchwork. A midi-skirted outfit topped with a floppy hat, for example, is strikingly modern when made with the pattern our grandmothers called Fanny's Fan *(right)*. A simple cotton fabric becomes an elegant evening dress in a pattern known as Thousand Pyramids *(page 101)*. And when a design dubbed Streak of Lightning is used for a cape and skirt *(overleaf)*, the result is pure Op Art, even though the pattern itself is a century or more old.

The colorful names of such patchwork designs, which add their own charm to the overall air of nostalgia, have become fixtures in American folklore. Many of the names came from the experiences of early settlers; some are pure whimsey. Schoolhouse, at right, celebrates the humble structure that was familiar in every community; but Delectable Mountains *(overleaf)* is only fancifully suggestive of its title. The number of patterns created during the last few centuries defies estimate—many patterns come in infinite variations under different names—and the possibilities for unique quilt-fabric creations today are equally limitless.

White House Steps

Oak Leaf

Schoolhouse

Streak of Lightning

Crazy Quilt

Delectable Mountains

Geometrics

Thousand Pyramids

The craft of piecing

Once upon a time all patchwork was used for bed covers; and piecing together the patches was a winter's project. The oldest form of piecing is the aptly named crazy quilt, made up of randomly shaped scraps assembled on a backing fabric. Today the most popular form is so-called geometric piecing, made from precisely cut triangles, squares and strips that can be combined in all manner of patterns and sewn directly to one another.

Patchwork now is also used for clothes, for which a mere handful of patchwork blocks may be needed. Tightly woven materials of medium weight are best, provided they are not stiff or ravelly. For dressmaking, machine stitches are strongest.

To minimize complications, prepare an oversized square or rectangle of patchwork, then cut it to the shape of the garment piece.

A PATCHWORK OF STRIPS

A CUTTING OUT THE STRIPS OF FABRIC

1. Press the fabric you plan to use.

2. If both selvages are intact, straighten the cut edges of the fabric in the following fashion: place the fabric on a flat surface and lay an L-shaped square on one corner with the short edge of the square aligned with the selvage. Then draw a line with a chalk pencil or lead pencil along the long edge of the square—at right angles to the selvage and as close to the original cut edge as possible. Moving the square as you go, continue the line across the fabric to the opposite selvage. Trim the fabric along this line.

3. If only one selvage is intact, straighten the two cut edges that adjoin it as described in Step 2. The remaining edge may be left as is unless you plan to use it as a marking guide for patches. In that case, draw a line between the two straightened edges at right angles to both of them and as close to the outside of the fabric as possible. Trim along this line.

4. If both selvages have been removed, draw a pencil square on the fabric close to the outside edges and parallel to the grain of the fabric. Be sure that the lines meet at right angles. Trim along the lines.

5. Decide what size you want the finished strips to be and add 1/2 inch to both the length and width to provide for 1/4-inch seam allowances all around.

6. With the fabric wrong side up, mark off the length or width for each strip you will need along the edges on opposite sides of the fabric.

7. Draw a line between each pair of marks and cut out the strips along the lines.

8. Repeat Steps 1-7 for each piece of fabric you are using.

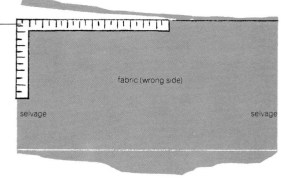

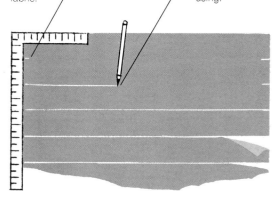

B JOINING THE STRIPS OF FABRIC

9. With the fabric wrong side down, arrange the strips attractively side by side into a row of the size you want.

10. Starting at one end of the row, turn the second strip wrong side up over the first strip.

11. Align the strips and insert pins, first at the corners and then at 4-inch intervals along the top edges.

12. If the strips are long or the fabric is slippery, baste 3/16 inch in from the edge and remove the pins.

13. Stitch the strips together by machine or by hand, leaving a 1/4-inch seam allowance. To sew them by hand, use a small running stitch, ending with a few backstitches, and cut off the thread. Remove the pins or basting. Spread the strips flat, wrong side up, and press the seam allowances toward the first strip.

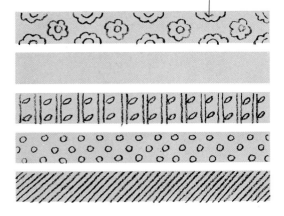

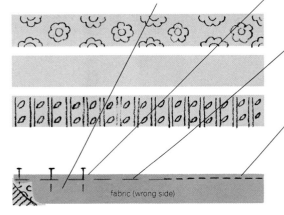

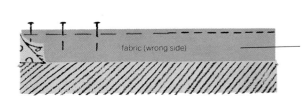

14. Turn the third strip in the row wrong side up on top of the second strip. Align the edge of the third strip with the unsewn edge of the second one. Then pin, baste and stitch the strips together, following the directions in Steps 11-13. Press the seam allowances toward the first strip.

continued

C FINISHING THE PATCHWORK

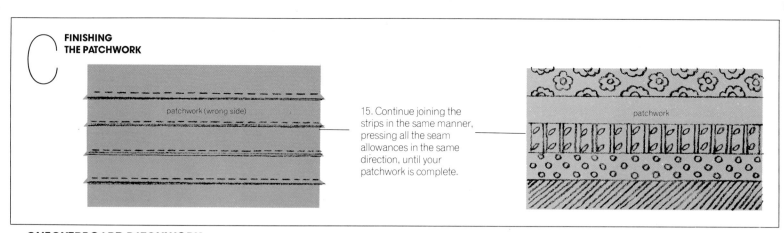

15. Continue joining the strips in the same manner, pressing all the seam allowances in the same direction, until your patchwork is complete.

CHECKERBOARD PATCHWORK

A MEASURING AND MARKING THE FABRIC

1. Press the fabric you plan to use and straighten the cut edges, following the instructions for a patchwork of strips, Steps 2-4.

2. Decide what size you want the finished squares to be and add 1/2 inch to provide a 1/4-inch seam allowance all around.

3. With the fabric wrong side up, mark along the edges on opposite sides of the fabric the distance figured in Step 2 for each row of squares you will need.

4. Draw a line between each pair of marks.

5. Make marks at the same interval along the two remaining edges of the fabric.

6. Draw lines to connect the marks.

B CUTTING OUT THE SQUARES OF FABRIC

7. Cut the fabric into strips along the lines you drew in Step 4.

8. Cut the strips into squares along the lines you drew in Step 6.

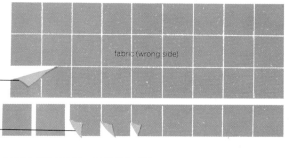

9. Repeat Steps 1-8 for each piece of fabric.

C JOINING THE SQUARES OF FABRIC INTO STRIPS

10. With the fabric wrong side down, arrange the squares attractively in a row of the desired length.

11. Starting at one end of the row, turn the second square wrong side up over the first square.

12. Align the edges to be joined and pin them at the corners. Pin large squares in the middle as well.

13. Stitch the squares together by machine or by hand, leaving a 1/4-inch seam allowance. To sew them by hand, use a small running stitch, ending with a few backstitches, and cut off the thread. Remove the pins. Press the seam allowance toward the first square.

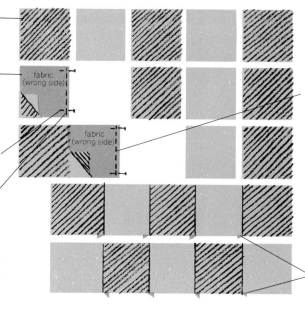

14. Open the joined squares and lay them flat, wrong side down. Place the third square, wrong side up, on top of the second square. Align the edges, then pin and stitch them, following the directions in Steps 12 and 13. Press the seam allowances toward the first square.

15. Continue joining the squares in the same manner, until the strip is the length you want.

16. Repeat Steps 10-15 for the second row of squares, pressing the seams all in the other direction—away from the first square.

D FINISHING THE PATCHWORK OF STRIPS

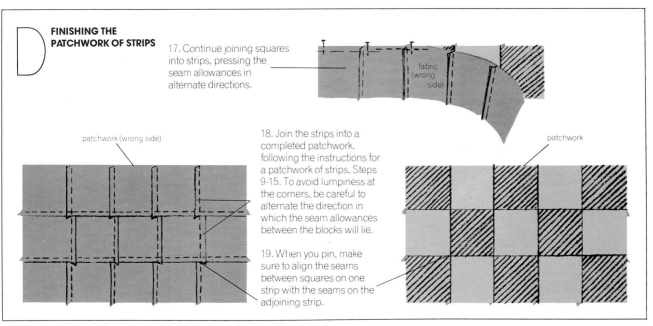

17. Continue joining squares into strips, pressing the seam allowances in alternate directions.

18. Join the strips into a completed patchwork, following the instructions for a patchwork of strips, Steps 9-15. To avoid lumpiness at the corners, be careful to alternate the direction in which the seam allowances between the blocks will lie.

19. When you pin, make sure to align the seams between squares on one strip with the seams on the adjoining strip.

patchwork (wrong side)

patchwork

A PATCHWORK OF LARGE AND SMALL SQUARES

A MEASURING AND CUTTING THE SQUARES OF FABRIC

1. To make a patchwork pattern that alternates large plain squares with equal-sized patchwork blocks of smaller squares, first decide on the size of the larger squares—4 inches for a vest or place mat, up to 12 or even 16 inches for bedcovers or draperies.

2. To determine the size of the small squares within the patchwork blocks, divide the length of one side of the large square by two for a four-square patchwork, by three for a nine-square patchwork.

3. Add 1/2 inch to the measurements of both the large and small squares to provide for a 1/4-inch seam allowance all around each piece. Press the fabric you plan to use and straighten the cut edges, following the instructions for a patchwork of strips, Steps 2-4.

4. Cut out as many of the large and small squares as you will need, following the directions for checkerboard patchwork, Steps 3-8.

5. With the fabric wrong side down, arrange small squares attractively into blocks of the size you want.

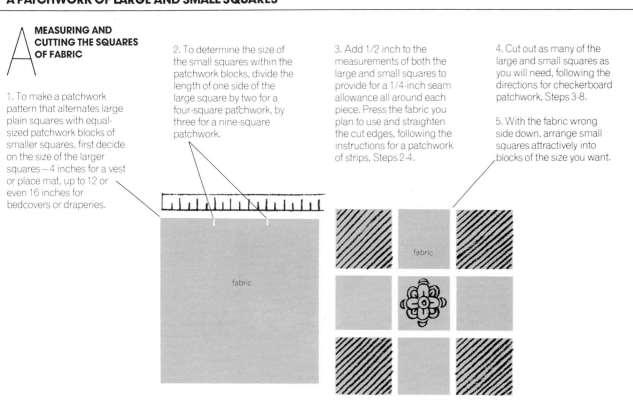

fabric

fabric

B JOINING THE SMALL SQUARES INTO BLOCKS

6. Assemble the small squares into strips, following the instructions for checkerboard patchwork, Steps 11-17.

7. Sew the strips into blocks, following the instructions for a patchwork of strips, Steps 9-14.

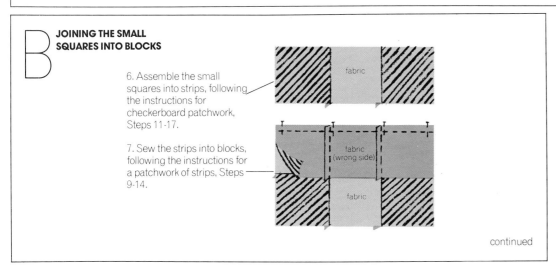

fabric

fabric (wrong side)

fabric

continued

JOINING THE PLAIN AND PATCHWORK SQUARES TOGETHER

8. Arrange the patchwork blocks alternately with the plain squares to form a strip of the length you want.

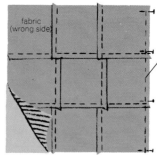

9. Then stitch the squares and blocks together, following the instructions for checkerboard patchwork, Steps 11-17.

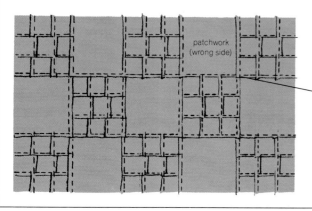

10. Join the strips into a completed patchwork, following the instructions for a patchwork of strips, Steps 9-15. When you pin, be careful to align the seams between the blocks and large squares on one strip with the seams on the adjoining strip.

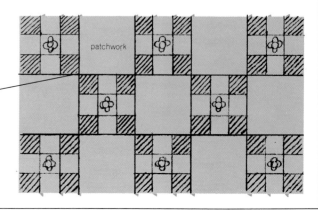

A PINWHEEL PATCHWORK OF RIGHT TRIANGLES

A MEASURING AND CUTTING THE TRIANGLES OF FABRIC

1. Press the fabric you plan to use, then straighten the cut edges, following the instructions for a patchwork of strips, Steps 2-4.

2. Decide how large you want the basic pinwheel to be—from 4 inches for a blouse or vest up to 16 inches for a floor-length skirt. The traditional pinwheel shown here is a square block made up of eight identical right-angle triangles with two sides of the same length. The triangles are stitched together in pairs to form four small squares. In this example the block is 8 inches square; the triangle sides are 4 inches long. To create larger or smaller blocks, figure that the length of one side of the pinwheel block will equal twice the length of one side of the finished triangle.

3. Draw a triangle of the size you need on a piece of cardboard or stiff paper, using a ruler to ensure that the two sides are the same length and that they meet at right angles.

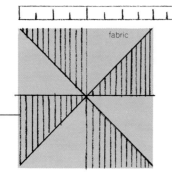

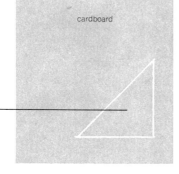

4. To provide for a 1/4-inch seam allowance all around the triangle, extend the lines that form each side by 5/8 inch.

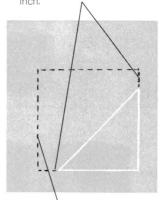

5. Squares are easier than triangles to mark on fabric, so draw lines from the triangle to form a square as shown.

6. Use the cardboard square as a pattern to determine marking intervals along the length and width of the fabric. Then mark and cut the fabric into squares, following the directions for checkerboard patchwork, Steps 3-8.

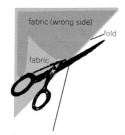

7. Fold each square in half diagonally and press, then cut along the folded edge to form two triangles of fabric.

8. Repeat Steps 6-7 for each piece of fabric.

B JOINING THE TRIANGLES INTO SQUARES

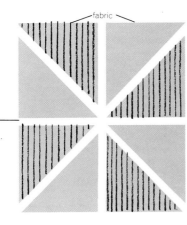

9. For each pinwheel, place eight triangles wrong side down on a flat surface and arrange them in an alternating pattern as shown.

10. To join two triangles together into a square, place one triangle wrong side down and set the adjoining one on top, wrong side up. Align the long edges.

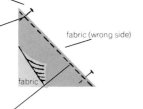

11. Pin the triangles together at both ends of the long edge. If the triangles are very large, baste them together 3/16 inch from the edge.

12. Stitch the triangles together by machine or by hand, leaving a 1/4-inch seam allowance. To sew them by hand use a small running stitch, ending with a few backstitches, and cut off the thread. Open the triangles, wrong sides up, and press the seam allowances to one side in either direction.

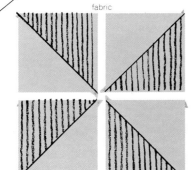

13. Repeat Steps 10-12 until all of your triangles are sewn into squares.

14. Stitch the squares into two strips, following the instructions for checkerboard patchwork, Steps 10-13. Be sure that all three seam allowances within the strip are pressed in the same direction.

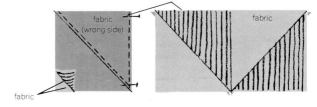

15. Join the strips into a completed pinwheel, following the instructions for a patchwork of strips, Steps 9-13. Be sure that the seam allowances on the top strip face in the opposite direction from those on the bottom strip.

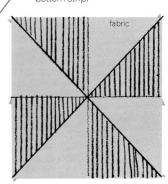

C JOINING THE PINWHEELS

16. Join the pinwheels into strips, following the instructions for checkerboard patchwork, Steps 10-17.

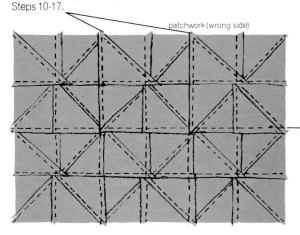

17. Join the strips of pinwheels into a completed patchwork, following the instructions for a patchwork of strips, Steps 9-15.

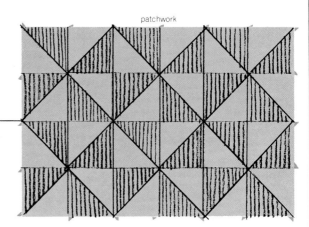

A PATCHWORK OF PYRAMIDS

A MAKING THE PATTERN

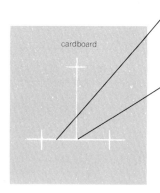

cardboard

1. On a piece of stiff cardboard, draw a line the length you want for the base of the triangle.

2. Starting at the center of the base line, draw another line of the same length at right angles to the base.

3. To complete the triangle, draw lines from the top of the center line to the ends of the base line.

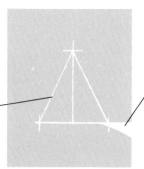

4. Cut the triangular pattern out of the cardboard along the lines.

B MARKING AND CUTTING THE FABRIC

5. Press the fabric you plan to use, then straighten the cut edges, following the instructions in a patchwork of strips, Steps 2-4.

6. With the fabric wrong side up, place the cardboard pattern base downward on the lower left-hand corner. To provide for 1/4-inch seam allowances all around the fabric triangle, the bottom left corner of the pattern should be 1/2 inch from the left side of the fabric and the base of the pattern should align with the crosswise grain of the fabric 1/4 inch above the cut edge.

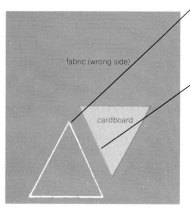

fabric (wrong side)

cardboard

7. Draw a line—which will be your seam line—on the fabric by tracing around the pattern with a pencil.

8. Turn the pattern around, base side up, and move it to the right so that the left side of the pattern is 1/2 inch away from, and parallel to, the right side of the first triangle you drew.

9. Slide the pattern upward until the tip of the triangle is 1/2 inch above the cut edge of the fabric. Align the base with the crosswise fabric grain and trace around the pattern.

10. Continue turning the pattern and tracing triangles until you complete one row.

11. Start a second row 1 1/2 inches above the tip of the first triangle.

12. Draw as many rows of triangles as you need. Cut out a new cardboard pattern if the first one becomes frayed.

13. To cut out the fabric triangles, start with the one in the lower left-hand corner. Make the first cut diagonally from the corner of the fabric to a point about 1/2 inch above the tip of the triangle, keeping the scissors parallel to the side of the triangle and 1/4 inch away from it for the seam allowance. Make the second cut diagonally from a point about 1/2 inch to the right of the bottom right-hand corner up to the end of the first cut.

14. To release the second triangle, make a diagonal cut from the bottom edge of the fabric to a point about 1/4 inch above the base. Then cut crosswise parallel to the base to leave a 1/4-inch seam allowance.

15. Repeat Steps 13 and 14 across the first row.

16. Make the first cut in the second row diagonally from a point about 1/2 inch directly below the tip of the triangle up to the left-hand edge of the fabric. The second cut should be from the same point to about 1/4 inch above the base. Cut crosswise to free the base, then repeat Steps 13 and 14 across the second row.

17. Continue row by row until all the triangles are cut out.

18. Repeat Steps 5-17 for each fabric you are using.

C JOINING THE PYRAMIDS INTO A STRIP

19. With the wrong side down, arrange the triangles in an alternating pattern in a row of the length you want.

20. Starting at one end of the row, turn the second triangle wrong side up and place it over the first triangle.

21. Align the seam lines of the edges that are to be joined, and pin the triangles together at the corners. If the triangles are large or the fabric is slippery, baste 3/16 inch outside the seam lines and remove the pins.

22. Machine stitch along the seam lines, or sew the triangles together by hand with a small running stitch, ending with a few back stitches. Cut off the thread, and remove the pins or the basting.

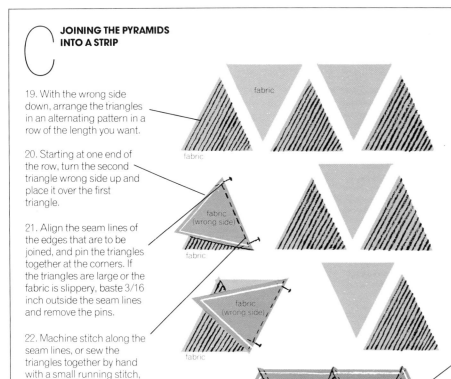

23. Open the joined triangles so that they are wrong side up. Press the seam toward the first triangle so that it will be out of the way of the next seam line you will be sewing.

24. Place the joined triangles on a flat surface, wrong side down, and set the third triangle in the row wrong side up on top of the second triangle. Then, to join the third triangle to the first two, pin, baste and stitch the seam lines, following the instructions in Steps 21-23.

25. Continue joining the triangles in the same manner until the strip is complete.

D JOINING THE STRIPS OF PYRAMIDS

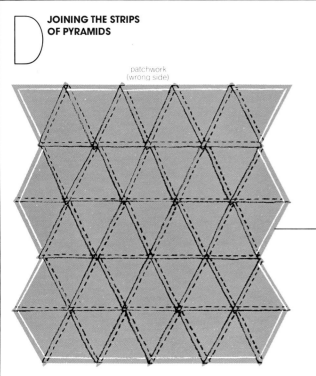

26. Continue joining triangles into strips as shown until you have all you need.

27. To make sure that the seams between the strips will lie flat and smooth, arrange the strips together wrong side up. Then check to see that adjoining seam allowances lie in opposite directions.

28. Join the strips of triangles into a completed patchwork, following the instructions for a patchwork of strips, Steps 10-15. To be sure that the points of the triangles on one strip will be perfectly aligned with those on the adjoining strip, hand stitch instead of machine stitching.

A COMPLEX GEOMETRIC PATCHWORK

A MAKING THE PATTERN

1. Decide what size you want the basic patchwork block to be—any size from 6 inches up to 16 inches would be appropriate. Then cut a square of that size out of stiff cardboard. Copy the design shown here inside the square, using a ruler and drawing the interior cross first, the triangles last.

2. Decide what fabric you want to use for each patch. Assign a number to each fabric and label it accordingly.

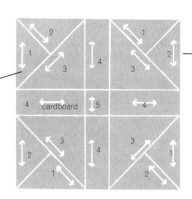

3. Number every part of the pattern design to correspond with the fabric, and draw an arrow representing the grain line on each different geometric shape; to ensure smooth, flat seams, no two adjoining edges should both be cut on the bias.

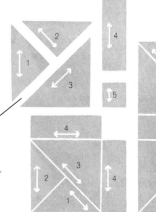
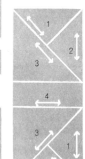

4. Cut the design apart to make one pattern piece for each geometric shape in every number. Save the uncut pieces as replacements for frayed pattern pieces.

B MARKING AND CUTTING THE FABRIC

5. Press the fabric you plan to use and straighten the cut edges, following the instructions for a patchwork of strips, Steps 2-4.

6. Place the fabric wrong side up and set the pattern piece of the corresponding number in one corner 1/4 inch in from the edges to leave enough fabric for seam allowances. Make sure the arrow runs in the same direction as the grain of the fabric.

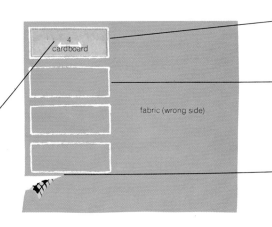

7. Draw a chalk or pencil line—which will be your seam line—on the fabric around the pattern piece.

8. Move the pattern piece 1/2 inch from the first outline and trace around it again. Continue moving and tracing the pattern piece until you have enough patches for the blocks you plan to make.

9. Cut out all the patches, leaving a 1/4-inch seam allowance beyond the lines all around each piece.

10. Repeat Steps 6-9 for each fabric and pattern piece you are using.

C JOINING THE TRIANGULAR PATCHES INTO SQUARES

11. Lay out all the patches for one block in the arrangement you want.

12. Join two small triangular patches first. Place them together, wrong sides out, and align the penciled seam lines on which they are to be joined. Pin the corners.

13. Hand stitch along the seam line with a small running stitch, ending with a few backstitches, and cut off the thread. Remove the pins.

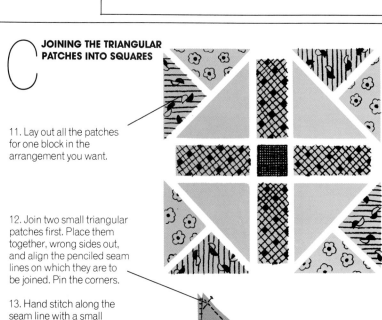

fabric (wrong side)

14. Open the joined triangles wrong side up and press the seam allowance toward triangle 2.

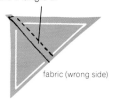

fabric (wrong side)

15. Turn the joined triangles wrong side down and place the large triangular piece on top of them, wrong side up. Align the seam lines and pin at the corners.

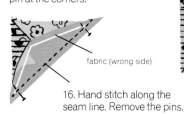

fabric (wrong side)

16. Hand stitch along the seam line. Remove the pins.

17. Now turn the square wrong side up and press the seam away from the two small triangles.

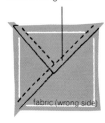

fabric (wrong side)

18. Repeat Steps 12-17 to join the other triangular patches into squares.

ASSEMBLING THE BLOCK

19. Connect pairs of small squares, each with a rectangular piece in between, to form two strips, following the instructions for checkerboard patchwork, Steps 10-15.

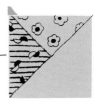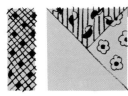

22. Join the strips into a block, following the instructions for a patchwork of strips, Steps 9-15.

20. Turn the strips wrong side up and press the two center seams toward each other.

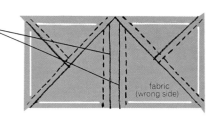

fabric (wrong side)

21. Connect the remaining two rectangular patches with the square, and press the two center seams away from each other.

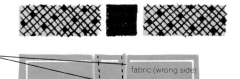

fabric (wrong side)

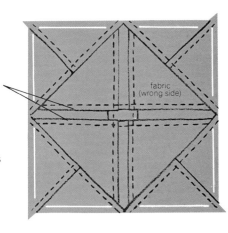

fabric (wrong side)

23. Turn the block over so that it is wrong side up and press the two center seams toward each other.

24. Repeat Steps 11-23 until you have sewn all the blocks you need. If the old pattern pieces become frayed, cut out new ones from the remaining cardboard design.

E

JOINING THE BLOCKS

25. Sew the blocks together into strips, following the instructions for checkerboard patchwork, Steps 10-17.

26. Sew the strips together into a completed patchwork, following the instructions for a patchwork of strips, Steps 9-15.

patchwork (wrong side)

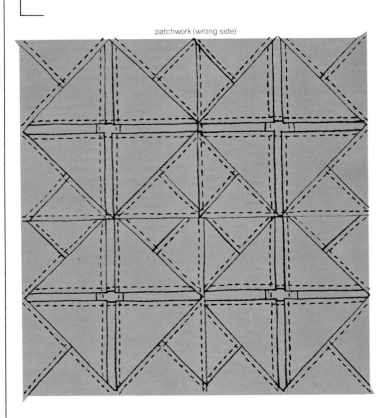

patchwork

A CRAZY-QUILT PATCHWORK

A — PREPARING THE BACKING FABRIC

1. Press the fabric you plan to use. For a crazy-quilt patchwork you will need not only patches, but also backing fabric for assembling the patches. Unbleached muslin is satisfactory for most purposes; wash the muslin to shrink it and remove the starch sizing before pressing.

2. Decide what size you want the basic block of patchwork to be; in most designs, the blocks are 8 to 18 inches square. Add 1/2 inch to both the width and length to provide a 1/4-inch seam allowance all around the block.

3. Using the measurement arrived at in Step 2 as your marking interval, mark and cut out as many blocks of backing fabric as you will need, following the instructions for checkerboard patchwork, Steps 3-8.

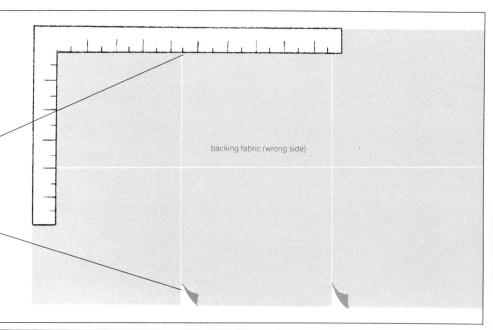

backing fabric (wrong side)

B — STARTING THE PATCHWORK

4. Arrange patches of fabric, wrong side down, on a square of backing, letting the edges of the patches overlap each other by at least 1/2 inch. Pin each patch in place with one or two pins.

5. Trim off the edges of any patches that extend beyond the edges of the backing.

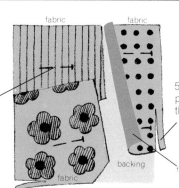

fabric · fabric · backing · fabric (wrong side)

C — ATTACHING THE PATCHES

6. Starting in the top left-hand corner of the block, pin the outside corner of the first fabric patch to the top and side edges of the backing. Fold back the overlapping edges of the adjoining patches to keep them out of the way.

7. Stitch along the top and side of the patch by machine, or by hand, 3/16 inch from the outside edges. To sew the patch by hand, use a small running stitch, ending with a few back-stitches. Cut off the thread. Remove the pins from the patch.

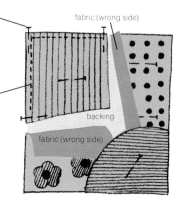

fabric (wrong side) · backing · fabric (wrong side)

8. With a pencil, lightly mark dots outside both sides of the lower left-hand corner patch 1/4 inch below the top edge of the patch.

9. Unpin the lower left-hand patch and turn it upside down and wrong side up over the upper left-hand patch. The bottom edge of the second patch should extend 1/4 inch below the pencil dots.

10. Pin along the edge where the two patches meet.

11. Sew the two patches to the backing along the pinned edge by machine or by hand, leaving a 1/4-inch seam allowance. Remove the pins.

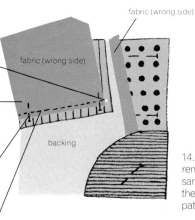

fabric (wrong side) · fabric (wrong side) · backing

12. Turn the second patch back into place, wrong side down, and press the seam flat.

13. Pin the patch to the backing along the outside edges and sew in place. Remove the pins.

14. Continue stitching the remaining patches in the same fashion, moving down the right-hand side of the patches already stitched.

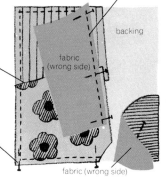

backing · fabric (wrong side) · fabric (wrong side)

D ATTACHING CURVED PIECES

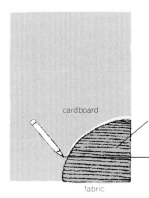

15. If you have a patchwork piece with a curved edge, unpin the patch from the backing and place it wrong side down on stiff cardboard.

16. With a pencil, trace around the edge of the patch. Remove the piece of fabric.

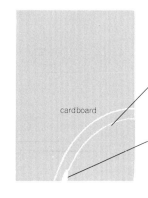

17. Draw a second curved line on the cardboard, freehand, 1/4 inch inside the curve of the pattern you traced.

18. Cut out the pattern piece along the second, or inner, curved line.

19. Turn the piece of fabric wrong side up. Place the cardboard pattern on the patch so that the curved edge of the pattern is 1/4 inch from the curved edge of the patch. Draw a line —which will be your seam line—on the fabric by tracing along the curved edge of the cardboard.

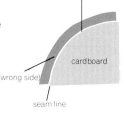

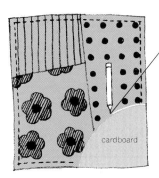

20. Using the pattern, draw a curved seam line on the partly finished patchwork block.

21. Place the curved patch, wrong side up, on top of the partly finished patchwork.

22. Align the center of the curved seam line on the patch with the center of the line drawn in Step 20 on the patchwork. Insert a pin to hold the seam lines together.

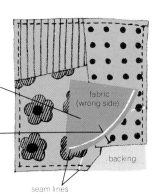

23. Starting in the center of the curve and working first in one direction, then in the other, pin the two curved seam lines together at 1/2-inch intervals. Ease the extra fullness of the fabric evenly into the seam along the curve as you go.

24. Hand stitch along the pinned seam with a small running stitch, ending with a few backstitches. Cut off the thread and remove the pins.

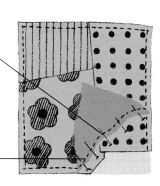

E FINISHING THE PATCHWORK

25. Turn the piece so that it is wrong side down and press the curved seam. Attach the outer edges as you did with the other pieces.

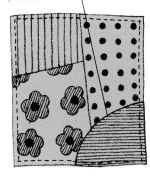

26. Repeat Steps 4-25 until you have all the blocks you need.

27. Join the blocks into strips following the instructions for a checkerboard patchwork, Steps 10-17.

28. Join the strips into a completed patchwork, following the instructions for a patchwork of strips, Steps 9-15.

The artistry of appliqué

Appliqué, which literally means applying one fabric to another, is a variety of patchwork: the designs are generally made with bits of leftover fabric. Unlike piecing, however, appliqué does not require that the scraps be fitted together jigsaw fashion. Therefore, they can be cut into any shape. Almost every sort of fabric is usable if it doesn't ravel; and the greater the variety of colors and designs, the brighter the effect.

Traditionally, appliqué is done by hand, but for garments that must be laundered frequently, zigzag machine stitching can be used.

The success of any appliqué design depends on meticulously maintaining the shapes of the pieces. For most shapes, running a row of machine stitches around the seam line of each piece before turning under the seam allowance will prevent raveling or stretching. For curves, clipping or notching the stitched edges will make it possible to turn the edges underneath as smooth arcs and corners so that the finished appliqué turns out as expected.

114

A BASIC APPLIQUÉ

A — MAKING A PATTERN FOR THE DESIGN

1A. To make a pattern for a design such as the flower shown here, draw each element of the design freehand on a piece of stiff cardboard or trace the design following the instructions in the Appendix.

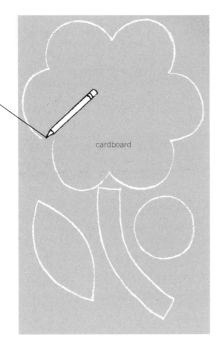

cardboard

1B. Alternatively, you can make a pattern for such symmetrical designs as the flower by folding and cutting paper. First cut a paper square the size you want the finished piece to be, then fold it into as many layers as you need for your design. (To make the flower, fold the square in half diagonally, then into thirds, as shown, to create the six layers needed for a six-petaled flower.) Then draw the shape you want for your design—a curve in this case —from one folded edge to the other, coming as close as possible to the open edges. Cut along the line, unfold the paper and, following the outline, draw the design on a piece of stiff cardboard.

2. Mark the top side of each cardboard pattern piece, then cut out the pieces.

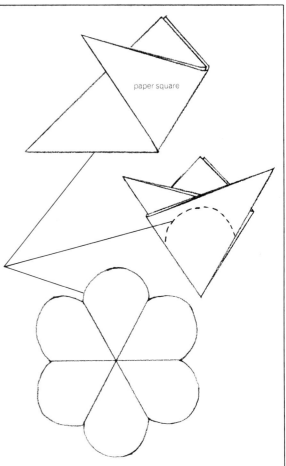

paper square

B — CUTTING OUT THE DESIGN

3. Press all fabric pieces and place them wrong side up on a flat surface.

4. Place the cardboard pattern pieces top-sides down on the fabric selected for each, allowing a margin of at least 1/4 inch on all sides.

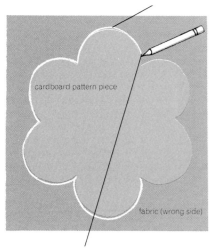

cardboard pattern piece

fabric (wrong side)

5. Draw a chalk-pencil or lead-pencil line around each pattern piece. This will become your seam line.

6A. If you plan to finish the edges of your appliqué pieces by machine with a zigzag satin stitch, cut out each piece along the seam-line marking made in Step 5.

6B. If you plan to sew your appliqué by hand, leave an extra 1/4 inch all around for seam allowances when you cut out the pieces. Skip to Box D.

continued

C | FINISHING AND ATTACHING THE APPLIQUÉ PIECES BY MACHINE

7A. Turn the appliqué pieces wrong sides down.

8A. Pin together any pieces that will be appliquéd one on top of the other—such as the flower and its center shown here.

9A. Set your machine for a zigzag satin stitch.

10A. Zigzag machine stitch around the edge of the smaller piece, attaching it to the piece underneath.

11A. As you stitch around curves, pivot the appliqué pieces frequently, making sure to pivot when the needle is on the outside of the curved edge. This will avoid gaps in the stitching.

12A. Remove the pins.

appliqué piece

appliqué piece

13A. Press the background fabric you want to use for the appliqué and place it wrong side down on a flat surface.

14A. Set the largest piece of the appliqué design into position and pin it to the fabric. Then arrange the smaller pieces of the design around the large one, pinning them in place as you go.

15A. Baste the appliqué pieces to the fabric with long stitches, as shown. Start with those pieces that will be at least partly covered by the edges of other pieces—in this case, the stem of the flower. Remove the pins.

16A. Stitch around the outer edge of each piece as shown in Step 11A. Remove the bastings.

17A. Skip to Box F.

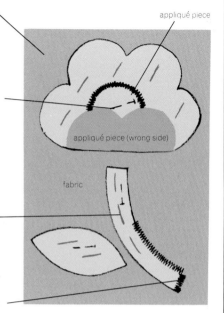

appliqué piece

appliqué piece (wrong side)

fabric

D | FINISHING THE EDGES OF THE APPLIQUÉ PIECES BY HAND

7B. Run a row of machine stitching all around the penciled seam line on the wrong side of each appliqué piece.

8B. Clip through the seam allowance at each sharp indentation, cutting up to but not into the line of machine stitching.

9B. Cut V-shaped notches up to the stitching line on all convex curves such as those on the petals of the flower shown.

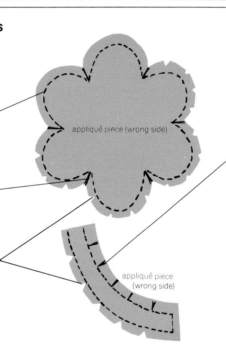

appliqué piece (wrong side)

appliqué piece (wrong side)

10B. Cut clips up to the stitching line around all concave curves—for example, the inside curve of the stem. If the edge is only slightly curved, space the clips 1 inch apart; if the curves are more pronounced, make clips at 1/2-inch or even 1/4-inch intervals.

11B. Turn the seam allowance over to the wrong side and baste, rolling the machine stitching made in Step 7B inside the edge so that it will not be visible on the finished appliqué. Make sure to keep the knotted ends of your basting threads on the side of the piece that will be visible in the completed appliqué so that they will be easy to remove later.

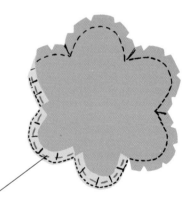

appliqué piece (wrong side)

12B. To form smooth edges at sharp points, such as the tips of a leaf, turn under and baste one complete side before doing the other.

13B. Pin together any pieces that will be appliquéd one on top of the other—such as the flower and its center shown here—making sure that the wrong sides of the pieces are down. Hand stitch the pieces together with a slip stitch (Appendix) or a decorative embroidery stitch (pages 132-135 and 193). Remove the pins.

ATTACHING THE APPLIQUÉ DESIGN TO BACKGROUND FABRIC BY HAND

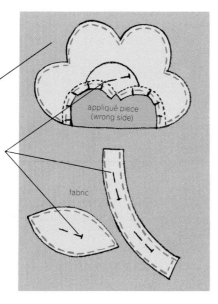

14B. Press the background fabric you want to use for the appliqué and place it wrong side down on a flat surface.

15B. Set the largest piece of the appliqué design into position and pin it to the fabric. Then arrange the smaller pieces of the design around the large one, pinning them in place as you go.

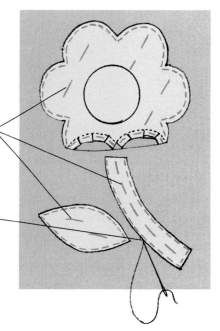

16B. Baste the appliqué pieces to the fabric with long stitches, beginning with those pieces that will be at least partly covered by the edges of other pieces —in this case, the stem of the flower. Remove the pins.

17B. Hand stitch each piece to the fabric with a slip stitch (*Appendix*) or a decorative embroidery stitch (*pages 132-135 and 193*). Remove the bastings.

PRESSING THE FINISHED APPLIQUÉ

18. Press the finished work on the appliquéd side. If the appliqué has been done by hand, take care not to flatten out the puffiness that is characteristic of hand work.

The technique
of quilting

In quilting, two layers of fabric are sewn together with a layer of cotton or polyester filler between them. The top layer, or covering, may be pieced or appliquéd patchwork or any firm, but mediumweight, fabric. The bottom layer, or backing, usually consists of plain cotton.

A systematic approach will keep the layers from shifting as they are sewn. Machine stitching must be done in alternately crisscrossing diagonal lines, following the bias of the fabric. Hand stitches may run in any direction, but they must start from the center. To keep the stitches even, hold the work in a hoop.

To make a coverlet, quilt the fabric first, as shown on the following pages, and then stitch 1-inch-wide bias tape or 2-inch-wide hemming tape around the edges. If the quilting is for clothing, cut out the pattern pieces before quilting them, leaving a 1-inch seam allowance to compensate for the quilting.

QUILTING A DIAMOND PATTERN

A PREPARING THE COVERING FABRIC

1. Fold the covering fabric in half diagonally with the wrong sides facing out.

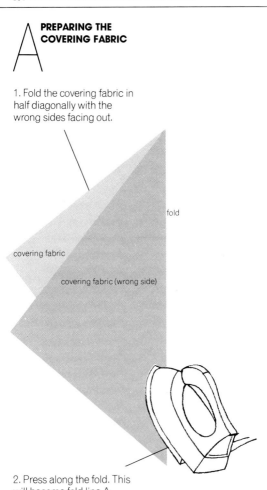

2. Press along the fold. This will become fold line A.

3. Open the fabric flat and fold it diagonally again in the opposite direction. Press along the fold. This will become fold line B.

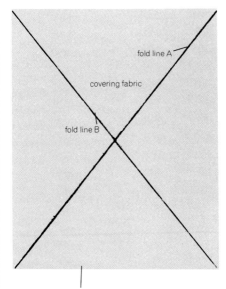

4. Open up the covering fabric and place it on a flat surface, wrong side down.

B MARKING THE COVERING FABRIC

5. Place a ruler on the fabric, aligning one edge with fold line A. Beginning where the ruler intercepts fold line B, make pencil dots along the outer edge of the ruler to one edge of the fabric. The dots should be at 2-inch intervals if you use cotton batting, at 3-inch intervals if you use polyester batting.

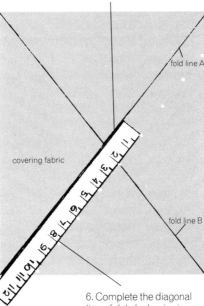

6. Complete the diagonal line of dots by beginning again at the point where the ruler intercepts fold line B, and make pencil dots along the outer edge of the ruler on the opposite side of the fabric.

7. Move the ruler to the opposite side of fold line A and make a similar diagonal line of dots, again making sure that you begin measuring at the point where the ruler intercepts fold line B.

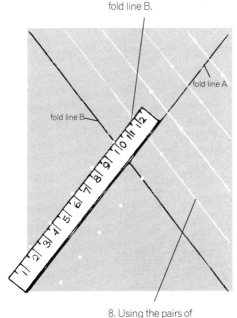

8. Using the pairs of penciled dots as guides, draw diagonal lines parallel to fold line B from one edge of the fabric to the other.

9. Now place the ruler on the fabric again, this time aligning one edge with fold line B, as shown. Repeat Steps 5 and 6 to create two diagonal rows of dots parallel to fold line B.

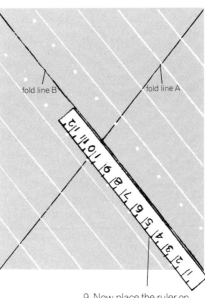

10. Using the pairs of penciled dots as guides, draw diagonal lines parallel to fold line A from one edge of the fabric to the other, thus creating a grid of diamonds.

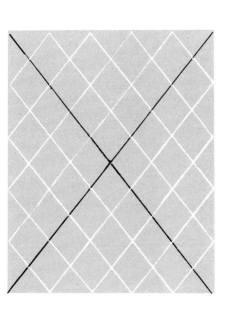

C ASSEMBLING THE FABRIC AND BATTING

11. Cut cotton or polyester batting and the fabric you plan to use to back the quilting. Both should be the same size as the covering fabric. The backing fabric may be pieced if necessary.

12. Place the backing fabric, wrong side up, on a flat surface and center the batting on top of it.

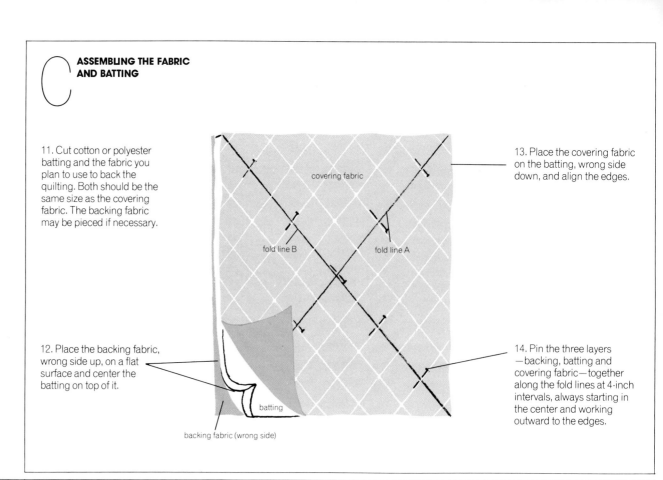

13. Place the covering fabric on the batting, wrong side down, and align the edges.

14. Pin the three layers —backing, batting and covering fabric—together along the fold lines at 4-inch intervals, always starting in the center and working outward to the edges.

D BASTING THE DIAMOND GRID

15. Baste the covering, batting and backing together by hand, starting from the center and sewing to the edge just outside one fold line so that you can later stitch directly on the fold line. Use oversized 1-inch-long stitches. Remove the pins.

16. Starting in the center again, baste alongside the other half of the fold line. Remove the pins.

17. Then to baste alongside the second fold line repeat Steps 15 and 16.

18A. If you plan to quilt by hand, repeat Steps 15-17 between the fold lines as shown.

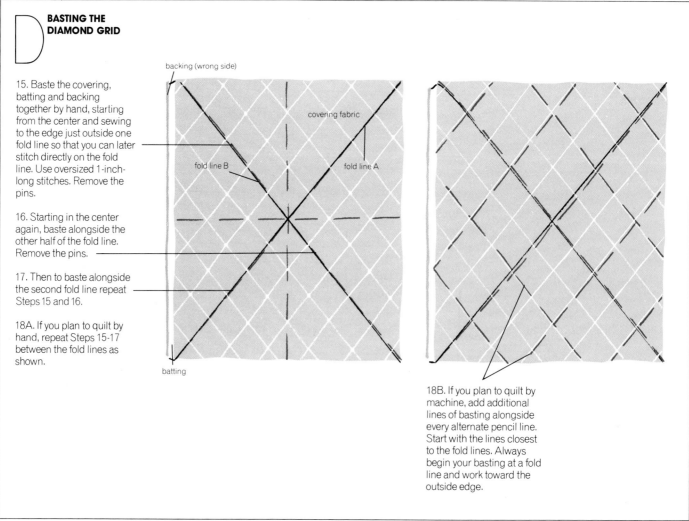

18B. If you plan to quilt by machine, add additional lines of basting alongside every alternate pencil line. Start with the lines closest to the fold lines. Always begin your basting at a fold line and work toward the outside edge.

QUILTING THE DIAMOND GRID BY HAND

19A. Center the quilting inside a large embroidery hoop with an adjustable screw or a quilting hoop 18 to 22 inches in diameter.

20A. Thread your needle with mercerized cotton or polyester-coated cotton thread. Alternately, you can use special quilting thread, which is waxed so that it is easy to work. Knot the thread at one end.

21A. Insert the needle into the center of the quilting from the backing side. To hide the knot, separate the threads of the backing fabric with the point of the needle and push the knot into the layer of batting.

22A. Push the needle through from the backing to the covering and pull the thread through where the fold lines meet. Insert the needle into the covering along one of the fold lines 1/8 inch from the center. Then push the needle through to the backing and make another short stitch. Repeat along one fold line until you reach the edge of the hoop, keeping the stitches as even as possible.

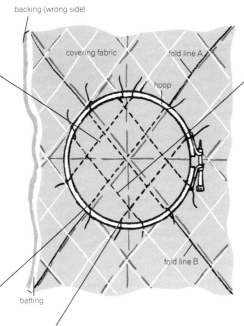

23A. At the edge of the hoop, pull the needle off the thread and leave the thread dangling so that you can pick it up later.

24A. Put a new length of thread in your needle; repeat Steps 21A-23A along the other fold lines and all marked lines.

25A. Move the hoop to an adjacent area where it will overlap the ends of some of the stitching lines you have started.

26A. Thread your needle with the loose threads, one at a time, and continue stitching along each line as shown.

27A. When a thread is almost used up, take a final stitch on the backing side of the quilting. Then point the needle diagonally into the backing and push it through the batting so that it emerges an inch or so away from the last stitch on the covering side of the quilting. Pull the thread taut and cut it off next to the surface of the covering fabric; the cut end will disappear back into the batting. When you reach the edge of the hoop, again pull the needle off the thread and leave the thread dangling.

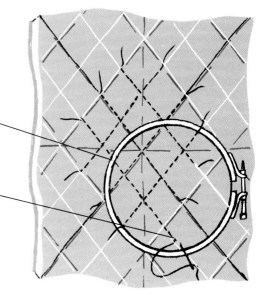

28A. Repeat Steps 25A and 26A until the entire piece is quilted.

29A. On corners and edges that cannot be clamped securely into the hoop, smooth the line of stitching with your fingers so that it will not pucker.

QUILTING THE DIAMOND GRID BY MACHINE

19B. Thread your machine with mercerized cotton or polyester-coated cotton thread, and set the machine at 6 stitches to the inch. A setting of 6 or 8 is generally used for quilting bed covers or pillows, but closer stitches—8 or 10 to the inch —are best for quilting garment pieces. Adjust the machine to the tension recommended for mediumweight wool.

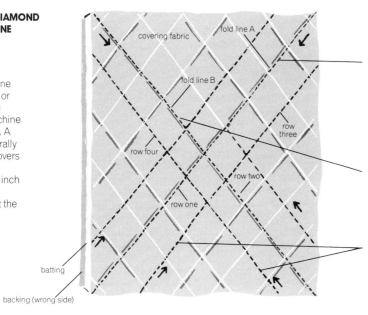

20B. To prevent the quilting from stretching out of shape, the first two crossed rows of machine stitching must be made from opposite edges of the fabric in the following fashion: starting at the top edge of the fabric covering, run the first row of machine stitching along fold line A.

21B. Again starting at the top edge of the fabric, run the second row of machine stitching along fold line B.

22B. Stitch along all the penciled lines, sewing first in one diagonal direction and then in the other as shown.

23B. Remove all of the bastings.

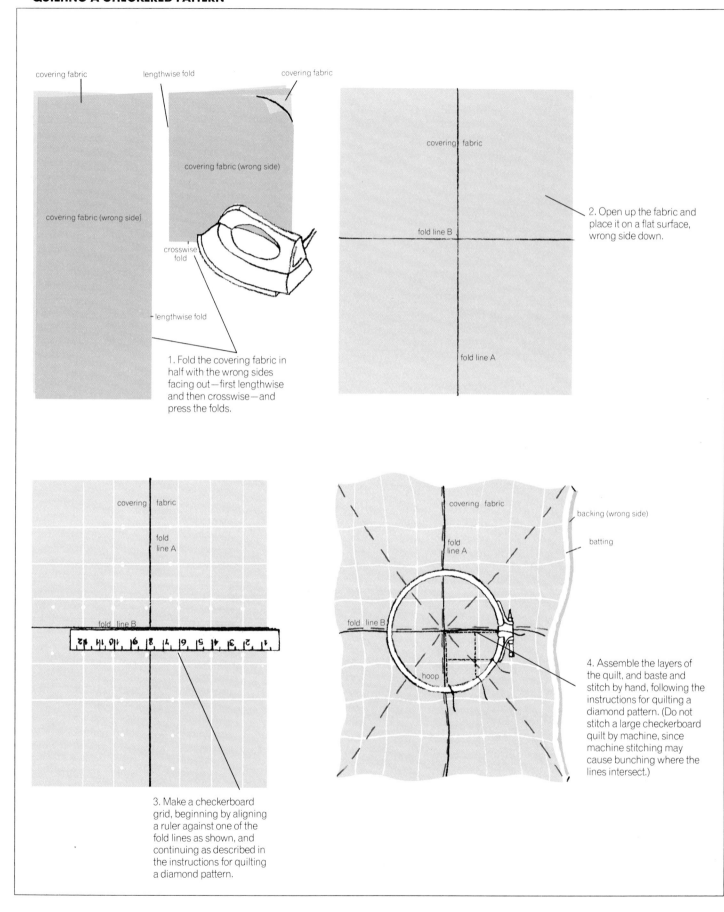

covering fabric

lengthwise fold

covering fabric

covering fabric (wrong side)

covering fabric (wrong side)

crosswise fold

lengthwise fold

1. Fold the covering fabric in half with the wrong sides facing out—first lengthwise and then crosswise—and press the folds.

covering fabric

fold line B

fold line A

2. Open up the fabric and place it on a flat surface, wrong side down.

covering fabric

fold line A

fold line B

3. Make a checkerboard grid, beginning by aligning a ruler against one of the fold lines as shown, and continuing as described in the instructions for quilting a diamond pattern.

covering fabric

backing (wrong side)

batting

fold line A

fold line B

hoop

4. Assemble the layers of the quilt, and baste and stitch by hand, following the instructions for quilting a diamond pattern. (Do not stitch a large checkerboard quilt by machine, since machine stitching may cause bunching where the lines intersect.)

QUILTING A PATCHWORK OR APPLIQUÉ PATTERN

A OUTLINING THE FIRST PATCH

1. Assemble the three layers of the quilt—the backing, the batting, and the patchwork or appliqué covering—following the instructions for quilting a diamond pattern, Steps 11-14.

2. Run intersecting lines of basting stitches through all thicknesses, following the instructions for quilting a diamond pattern, Steps 15-18A. This will hold the quilt together when you do the outline stitching.

3. Decide what patches you want to outline, keeping in mind that the lines of stitches should be 2 inches apart if the batting is cotton, and 3 inches apart if the batting is polyester.

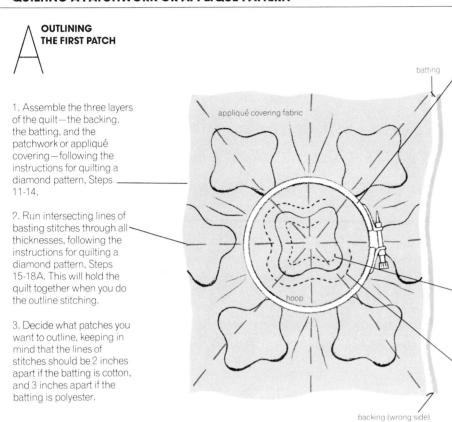

appliqué covering fabric

batting

hoop

backing (wrong side)

4. Center the quilting inside an embroidery hoop with an adjustable screw or—for large pieces—a quilting hoop 18 to 22 inches in diameter.

5. Thread your needle with mercerized cotton, polyester-coated cotton or special quilting thread. Knot one end.

6. Insert the needle from the backing side 1/8 to 1 inch from the edge of a patch. Hide the knot by separating the threads of the backing fabric with the point of the needle and push the knot into the layer of batting.

7. Using small, even stitches, sew all around the edge of the patch 1/8 to 1 inch in from the edge.

8. Make another line of outline stitches outside the edge of the patch, 2 to 3 inches away from the first line.

B COMPLETING THE QUILT

9. To finish the stitches, push the needle up from the backing side of the quilting. Then point the needle diagonally into the backing and push it through the batting so that it emerges an inch or so away from the last stitch on the covering side of the quilting. Pull the thread taut and cut it off next to the surface of the covering fabric; the cut end will disappear back into the batting.

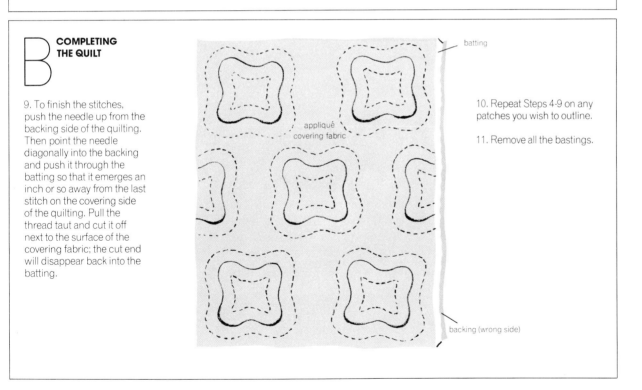

batting

appliqué covering fabric

backing (wrong side)

10. Repeat Steps 4-9 on any patches you wish to outline.

11. Remove all the bastings.

4
TRADITIONAL
NEEDLECRAFTS

With pride, an engineer in San Ramon, California, drafts his own patterns and knits sweaters for his wife and himself. A prominent entertainer on tour enriches the long hours in hotel rooms crocheting afghans, scarves and shawls for her friends. A Brooklyn priest, seeking new artistic outlets for his young ghetto charges, enrolls in a natural-dyes workshop.

These newly minted craftsmen are typi-

THE PLEASURES OF USING OLD SKILLS

cal of the ever-growing number of Americans who have immersed themselves in traditional yarn skills. Their reasons for doing so may range from high-minded social protest to a simple desire to avoid smoking. But virtually all these embryo spinners and knitters and dyers find that beyond these reasons—and the fun of using their hands —lies a subtler satisfaction. They have found a way to introduce into Space Age lives some of the creativity and self-reliance of their ancestors. And the deeper these craftsmen go in exploring the old skills, the more their respect increases for the toughness and virtuosity with which the first Americans took charge of their lives.

In the frontier household, a woman's skill with spinning wheel and needle was as vital as her husband's ability to wield his ax and musket. From her own field of flax, she laboriously—and meticulously—produced a durable linen called homespun. The process often took 16 months from the time of planting until the cloth came off the loom. For a flax stalk, our forebears discovered, does not surrender its fibers without a struggle. Retting, scutching, and hackling are arcane words now; once every householder knew them—all too well—as the stages by which flax stalks were rotted, pounded, scraped and combed into submission. Repeated washing, drying and bleaching were also necessary before the fiber could be spun into thread and woven.

Producing yarn from wool fleece was only slightly less laborious than turning out homespun linen. Sometimes wool could be bought, but usually it came off the backs of the family's sheep. After the menfolk had finished shearing, the housewife scoured the wool in a soap-and-alkali solution to remove grease, dried sweat and the inevitable twigs and burrs. Next she rubbed it with an oil such as melted hog fat to lubricate the fibers and pulled the wool through the wire teeth of carding combs. Finally she spun her rolls of carded wool into yarn on the large wool wheel. Spinning became second nature to the women of every family, and an unmarried daughter usually found herself shouldering more and more of this monotonous task—in short, turning into a spinster.

To dye her yarns the early housewife relied on plants like indigo—preferably *Indigofera tinctoria*, the variety she called true blue to distinguish it from less-reliable types. A universal favorite because it yielded tints that were colorfast, indigo thus became the source of the beautiful blues that predominate in early American crewel embroidery. By varying the time she immersed her wool in the indigo pot, the dyer was able to create shades from the palest sky tints to a deep midnight hue.

Contemporary craftsmen feel a justifiable wonder at the long hours that went into these traditional tasks. Though a woman could sit as she spun thread on the small flax wheel, she had to stand up to use the large wool spinning wheel; indeed, she might walk 10 miles a day as she trod back and forth winding the yarn. And many jobs were messy and noisome. The dye pots often reeked of chamber lye—in plain language, urine—the most common fixative available for some dyeing.

Under the circumstances, the evident pleasure and possessive pride our ancestors took in refining and beautifying their primitive handiwork is all the more striking. One legendary New England lady is symbolic of these attitudes. Like most early needlewomen, she was an indefatigable searcher for ever-new shades to dye her crewel yarns. Reds and pinks were especially elusive, and when she developed a particularly enchanting pink, it excited enormous admiration and envy among her neighbors. But so jealous was she of the prized formula, she refused to confide it to anyone and took the secret to her grave. Thereafter the color bore the name of the town in which she had lived: Wyndam pink.

Treasured forms of embroidery

An issue of the Boston Gazette of 1749 carried this notice: "On the 11th of Nov. last, was stolen out of the yard of Mr. Joseph Coit, Joiner in Boston, living in Cross Street, a woman's Fustian Petticoat, with a large work'd Embroider'd Border, being Deer, Sheep, Houses, Forrest, & c., so worked. Whoever has taken the said Petticoat, will return it to the Owner thereof, or to the Printer, shall have 40s. old Tenor Reward and no Question ask'd."

The value which Mr. Coit placed on this obviously fetching garment would have surprised none of the paper's readers. Because of its elaborately wrought band of embroidery, everyone would have recognized the petticoat as a genuine treasure, understandably cherished by the lady of the house. Like many other New England women of the day, Mrs. Coit had probably stitched it herself as part of her trousseau, to be handed on in time to her daughter.

Because printed textiles were scarce and expensive in rural America, embroidery was the chief means of enlivening homes and personal apparel with colorful designs. For the colonists, and their successors on the moving frontier, finding time to embroider can never have been easy; too much essential sewing and mending and knitting had prior claim on the housewife's needle. But the joy she took in working with her varicolored crewels is evident in the freshness and vigor of her designs—the hills, fields, animals, birds and flowers of her new world.

Though she based her style on actual or remembered English models, her work had a notable ingenuity and freedom. Ultimately she decorated everything from cupboard cloths to house slippers, but her first and most extensive efforts were lavished on the bed hangings. Bedspreads, valances, and curtains that could be drawn to enclose the bed like a small room all proudly displayed embroidery. The drapery was not for show alone: bed hangings kept out drafts during the cold New England winters.

In creating her designs, the colonial housewife rarely used more than four or five stitches. Her favorite was the Romanian stitch, sometimes called the economy stitch because it filled in a large area while leaving a minimum amount of yarn on the back of the material. As a substitute for a pattern book, a rarity in the early days, she consulted her sampler—the rolled-up length of linen on which she had recorded useful examples of stitchery for future reference.

Around 1640, the young daughter of Pilgrim Captain Myles Standish worked the earliest American sampler known to us: it bears the simple, touching inscription,

Loara Standish is my name/Lord guide my heart that I may do Thy will. . . . Like all early samplers, Loara's was long and narrow because of the narrowness of 17th Century looms. When looms grew wider, samplers acquired the shorter, broader shape more familiar to us today. At the same time, sampler-making developed into an educational discipline for the young, a kind of obligatory diploma in needlework, which, talented or not, girls were expected to produce as a mark of genteel accomplishment. During the last years of the American Revolution, samplers took on a bright, pictorial aspect as girls embroidered likenesses of their homes and surroundings and some-times framed the composition in a border of flowers. Occasionally the sampler served as a register of births, marriages and deaths, much like the family Bible, and in Virginia the charming custom arose of giving samplers as engagement or wedding presents.

Today, a sampler still makes a uniquely precious gift to mark a special occasion; and a crewelwork frame can transform a common household item into a work of art. For the modern embroiderer, stitchery is a labor of love. Gone is the duress which prompted a young rebel of nearly two centuries ago to sign her work: "Patty Polk did this and she hated every stitch she did in it. She loves to read much more."

In the needlework curriculum of every Victorian schoolgirl was at least one sampler—a yarn composition made with samples of embroidery stitches. The one above, completed by 17-year-old Anne Williams in 1862, includes the standard flower border and alphabet and a stylized schoolhouse. Such samplers, though no longer used as teaching tools, still provide opportunities to develop—and display—skill with yarn and needle.

Natural beauty dyed in the wool

The soft, subtle yarn colors of early American embroidery owe their beauty to Nature. From plants like those shown at right with their correspondingly colored wool skeins, the colonial housewife extracted her own dye. Some recipes were simple: black walnut hulls needed only to be soaked and then boiled to produce a colorfast brown dye. But most vegetable substances, to yield more than a fugitive stain, required mordanting: the addition of an agent like alum or iron to act as a chemical bond fusing color to fiber.

Before immersing wool yarn in an onion-skin dye, for example, the home dyer had to simmer the yarn in an alum solution. Indigo required still another process: its dye pigment did not dissolve in water and had to be broken down with bacteria in a fermentation vat—the so-called blue-pot of early American kitchens.

Never an exact science, natural dyeing almost disappeared after the discovery of synthetic aniline dyes in the 19th Century. Yet today craftsmen in growing numbers are relearning the old skills—and for the very reason they were once abandoned. The home methods produce unpredictable colors that are impossible to duplicate, and as infinitely variable as Nature herself.

Walnut hulls dye wool a lasting brown without mordants.

With alum added, dry onionskins produce a bright yellow.

Leaves of the indigo plant can produce a wide range of blues.

Rust-hued logwood chips yield both lavender and blue black.

Rhododendron leaves with an iron mordant create a gray dye.

Madder root is the best plant source of red or burnt orange.

With an alum mordant, sumac berries dye wool a soft gold.

The bright purple juice of the pokeberry yields a peach tint.

A repertoire of colonial stitchery

Crewel, like any other type of embroidery, depends for its subtle textures on decorative stitches, combined artistically. The eight stitches shown at right and on the following pages were among the most popular of all the hundreds in the repertoire of a knowledgeable 17th Century crewel worker. Each of the eight still warrants learning today because each creates a distinctive effect.

The backstitch at right, for example, forms a delicate outline, specially useful for tracing curves. The open buttonhole stitch *(overleaf)* defines a bold, broad outline and ornaments the edge it silhouettes.

All of these stitches turn out neater and more uniform in size when the work is secured by an embroidery hoop, either handheld or on a stand. The yarn recommended nowadays is Persian wool; one strand replaces the classic—but hard to find—2-ply crewel wool.

As for needles, they must have wide eyes to accommodate the yarn comfortably. Either Size 3 or Size 4 embroidery/crewel needles meet that need and both of them are thick enough so that they help to prevent the yarn from breaking in midstitch.

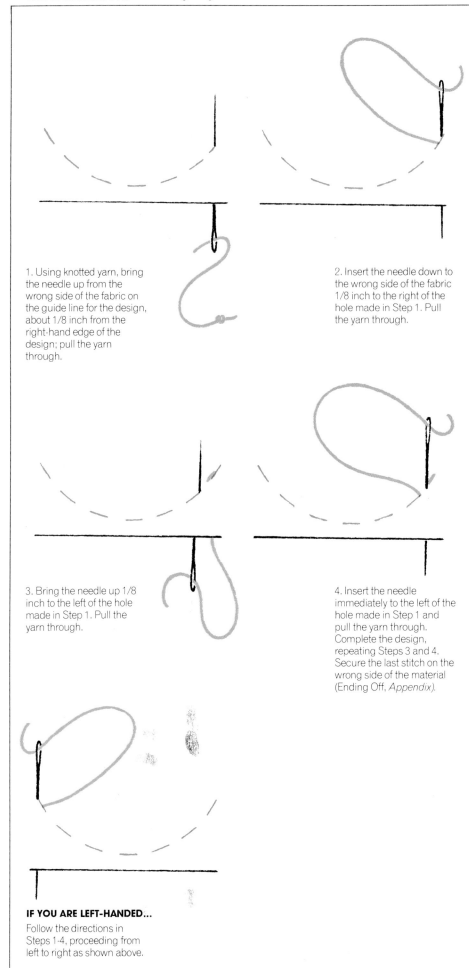

1. Using knotted yarn, bring the needle up from the wrong side of the fabric on the guide line for the design, about 1/8 inch from the right-hand edge of the design; pull the yarn through.

2. Insert the needle down to the wrong side of the fabric 1/8 inch to the right of the hole made in Step 1. Pull the yarn through.

3. Bring the needle up 1/8 inch to the left of the hole made in Step 1. Pull the yarn through.

4. Insert the needle immediately to the left of the hole made in Step 1 and pull the yarn through. Complete the design, repeating Steps 3 and 4. Secure the last stitch on the wrong side of the material (Ending Off, *Appendix*).

IF YOU ARE LEFT-HANDED...
Follow the directions in Steps 1-4, proceeding from left to right as shown above.

THE SEED STITCH: To make flower centers or shading effects

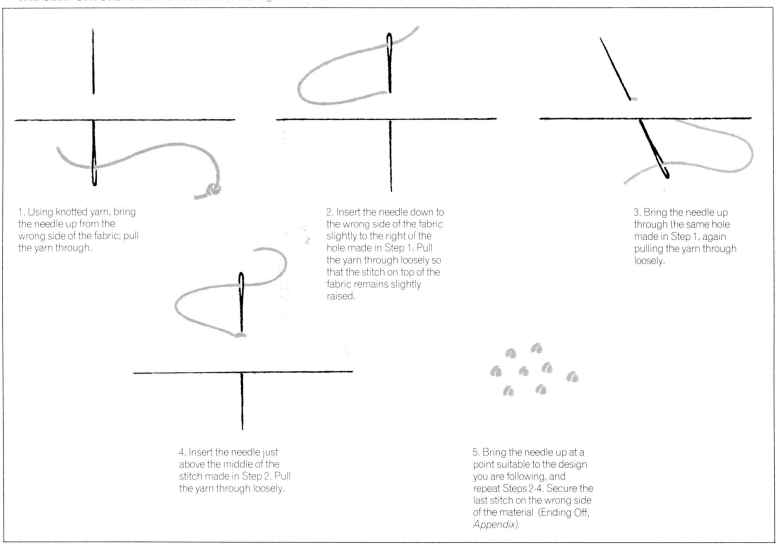

1. Using knotted yarn, bring the needle up from the wrong side of the fabric; pull the yarn through.

2. Insert the needle down to the wrong side of the fabric slightly to the right of the hole made in Step 1. Pull the yarn through loosely so that the stitch on top of the fabric remains slightly raised.

3. Bring the needle up through the same hole made in Step 1, again pulling the yarn through loosely.

4. Insert the needle just above the middle of the stitch made in Step 2. Pull the yarn through loosely.

5. Bring the needle up at a point suitable to the design you are following, and repeat Steps 2-4. Secure the last stitch on the wrong side of the material (Ending Off, *Appendix*).

THE DETACHED FLY STITCH: For filling in open areas and anchoring other stitches

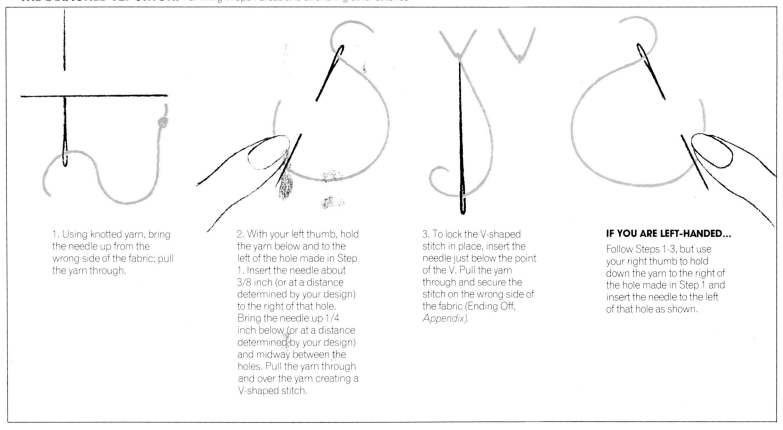

1. Using knotted yarn, bring the needle up from the wrong side of the fabric; pull the yarn through.

2. With your left thumb, hold the yarn below and to the left of the hole made in Step 1. Insert the needle about 3/8 inch (or at a distance determined by your design) to the right of that hole. Bring the needle up 1/4 inch below (or at a distance determined by your design) and midway between the holes. Pull the yarn through and over the yarn creating a V-shaped stitch.

3. To lock the V-shaped stitch in place, insert the needle just below the point of the V. Pull the yarn through and secure the stitch on the wrong side of the fabric (Ending Off, *Appendix*).

IF YOU ARE LEFT-HANDED...
Follow Steps 1-3, but use your right thumb to hold down the yarn to the right of the hole made in Step 1 and insert the needle to the left of that hole as shown.

THE ATTACHED FLY STITCH: For making wheat, fern or other patterns

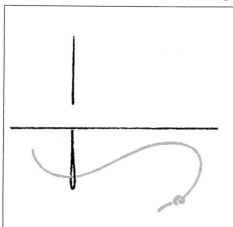

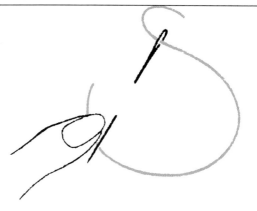

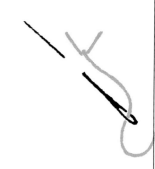

1. Using knotted yarn, bring the needle up from the wrong side of the fabric; pull the yarn through.

2. With your left thumb, hold down the yarn below and to the left of the hole made in Step 1. Insert the needle about 3/8 inch (or at a distance determined by your design) to the right of that hole. Bring the needle up 1/4 inch below and midway between the holes made in Steps 1 and 2. Pull the yarn through the fabric over the yarn, creating a V-shaped stitch.

3. To lock the V-shaped stitch in place and form the beginning of a stem, insert the needle about 3/8 inch (or the desired distance) below the point of the V. Then slant the needle up and to the left and bring it up about 1/4 inch directly below the upper left edge of the stitch made in Step 2. Pull the yarn through.

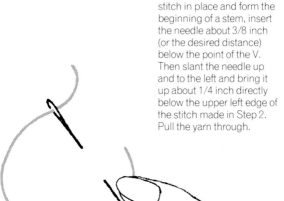

4. Complete the design, repeating Steps 2 and 3. Secure the last stitch on the wrong side of the fabric (Ending Off, *Appendix*).

IF YOU ARE LEFT-HANDED...

Follow Steps 1-4, but hold down the yarn with your right thumb to the right of the hole made in Step 1; insert the needle to the left of that hole; and slant the needle down and to the right, as shown.

THE OPEN BUTTONHOLE STITCH: For outlining and filling in designs

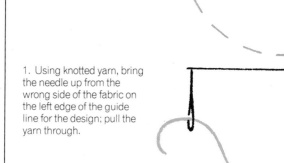

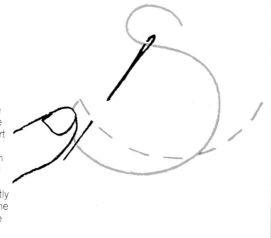

1. Using knotted yarn, bring the needle up from the wrong side of the fabric on the left edge of the guide line for the design; pull the yarn through.

2. With your left thumb, hold the thread below the guide line to the left of the hole made in Step 1. Insert the needle the desired distance above the design line and to the right of the hole made in Step 1, and bring the needle up directly below this on the guide line and over the yarn; pull the yarn through.

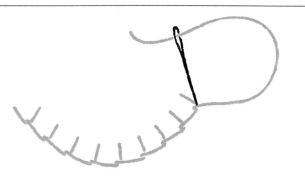

3. Complete the design by repeating Step 2. The distance between the stitches is arbitrary, but should be constant. Secure the last stitch on the wrong side of the material (Ending Off, *Appendix*).

IF YOU ARE LEFT-HANDED…

Follow Steps 1-3, working from right to left and holding the thread with your right thumb on the right side of the hole.

THE ROMANIAN STITCH: For filling in designs

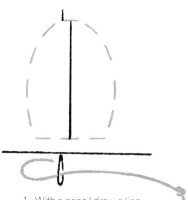

1. With a pencil draw a line down the center of the design to be filled in. Using knotted yarn, bring the needle up from the wrong side of the fabric about 1/8 inch, depending on the design, to the left of center at the top of the design; pull the yarn through.

2. Insert the needle down to the wrong side of the fabric about 1/8 inch to the right of center at the top of the design. Make sure that the holes made in Steps 1 and 2 are equidistant from the center line.

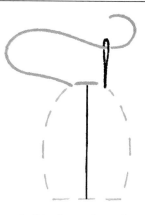

3. Bring the needle up at a point on the guide line for the design to the left and just below the hole made in Step 1; pull the yarn through. Then insert the needle at a point on the guide line to the right and just below the hole made in Step 2. Pull the yarn through.

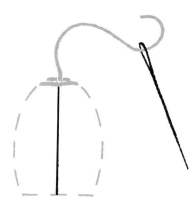

4. Bring the needle up slightly to the right of center just above the stitch made in Step 3. Pull the yarn through.

5. Insert the needle slightly to the left of center just below the stitch made in Step 3. Pull the yarn through, thus forming a diagonal lock stitch.

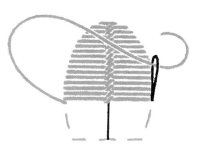

6. Complete the design, repeating Steps 3-5, making sure there is no space between the horizontal stitches and that the diagonal stitches are in a vertical row. Secure the last stitch on the wrong side of the material (Ending Off, *Appendix*).

LAID WORK TIED WITH THE DETACHED FLY STITCH: To fill in a leaf or petal

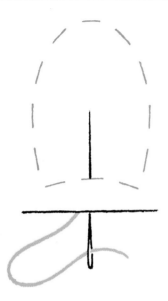

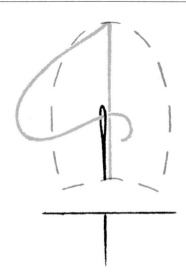

1. Using knotted yarn, bring the needle up from the wrong side of the fabric in the center of one end of the design as shown; pull the yarn through.

2. Insert the needle down to the wrong side of the fabric in the center of the opposite end of the design. Pull the yarn through.

3. Bring the needle up at a point on the guide line for the design immediately to the left of the hole made in Step 2. Pull the yarn through. Then insert the needle immediately to the left of the hole made in Step 1 and pull the yarn through.

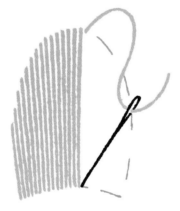

4. Continue to make long parallel stitches across the design until the left half is filled. Bring the needle up to the right of the center stitch and complete the right half of the design. Secure the last stitch on the wrong side of the material (Ending Off, *Appendix*).

5. Secure the vertical stitches with four or more detached fly stitches *(page 133)*, depending on the size of the design. Scatter them at random or arrange them in a pattern, but however they are placed, they should tie down every stitch of the laid work at some point.

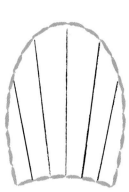
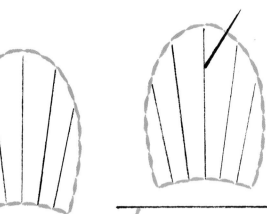
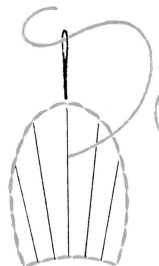
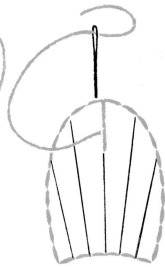

1. Draw a line down the center of the design with a pencil, then draw radiating vertical lines at equal distances on either side of the center line to guide you in making the stitches. Outline the design with the backstitch *(page 132)*.

2. Using knotted yarn, bring the needle up from the wrong side of the fabric along the center guide line at a distance from the top equal to the desired length of the long part of the stitch and pull the yarn through. The length of the long stitch is arbitrary but should remain constant throughout the design.

3. Insert the needle down to the wrong side of the fabric just above the outline stitches in a line with the hole made in Step 2. Pull the yarn through.

4. Make the short part of the stitch by bringing the needle out to the left of the center stitch at a shorter distance from the top and pull the yarn through. The length of this short part of the stitch is arbitrary but should remain constant throughout the design. Insert the needle just above the outline stitch and to the immediate left of the hole made in Step 3 and pull the yarn through.

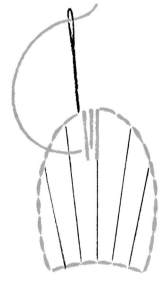
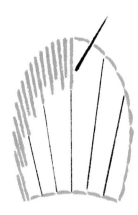
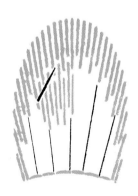
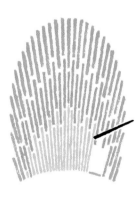

5. Continue to make alternating long and short stitches around the left half of the design, forming an outer row of radiating stitches. Slant the stitches in the direction of the penciled guide lines. Secure the last stitch on the wrong side of the material (Ending Off, *Appendix*).

6. Using knotted yarn, bring the needle up from the wrong side of the material to the right of the long center stitch to make a short stitch. Pull the yarn through. Repeat Steps 3-5 until the outer row of the right half of the design is completed. Secure the last stitch on the wrong side of the material (Ending Off, *Appendix*).

7. To make a second row of stitches, bring the needle up from the wrong side of the fabric through the base of the center stitch; pull the yarn through. Insert the needle directly below at the desired distance from the top row; all stitches in this row will be of equal length. Completing first the left side of the design, bring the needle out through the base of each stitch in the row above and insert it directly below. Then start at the base of the stitch to the right of the center stitch and complete the right side of the design.

8. Complete the bottom of the design with a final row of stitches of whatever length is required to fill the remaining spaces. Start at the left edge of the design and work toward the right, inserting the needle just below the outline. Secure the last stitch on the wrong side of the material (Ending Off, *Appendix*).

Reflections on the Tree of Life

The fanciful embroidery framing the mirror at right is a modern American version of a traditional design called the Tree of Life. One of mankind's oldest and most universal symbols, it stands for growth, proliferation, generation and regeneration—and, ultimately, immortality. *Genesis* records that the Tree of Life grew in the Garden of Eden, and indeed it is easy to imagine Adam and Eve strolling under such a tree as the one opposite, so much does it evoke the delight of an earthly paradise.

During the 16th and 17th centuries, the Tree of Life became a favorite embroidery motif of English ladies, who copied it from the palampores (painted or printed cotton hangings) brought back from the Orient by merchants connected with the East India Company. The ladies worked these fairy-tale flowers and fruits, buds and berries in crewels, a term for sturdy worsted yarns. Their handiwork proved so appealing that "crewel work" still connotes for most people these designs characteristic of 17th Century England.

Transplanted to Colonial America, crewel work took on a freer, less conventionalized air. This Tree of Life is recognizably American in the lightness and gaiety of its effect; English symmetry, with its characteristically formal repetition of motifs, has here given way to a free-flowing arrangement of ever-new images, worked in a rich variety of stitches and a profusion of sumptuous colors. Instructions for embroidering the mirror frame appear overleaf.

Instructions for embroidering the Tree of Life

To make the embroidered frame you will need a large crewel needle (Size 3 or 4), one-ounce skeins of Persian wool in the colors indicated on the chart at right and a square piece of not too tightly woven cloth – preferably linen, homespun, linen twill or antique satin. The amount of the cloth will depend on the size frame you want. But to allow ample scope to the stitchery as well as adequate space for a mirror, a finished size no smaller than 17 1/2 inches tall and 17 inches wide is recommended. When cutting out your fabric be sure to allow a margin of at least 5 inches outside the embroidered area on all sides.

Transferring the design: Follow the instructions for this technique given in the Appendix.

Selecting colors and stitches: Yarn colors used are shown in the chart at right. These can be matched to the color photograph of the frame on the preceding pages. All stitches are keyed by letter on the diagram opposite.

Stitching the design: Using 1 strand of Persian wool, begin by working the flowers, nuts, berries, butterfly and peacock, finishing each completely before moving to the next. Work from top to bottom and from left to right. Embroider stems and leaves next, top to bottom, then the tree trunk and lower branches. Embroider the mounds of earth last, working from the center out.

Pressing the finished work: Place the finished embroidery wrong side up on top of four layers of soft dry toweling. Then press with a dry iron and a wet cloth.

light blue

peacock blue

navy

light green

medium green

moss green

blue green

thalo green

pale pink

medium pink

deep pink

rose

lavender

periwinkle

turquoise

wheat

ochre yellow

gold

antique gold

tan

rust

brown

All stems and tendrils in the diagram above are worked in the stem stitch; the peacock's breast and the tree trunk are worked in alternating rows of chain stitches and stem stitches. Stitches to be used for all other areas are keyed by letter at right.

A Attached fly stitch
B Backstitch
C Chain stitch
D Detached fly stitch
E French knot

F Laid work
G Long and short stitch
H Open buttonhole stitch
I Romanian stitch
J Satin stitch

K Seed stitch
L Stem stitch
M Squared filling stitch

Age-old designs for hook and needle

Any woman lucky enough to own a genuine Scandinavian ski sweater has probably not bought it solely to keep warm. Consciously or not, she values it for its vigorous folk art, the knit-in traditional motifs that embellish it with so much charm. The designs may seem as familiar to her as her own childhood. The antlered deer are part of the nights she lay listening for the jingle of sleigh bells as Santa's team swept across the December sky. The fir tree is the tall evergreen that came indoors each Yuletide, exhaling a mysterious forest magic. The star and the snowflake too are emblems of a winter world of pageant and celebration.

At their heart, such symbols represent a deep response to nature that stretches far back into our pagan past. More immediately, they are our inheritance from Scandinavian peasants who carved and painted and embroidered these motifs on household furnishings—and knitted them into superb cold-weather garments whose primitive beauty delights us still.

In the traditional pastoral life of Norway, Sweden, Finland and Denmark, knitting was an integral part of every farmwife's *husflidsarbeide,* as the Norwegians put it—her "house-diligence-work." During the long arctic winters, and during the equally long "light-nights" of summer when she helped with the crops or watched the herds, her needles and yarn were always within reach.

The designs that grew under her flying fingers were stylized, simple and bold. Their subjects came from the life around her. Looking out on her frosted landscape, the Scandinavian woman saw herds of reindeer, forests of fir trees and, often, soft clouds of falling snow. Raising her eyes to a sky unmarred by smog, she beheld the bright stars of the northern sky. It is not hard to understand how these four motifs—the reindeer, fir tree, snowflake and star—came to predominate in Scandinavian stockings, sweaters, mittens and caps.

But folk art involves more than simply copying one's surroundings. Certain cherished designs pass from generation to generation because they are rich in symbolic and often religious associations. The tree, for example, is an ancient and universal emblem of life and regeneration. In Scandinavian mythology, the great ash tree Yggdrasil was believed to support the whole universe. In the Judeo-Christian story of creation, a bite of an apple from the Tree of Knowledge led to the fall of man.

The eight-pointed star, perhaps the most frequently used of all Nordic motifs, is a sign of divine guidance. The reindeer, like other animals with horns, stands for power and strength. Only the snowflake seems never to have acquired a specific symbolic meaning, but it has been used in many variations in Scandinavian design for its beauty alone.

Not all folk motifs are direct images of the natural world, though they may have had their original inspiration there; many have evolved as abstract geometrical designs. Whether discreetly bordering a mitten cuff or a warm cap or slashing across a sweater front, such motifs are a characteristic and essential part of Scandinavian knitwear. And geometric design is what animates an even more primitive and humble needlecraft, the crocheted granny square.

Like the old-fashioned patchwork quilt, the granny square began as a salvage art. The thrifty housewife found she could put scraps of leftover yarn to good use by crocheting them into individual squares, then assembling the squares into a shawl or an afghan. The repeated geometry of the squares created a satisfying rhythm, and gave unity to what otherwise might have been an optical hodgepodge. Today, when yarn color can usually be preplanned, even more striking geometric effects can be achieved with granny squares.

The satisfaction of being able to create such handsome designs—whether it be knitting the ski sweater on page 146 or crocheting the hooded cape on pages 160-161 —has many sources. Not the least of them is a feeling that, across the chasm of the Industrial Revolution and mass-produced clothes, one is making contact with our forebears, and with the simpler world they lived in and interpreted in their work.

Reindeer impressions from an ancient Lapp sorcerer's magical deerskin drum reflect the northmen's reverence for the animal on which they relied for food, transportation and warm clothing. In ages past these hardy people revered the creature as a kind of nature-god and etched or painted reindeer figures as lucky symbols on ritual implements and hunting gear. Today modern Scandinavians still knit the images into their apparel.

Traditional Scandinavian motifs

Although the symbols on these swatches are Nordic in origin, Americans of every origin have happily assimilated them into their melting-pot heritage. By now, the fir tree, reindeer and snowflake are familiar emblems of wintertime. Knitted into sweaters or dresses *(overleaf),* they give to simple, classic shapes the lively charm of folk art. Because of their size—each of the swatches here is 7 inches high and composed of 35 rows—these three natural motifs are most appropriate on garments where a bold accent can be displayed to advantage.

Even more versatile are the six border designs shown in double tiers on the remaining three swatches. Their patterns are more stylized and take only 15 rows each to execute. Because of their smaller scale, they are an ideal way to add a tasteful flair to otherwise plain caps, mittens and scarves. Diagrams for knitting the three patterns and six borders pictured here are shown and explained on pages 148-149.

Border designs 1 and 2

Snowflake Motif

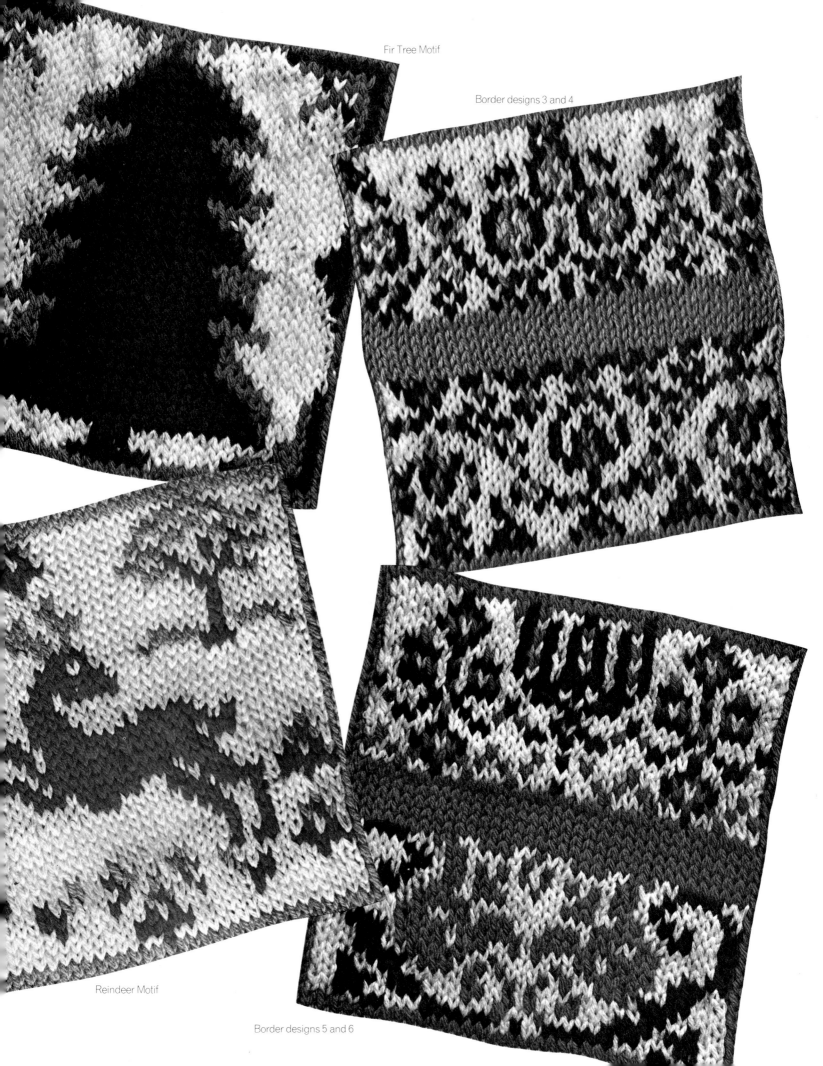

Fir Tree Motif

Border designs 3 and 4

Reindeer Motif

Border designs 5 and 6

A blizzard of knitted flakes

The serene refreshment of snow falling in northern forests served as inspiration for the sweater, dress and cap at left, knit in a soft lichen green accented with a moss green and white. A blizzard of steadily growing flakes culminates on the sweater and dress in a band of huge snow crystals—a traditional Nordic motif illustrated on the preceding pages. All of these garments are simply shaped, having been knit in a basic stockinette pattern with ribbed edgings. They use no more than three colors of yarn, giving them an ease of construction that belies their intricate look. Both the man's medium-weight ski sweater and the woman's dress are knitted on two straight needles, have set-in sleeves, and are seamed up the sides and underarms. Full instructions for making all three garments begin on page 150.

How to knit the Scandinavian motifs

The handsome designs pictured on pages 144 and 145 can be executed in a simple pattern called the stockinette, which is nothing more than alternating rows of knit and purl stitches (*Appendix*). These designs are knitted with three colors. At right, each design is shown with its color scheme plotted to indicate exactly where the knitter switches yarns. Designs are begun in each case at the lower right and worked from bottom to top. The detailed instructions overleaf for incorporating the snowflake motif in a man's sweater or a woman's dress can serve as a model for using either the fir tree or the reindeer motif.

In general, if a yarn color will be needed again within five stitches, it is carried along the back of the knitting and picked up when required. If, however, more than five stitches will elapse before the yarn color is needed once more, it is broken off and the loose end later worked into the wrong side of the garment. Techniques for weaving in the loose ends and joining a new yarn color, whether at the beginning or in the middle of a row, are shown in the project instructions that follow.

Border designs 1 and 2: ■ dark tone ● light tone □ white

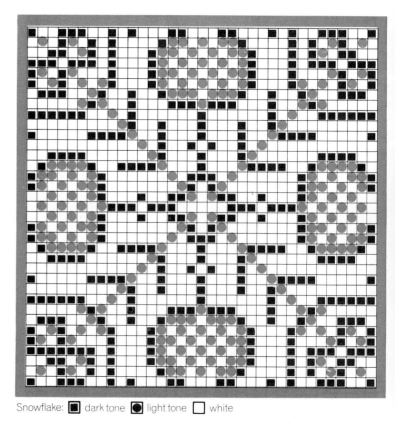

Snowflake: ■ dark tone ● light tone □ white

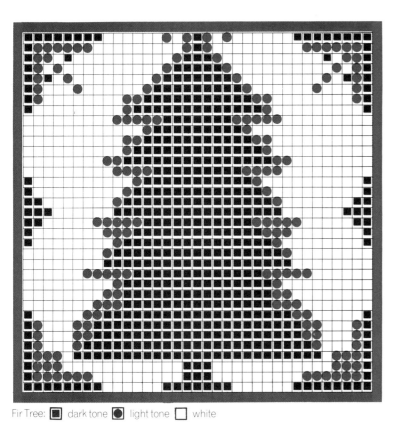

Fir Tree: ■ dark tone ● light tone □ white

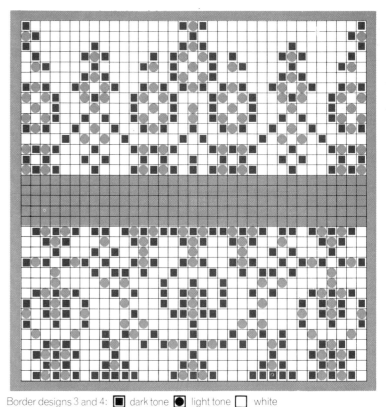

Border designs 3 and 4: ■ dark tone ● light tone □ white

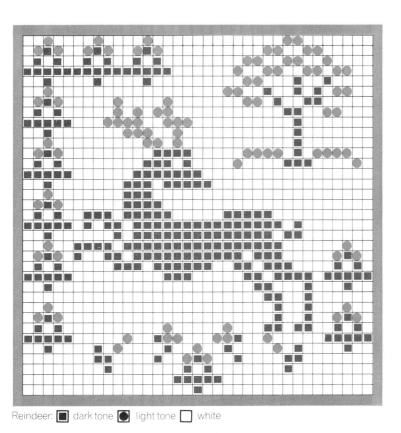

Reindeer: ■ dark tone ● light tone □ white

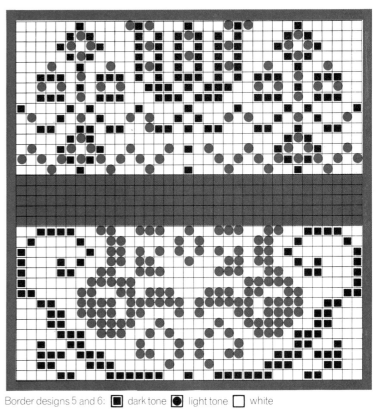

Border designs 5 and 6: ■ dark tone ● light tone □ white

Instructions for knit projects

The knitting instructions that follow explain in simple terms the projects shown in this book. However, since you may want to try different projects described in other publications—which use a knitter's shorthand for their instructions—a translation of these terms is included below.

KNITTING ABBREVIATIONS

K—knit	**REP**—repeat
P—purl	**PAT**—pattern
ST—stitch	**SL**—slip stitch
YO—yarn over	**PSSO**—pass slipped stitch over

—starting point for a repeated sequence of steps: when instructions tell you to "rep from," read back to find the point (*) where you must begin to repeat.

CHECKING THE GAUGE

A stitch gauge precedes all knit instructions. This gauge specifies the number of stitches to an inch (and often how many rows to an inch) you must have if your project is to come out the proper size. Check the gauge—to make sure your needles and yarn provide the desired number of stitches to an inch—by knitting a sample swatch before beginning your project. The swatch should measure at least 4 by 4 inches and be made with the yarn and needles recommended in the pattern. If two sizes of needles are required, i.e., a smaller one for a ribbed edging and a larger one for the main part of the garment, measure the gauge using the larger needles.

Remove the sample swatch from the needles without binding off. Then lay the piece on a flat surface and count the number of stitches to an inch, measuring them with a ruler, not a tape measure. If the gauge that is indicated for your project calls for more stitches to an inch, change to smaller needles. If the gauge calls for fewer stitches to an inch, use larger needles. This change of needle size will also adjust the row-to-an-inch gauge.

BLOCKING THE FINISHED WORK

Press, or block, each completed garment, by laying the work on a flat surface; then cover it with a damp cloth, and press very lightly with a warm iron. Do not pin the garment to the pressing surface or let the iron rest too long in one area lest you leave marks. Enlarge or reduce the size of the garment a little by dampening lightly, then pushing or stretching the work as you lay the garment out.

KNITTING THE SWEATER, DRESS AND CAP

The following instructions are for knitting the man's sweater, the woman's dress and the cap pictured on pages 146-147. The directions for the man's sweater are for small sizes (36-38); the changes in the number of stitches necessary for medium (40-42) and large (44-46) follow in parentheses in that order. The directions for the woman's dress are for size 10; changes for sizes 12, 14, 16 and 18 follow in parentheses in that order. The number of skeins of yarn needed for the sweater are for the small size; the number of skeins needed for medium and large follow in parentheses in that order. The number of skeins of yarn needed for the dress are for size 10; the number of skeins needed for sizes 12, 14, 16 and 18 follow in parentheses in that order. The directions for the cap are for all sizes. Basic knitting stitches and procedures are set forth in the Appendix; additional knitting techniques needed for these projects follow in the instructions.

THE SWEATER

For color A (light green in the picture on page 146), you will need 3 (3,4) four-ounce skeins of knitting worsted; 1 (1,1) four-ounce skein for color B (darker green); 1 (1,2) four-ounce skein for color C (white). Use straight knitting needles Sizes 7 and 10, an aluminum crochet hook Size E for weaving in loose threads, and a tapestry needle for sewing seams and embroidering the snowflakes. Knit a sample swatch to check the gauge: 4 stitches and 5 rows to an inch on Size 10 needles.

The front: With Size 7 needles and color A, cast on 77 (85,93) stitches. Knit 1, purl 1 to make a 3-inch ribbing. Change to the Size 10 needles, and work alternating rows of knit and purl stitches, until the piece measures 11 inches. Beginning on a knit row, start to work the band of snowflakes across the front of the sweater. All sizes will have one complete snowflake design at the center of the band, but only a portion of the design on either side. The width of this portion will vary with the size of the sweater; use the partial diagrams, opposite, as well as the main diagram on page 148 to position the snowflake design correctly for your size. Follow the instructions on page 155 for joining yarn and working with more than one yarn color. On the first row, working on 77 (85,93) stitches, start with the top diagram on the opposite page. Follow the bottom row from right to left beginning at the place indicated for your size, and knit the 21 (25,29) stitches needed for your size. Then use the bottom row of the main diagram (where color A is the light tone, color B is the dark tone and color C is white). Follow it in the same manner, and knit the 35 stitches. Finally use the bottom row of the lower diagram on the opposite page, still working from right to left, and knit the necessary 21 (25,29) stitches, ending at the place indicated for your size.

Purl across the next row following the second row of the three diagrams in reverse order (left to right). Continue until you have completed the 35 rows of the snowflake design. Break off colors B and C, and work 1 purl row using color A. The piece should now measure about 18 inches.

The armholes: Begin shaping the piece for the armholes; at the same time start the first falling-snow pattern—12 rows in all. (As you decrease, always make sure that the first stitch with color C is centered over the color A unit on the previous pattern row.) On the first row, using color A, bind off 4 (4,5) stitches. Knit 1 stitch with color A. Attach color C and knit 1 stitch. Continue knitting across the row, alternating 1 stitch in color A and 1 stitch in color C. Break off color C at the end of this and every pattern row and re-attach the yarn at the beginning of the next pattern row.

On the following row, using only color A, bind off 4 (4,5) stitches and purl across the row. On the next row, using color A, decrease 1 stitch by knitting 2 stitches together. Attach color C and knit 1 stitch. Then knit 1 stitch in color A. Continue knitting across the row alternating 1 stitch in color A and 1 stitch in color C; decrease 1 stitch at the end

right side

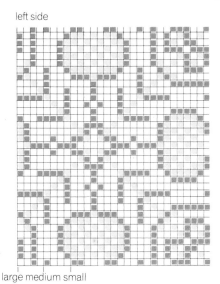

small medium large

left side

large medium small

of the row by knitting 2 stitches together. Purl across the next row using only color A. Repeat the last 2 rows 2 (3,4) more times until 63 (69,73) stitches remain.

Work the first falling-snow pattern 2 (1,0) more times without decreasing stitches. End with a purl row.

Now begin the 18 rows of the second falling-snow pattern. On the first row, knit 3 stitches with color A. Attach color C and knit 1 stitch. Continue knitting across the row in this pattern. Purl across the following row using only color A. On the next row, knit 1 stitch with color A. Attach color C and knit 1 stitch. Knit 3 stitches with color A. Continue across the row in the pattern. Purl across the following row using only color A. Repeat these 4 rows 3 more times—16 rows in all. Then repeat the first 2 rows of the pattern 1 more time, ending on a purl row.

On the next row, begin the third falling-snow pattern. Knit 1 stitch with color C and then knit 5 stitches with color A. Continue knitting across the row in this pattern. Purl across the next row using only color A. On the next row, knit 3 stitches in color A and 1 stitch in color C. Knit 5 stitches with color A. Continue across the row in the pattern. Purl across the following row using only color A. Repeat the 4 rows of this pattern until the piece measures 6 1/2 (7,7 1/2) inches above the start of the armhole edge.

The neck: Still working in the third falling-snow pattern, knit across 23 (25,27) stitches. Attach another ball of color A and bind off 17 (19,19) stitches at the center; then knit across the remaining 23 (25,27) stitches. On the next row, using only color A and working on both sides of the front at once, purl across the row, decreasing 1 stitch at each inner, or neck edge. Repeat the decreases at the neck edges every other row until 20 (22,24) stitches remain at each side of the neck. Then continue in the third falling-snow pattern on the 40 (44,48) stitches until the two pieces measure 8 1/2 (9,9 1/2) inches above the start of the armhole edge. The shoulders: Bind off 10 (11,12) stitches at the beginning of the next knit row. Continue knitting across the row still working in the third falling-snow pattern. On the next row, bind off 10 (11,12) stitches. Continue to purl across the row using only color A. Repeat these two rows 1 more time to complete the front.

The V-shaped stitches: To make the large and small V-shaped stitches, thread a double strand of color C through a tapestry needle and knot the ends leaving 3-inch-long loose threads. Make about 25 stitches, varying in length from 1 1/4 inches to 1/2 inch, at random over the falling-snow patterns. Loosen the knots and weave in the loose threads as instructed on page 155.

The back: Work the back the same way you did the front until the piece measures 11 inches. At this point, begin the 12 rows of the first falling-snow pattern for the back. On the first row, attach color C and knit 1 stitch. Knit 23 stitches with color A. Continue knitting across the row in this pattern. Using only color A, work 5 alternating rows of knit and purl stitches. On the next row, knit 12 stitches with color A. Attach color C and knit 1 stitch. Knit 23 stitches with color A. Continue across the row in the pattern. Using color A, work 5 alternating rows of knit and purl stitches.

Now begin the 12 rows of the second falling-snow pattern. On the next row, attach color C and knit 1 stitch. Knit 11 stitches with color A. Continue across the row in this pattern. Using color A, work 5 alternating rows of knit and purl stitches. On the next row, knit 6 stitches with color A, then knit 1 stitch with color C. Knit 11 stitches with color A. Continue knitting across the row in the pattern. Using only color A, work 5 alternating rows of knit and purl stitches.

Now begin the 30 rows of the third falling-snow pattern. On the first row, knit 1 stitch with color C. Then knit 5 stitches with color A. Continue knitting across the row in the pattern. Using only color A, work 5 alternating rows of knit and purl stitches. On the next row, knit 3 stitches with color A, then 1 stitch with color C. Knit 5 stitches with color A. Continue across the row in the pattern. Using color A, work 5 more alternating rows of knit and purl stitches. At this point, the piece should measure about 18 inches, or the same as the front measured to the underarm edge.

The armholes: Shape the armholes as you did on the front until 63 (69,73) stitches remain. At the same time, continue working 18 more rows in the third falling-snow pattern.

Now begin the 20 rows of the fourth falling-snow pattern. Knit 5 stitches with color A, then 1 stitch with color C. Continue across the row in the pattern. Using only color A, work 3 alternating rows of knit and purl stitches. On the next row knit 2 stitches with color A, 1 stitch with color C, then 5 stitches with color A. Continue across the row in the pattern. Using only color A, work 3 alternating rows of knit and purl stitches. Repeat these 8 rows 1 more time, then repeat the first 4 rows 1 more time.

Now begin the fifth falling-snow pattern. On the first row, knit 1 stitch with color C. Knit 5 stitches with color A. Continue across the row in the pattern. Using color A, purl across the next row. On the following row, knit 3 stitches with color A, 1 stitch with color C, then 5 stitches with color A. Continue across the row in the pattern. Purl across the next row using color A. Continue to work the fifth pattern in this manner until the piece measures the same as the front from the armhole to the shoulders—8 (9,9 1/2) inches.

Shape the shoulders as you did on the front, still working in the fifth falling-snow pattern, then loosely bind off the remaining 23 (25,25) stitches for the back of the neck. Embroider about 60 large and small V-shaped stitches as you did on the front.

The sleeves: With Size 7 needles and using color A, cast on 38 (42,46) stitches. Knit 1, purl 1 to make a 2 1/2-inch ribbing. Change to Size 10 needles. Using color A, work alternating rows of knit and purl stitches for 1 inch. On the next row, increase 1 stitch at the beginning and end of the row. Continue alternating knit and purl rows, increasing 1 stitch at the beginning and end of a row 7 more times at 1-inch intervals. When the piece measures 11 inches, begin the falling-snow patterns, working them in the same order and sequence as you did on the back. Remember to center the first color C stitch over the color A unit on the previous row. At the same time, continue to increase 1 stitch at the beginning and end of a knit row at 1-inch intervals until there are 60 (64,68) stitches on the needles. Work in the fall-ing-snow patterns until the piece measures 18 inches.

The sleeve cap: Continue the falling-snow patterns as on the back. Bind off 4 (4,5) stitches at the beginning of the next 2 rows. Then decrease 1 stitch at the beginning and end of every other row for 5 1/2 (6,6 1/2) inches. Bind off 2 stitches at the beginning of each of the next 4 rows. Bind off the remaining stitches. Repeat the preceding steps on the other sleeve, and embroider 35-40 large and small V-shaped stitches—as you did on the front.

The finishing touches: Place the back and the front together, wrong sides out, with the front facing up. Sew the left shoulder seam. Form the neckband by spreading the two pieces apart, wrong sides down. Using Size 7 needles and color A yarn, pick up 88 (92,96) stitches around the neck edge as instructed on page 155.

Knit 1, purl 1 to make a 1 1/2-inch ribbing; then bind off loosely in the ribbing pattern. Place the pieces together, wrong sides out, and sew all seams. Block, following the instructions on page 150.

THE DRESS

For color A (light green in the picture on page 147), you will need 5 (6,7,8,9) four-ounce skeins of knitting worsted; 1 (1,1,2,2) four-ounce skeins for color B (the darker green) and 2 (3,3,4,4) four-ounce skeins for color C (white). Use straight knitting needles Sizes 7 and 10, an aluminum crochet hook Size G and a tapestry needle for sewing the seams and embroidering the snowflakes.

Knit a sample swatch to check the gauge: 4 stitches and 5 rows to an inch on Size 10 needles.

The back: With Size 7 needles and color A, cast on 103 (107,111,115,119) stitches. Work alternating rows of knit and purl stitches for 6 rows, ending with a purl row. Purl across the following row to form the hemline. Purl the next row. Change to Size 10 needles and work 6 alternating rows of knit and purl stitches. Beginning on a knit row, start to work the 35 rows of the band of snowflakes using the diagrams (opposite), the main diagram on page 148 and the instructions included for the front of the man's sweater to position the designs correctly. Follow the instructions on page 155 for joining yarn along a row and for working with more than one yarn color.

On the next row, using only color A, decrease 1 stitch at the beginning of the row. Purl across the row, and decrease 1 stitch at the end of the row. Continue decreasing every fourth row 17 more times and at the same time start the first falling-snow pattern—12 rows in all. (As you decrease, always make sure that the first stitch with color C is centered over the color A unit on the previous pattern row.) On the first row, knit 1 stitch with color A. Attach color C and knit 1 stitch. Continue across the row in this pattern. Break off color C at the end of this and every other falling-snow pattern row and reattach the yarn at the beginning of the next pattern row.

Purl across the next row using color A. On the next row, knit 1 stitch with color C, then 1 stitch with color A. Continue knitting across the row in this pattern. Purl across the next row using color A, decreasing 1 stitch at the beginning and end of the row. Repeat this pattern 2 more times.

Begin the 20 rows of the second falling-snow pattern on the next row. On the first row, knit 3 stitches with color A, then 1 stitch with color C. Continue across the row in this pattern. Purl across the next row using only color A. On the following row, knit 1 stitch with color A. Knit 1 stitch with color C, then knit 3 stitches with color A. Continue across the row in the pattern. Purl across the next row using only color A, decreasing 1 stitch at the beginning and end of the row. Repeat this pattern 4 more times, again centering the first stitch with color C over the color A unit of the previous row.

Working now on 85 (89,93,97,101) stitches, begin the 18 rows of the third falling-snow pattern. On the first row, knit 5 stitches with color A, then knit 1 stitch with color C. Con-

right side

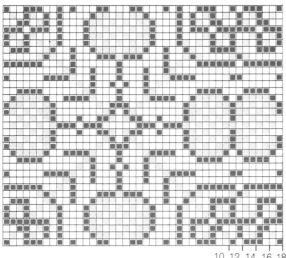

10 12 14 16 18

left side

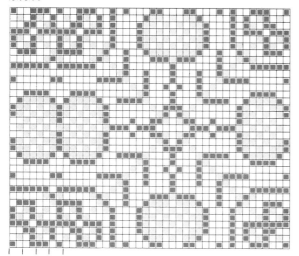

18 16 14 12 10

tinue across the row in this pattern. Purl across the next row, using only color A. On the following row, knit 2 stitches with color A. Knit 1 stitch with color C, then 5 stitches with color A. Continue across the row in the pattern. Purl across the next row, using only color A, decreasing 1 stitch at the beginning and end of the row. Repeat these 4 rows 3 more times. On the following row, knit 1 stitch with color C, then knit 5 stitches with color A. Continue across the row in this pattern. Purl across the next row using only color A. There are now 77 (81,85,89,93) stitches on the needles.

Now begin the 12 rows of the fourth falling-snow pattern. On the first row, knit 3 stitches with color A. Knit 1 stitch with color C, then knit 5 stitches with color A. Continue across the row in this pattern. Work 3 alternating rows of knit and purl stitches using only color A and decreasing at the beginning and end of the third row. On the next row, knit 1 stitch with color A, then 1 stitch with color C. Knit 5 stitches with color A. Continue across the row in the pattern. Work 3 alternating rows of knit and purl stitches using only color A and decreasing 1 stitch at the beginning and end of the third row. On the next row, knit 3 stitches with color A, then 1 stitch with color C. Knit 5 stitches with color A. Continue across the row in the pattern. Repeat the previous 3 rows 1 more time. There are now 71 (75,79,83,87) stitches on the needles. Now begin the 18 rows of the fifth falling-snow pattern. Knit 5 stitches with color A, then knit 1 stitch with color C. Continue knitting across the row in the pattern. Purl across the next row using only color A. Knit across the following row using only color A. Purl across the next row, using only color A and decreasing 1 stitch at the beginning and end of the row. Knit across the next row using only color A. Purl across the following row using only color A.

On the next row, knit 1 stitch with color A. Knit 1 stitch with color C, then knit 5 stitches with color A. Continue across the row in the pattern. Purl across the following row, using only color A and decreasing 1 stitch at the beginning and the end of the row. Work 3 alternating rows of knit and purl stitches using only color A. On the next row, purl across the row using only color A and decreasing 1 stitch at the beginning and end of the row, thus completing the 18 decrease rows. There are now 65(69,73,77,81) stitches on the needles.

On the next row, knit 2 stitches with color A, then 1 stitch with color C. Knit 5 stitches with color A. Continue across the row in this pattern. Beginning with a purl row, work 5 alternating rows of knit and purl stitches using only color A.

Now begin the 7 rows of the sixth falling-snow pattern. Knit 5 stitches with color A. Knit 1 stitch with color C, then knit 11 stitches with color A. Continue across the row in the pattern. Starting with a purl row, and using only color A, work 5 alternating rows of knit and purl stitches. On the next row, knit 11 stitches with color A then knit 1 stitch with color C. Continue knitting across the row in the pattern. This row completes the sixth falling-snow pattern. Using only color A, work alternating rows of knit and purl stitches until the piece measures 28 inches from the purl row marking the hemline.

The armholes: Bind off 4(4,5,5,5) stitches at the beginning of each of the next 2 rows. Decrease 1 stitch at the beginning of the next row by knitting 2 stitches together; then knit across the row decreasing 1 stitch at the end of the row. Purl across the next row. Repeat the last 2 rows 3(3, 3,3,4) more times. Work on 49(53,55,59,61) stitches until the piece measures 7 (7 1/4,7 1/2,7 3/4,8) inches above the start of the armhole edge.

The shoulders: Bind off 8(9,9,10,10) stitches at the beginning of each of the next 2 rows. Then bind off 8(8,9,9,10) stitches at the beginning of each of the following 2 rows. Loosely bind off the remaining 17(19,19,21,21) stitches for the back of the neck. Embroider about 120 V-shaped stitches as instructed in the directions for the man's sweater.

The front: Work the front the same way you did the back until the piece measures 5 (5 1/4,5 1/2,5 3/4,6) inches above the start of the armhole. End with a purl row. Shape the neck by knitting across 19(20,21,22,23) stitches. Join another ball of color A and bind off 11(13,13,15,15) stitches at the center. Then knit across the remaining 19(20,21,22, 23) stitches. On the next row, working on both sides of the front at once, purl across the row, decreasing 1 stitch at each inner, or neck, edge. Repeat the decreases at each neck edge on every other row 2 more times. Work now on the 16(17,18,19,20) stitches at each side of the neck. When the front measures the same as the back from the underarm to the shoulders, shape the shoulders as you did on the back. Embroider about 150 V-shaped stitches as instructed in the directions for the man's sweater.

The sleeves: With Size 7 needles and using only color A, cast on 32(34,36,38,40) stitches. Knit 1, purl 1 to make a 1 1/2-inch ribbing. Change to Size 10 needles and work alternating rows of knit and purl stitches for 1 inch. Then increase 1 stitch at the beginning and at the end of the next row. Repeat this increase every 1 1/2 inches 6 more times. Work now on 46(48,50,52,54) stitches until the sleeve piece measures 18 inches.

The sleeve cap: Bind off 4(4,5,5,5) stitches at the beginning of each of the next 2 rows. Then decrease 1 stitch at the beginning and end of every other row for 4(4 1/4,4 1/2,4 3/4, 5) inches. Bind off 2 stitches at the beginning of each of the next 4 rows. Bind off the remaining stitches. Repeat the preceding steps on the other sleeve.

The finishing touches: Place the back and the front sections together, wrong sides out, with the front piece facing up. Sew the left shoulder seam. Form the neckband by spreading the two pieces apart, wrong sides down. Using Size 7 needles and color A, pick up 68(72,76,80,84) stitches around the neck edge following the diagram and instructions on page 155. Knit 1, purl 1 to make a 1-inch ribbing and bind off loosely in the ribbing pattern. Place the pieces together wrong sides out again, and sew all seams.

Turn under the bottom of the dress at the purl row forming the hemline. Sew the hem in place using an overcast stitch (Appendix). With the crochet hook and color A, pick up the purl stitches marking the hem and work 1 row of single crochet stitches (Appendix) around the bottom of the dress. Block, following the instructions on page 150.

THE CAP

For color A (light green in the picture on page 146), you will need 2 four-ounce skeins of knitting worsted and 1 skein of white knitting worsted for color C (white).

Use straight knitting needles Sizes 7 and 10, and a tapestry needle for sewing the seams and embroidering the snowflake designs.

Knit a sample swatch to check the gauge: 4 stitches and 5 rows to an inch on Size 10 needles.

The cuff: With Size 7 needles and color A, cast on 84 stitches. Knit 1, purl 1 to make a 5-inch ribbing.

The crown: Change to Size 10 needles. At the beginning of the next row, using only color A, knit 12 stitches. Knit 2 stitches together to decrease. Continue to knit across the row, decreasing every thirteenth stitch for a total of 6 decreases. Working on 78 stitches and using color A, purl across the following row.

At the beginning of the next row, start the falling-snow pattern. Knit 3 stitches with color A. Attach color C and knit 1 stitch. Knit 3 stitches with color A. Continue across the row in this pattern. Purl across the following row using only color A. On the next row, using color A, knit 11 stitches. Knit 2 stitches together to decrease. (As you decrease, always make sure that the first stitch with color C is centered over the color A unit on the previous pattern row.) Continue across the row, decreasing every twelfth stitch for a total of 6 decreases. Purl across the next row, on 72 stitches, using only color A. On the following row, knit 2 stitches with color A. Knit 1 stitch with color C. Knit 3 stitches with color A. Continue to knit across the row in the falling-snow pattern. Purl across the next row using only color A. At the beginning of the next row, knit 10 stitches with color A. Knit 2 stitches together to decrease. Continue across the row, decreasing every eleventh stitch for a total of 6 decreases. Purl across the next row on 66 stitches using only color A. On the next row knit 1 stitch with color A. Knit 1 stitch with color C, then knit 3 stitches with color A. Continue to knit across the row in the falling-snow pattern. Purl across the next row using only color A. Continue to work in this manner until 48 stitches remain: decrease 6 times at evenly spaced intervals on a knit row—knitting 1 less stitch between the decreases each time the row is repeated; purl the next row; work the next knit row in the falling-snow pattern, centering the first color C stitch over the color A unit of the previous row; and purl the next row. Then using color A only, work alternating rows of knit and purl stitches, decreasing 6 evenly spaced stitches in every knit row until 6 stitches remain. Bind off, leaving a long strand of yarn measuring at least 15 inches.

The V-shaped stitches: Embroider approximately 18 V-shaped stitches as instructed in the directions given for the man's sweater.

The finishing touches: Block, following the instructions on page 150. Then thread the long strand of yarn left at the crown through a tapestry needle and weave the needle through the 6 bound-off stitches. Using the same strand of yarn, sew up the back seam. Form a peak on the cap by twisting the top slightly and sewing it in place.

JOINING YARN

To introduce a new ball or color of yarn at any point along a row, wrap it around the working needle, leaving 2- or 3-inch-long ends, and use the new yarn to knit the next stitch *(drawing 1)*. When you have knitted 2 or 3 rows, weave the loose ends *(drawing 2)* through nearby stitches on the wrong side of the piece, using a crochet hook. When working with more than one yarn color, carry a second color up from row to row—or loosely across the back of the work —for a maximum of 5 stitches, always picking up the new color from underneath the color you are dropping. If more than 5 stitches occur before the yarn is needed again, break off the color you are working with and attach the new color as shown here.

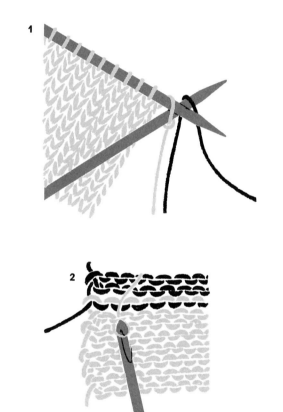

PICKING UP STITCHES AT AN EDGE

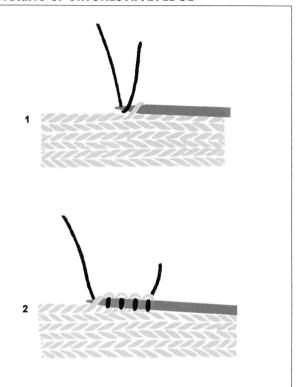

To form a new row of stitches at a neck or armhole edge for a collar, neckline ribbing or sleeve, insert a needle from right to left into the first stitch to be picked up. Wrap a new strand of yarn around the needle and draw it through the stitch at the edge *(drawing 1)*. Continue in this manner along the row of stitches to be picked up, drawing the yarn through each successive stitch *(drawing 2)*.

Cubes

Parallels

Hourglasses

156

Quadrate

Variations on the granny patch

The name of the innovative genius who first crocheted precious scraps of leftover yarn into a square has been forgotten, but the technique she—or he—devised is still a favorite one with crocheters the world over. The task is easy, the work supremely portable, and it can be dropped and resumed at whim.

As squares accumulate, they can be sewn together in pieces as small or as large as wanted. The sober economy of granny patchwork appeals to the thrifty, its ad-lib air pleases the playful. No wonder this simple and satisfying art—as perfect in its way as the wheel or the pigtail—has survived for centuries.

Contemporary granny squares, like those pictured here, differ from grandmother's in that they are a bit more calculated. Modern granny patchers seek to exploit the use of multiple yarn hues by developing sophisticated design plans. For a look at the unplain geometry that can result, turn the page.

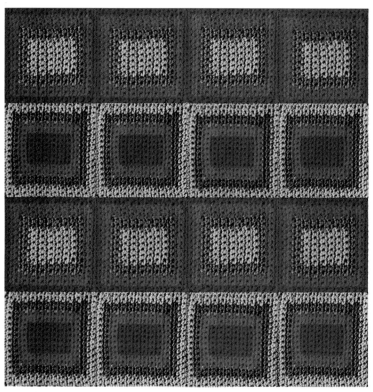

Planning the way in which individual granny squares will be sewn together, to form anything from a car robe to a horse blanket, is a stimulating exercise in artistic imagination. Each design offers a variety of color and pattern options. The Cubes above are shown in two versions of the same warm-hued color scheme. Whether the two are arranged in alternating horizontal rows *(left)*, or as a checkerboard *(right)*, the result is a strikingly dynamic design. Both would be effective in dramatic fashions such as a full-length skirt or sleeveless coat.

A careful choice and combination of color harmonies running from deep rose to soft lavender, as illustrated in the Parallels design above, can lead to allover patterns that range from a broken-striped honeycomb *(left)* to a vigorous diagonal zigzag *(right)*. Composed entirely of stripes, Parallels is one of the easiest of the granny square designs to execute because the switches of yarn color occur only at the beginning of the row. Thus this particular pattern makes a good vehicle for a family project in which all ages can join.

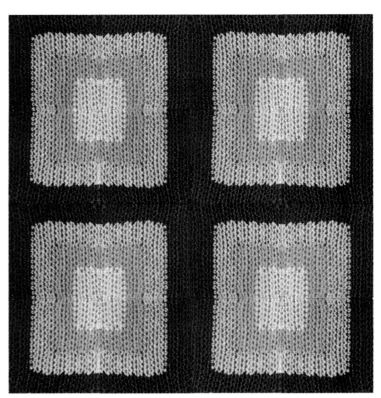

The soft-hued Qradrate above is close kin to the vivid Cubes at left; both are constructed on the principle of the square. In the Quadrate, however, the corner positioning of the small square opens up exciting alternatives in total design. With greatly differing effect,

the individual patches can be combined in bricklaying fashion *(left)*, or arranged to form a four-paned "window" *(right)*—a design used for the hooded cape shown on pages 160-161. Quadrate would be equally handsome as a cover for couch pillows or large floor cushions.

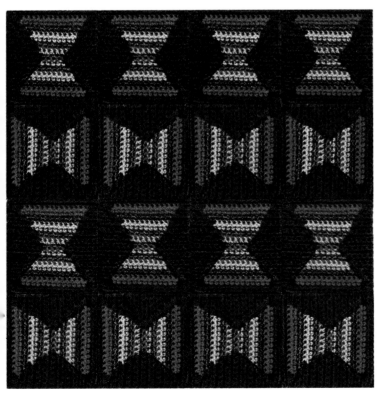

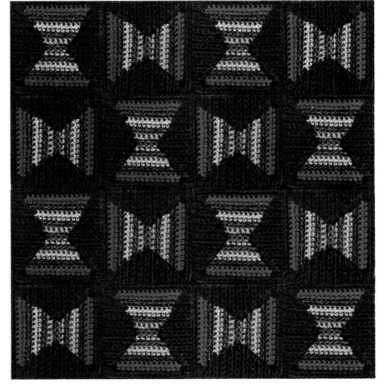

The hourglass figure in the designs above is an integral part of each square, crocheted directly into the work and then outlined with an embroidered running chain stitch. Yet the effect is that of appliqué patches cut from a bright striped fabric and superimposed on a plain

background. When the individual granny squares are combined in symmetrical rows *(left)*, or in alternating directions *(right)*, they create patterns reminiscent of patchwork quilts, making Hourglass particularly suitable for afghans, bed covers and throws.

A hooded cape of quadrates

Thanks to the straightforward geometry of the Quadrate granny-square *(page 157)*, this Little Blue Riding Hood cape looks as bright and contemporary as the girl wearing it. Shown in both back and front views, the cape consists of 36 artfully arranged Quadrates. When joined, the squares can serve just as enchantingly in any other garment whose design calls for bold but simple lines and straight-edged pieces.

Of the 36 squares, four constitute the hood and the other 32—grouped into eight blocks of four squares each—form the cape. Making each square requires only the single and half double crochet stitches, but finishing the cape involves three more: the triple crochet stitch and the slip stitch for framing the blocks, and the simple chain stitch for the neck cord.

The instructions for the hooded cape appear on pages 163-164.

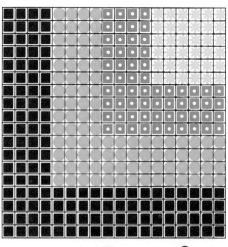

quadrate: dark tone ■ neutral tone ●
medium tone ◨ light tone ✱

Instructions for the crocheted cape

The modern granny squares on pages 156-157 can be crocheted by following the color-keyed diagrams shown here and using the stitches described below.

The Quadrate pattern *(top right)* is worked in alternating rows of single and half double crochet stitches at a gauge of 3 stitches and 3 rows to an inch; the other squares, in single crochet at a gauge of 3 stitches and 4 rows to an inch. Because of the gauge difference, it takes 18 rows to make a 6-inch Quadrate square, but 24 rows to make the other squares —hence, the elongated diagrams.

Instructions for combining the Quadrate squares to make the hooded cape pictured on pages 160-161 begin on the opposite page.

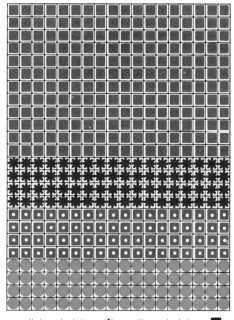

parallels: dark tone ✱ medium dark tone ■
medium tone ◨ light tone ●

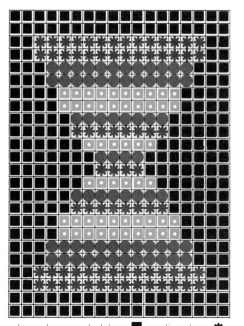

hourglasses: dark tone ■ medium tone ✱
neutral tone ● light tone ◨

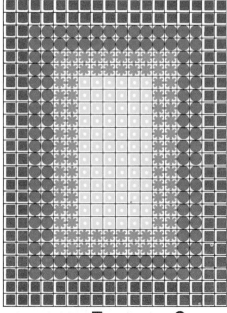

cubes: dark tone ■ medium tone ●
neutral tone ✱ light tone ◨

CROCHETING ABBREVIATIONS

The following instructions describe in simple terms the project in this book. Below are the standard needlework codes for adapting these techniques to other projects.

SC—single crochet   **HDC**—half double crochet
CH—chain   **DC**—double crochet
HK—hook   **TRC**—triple crochet
ST—stitch   **SK**—skip
REP—repeat   **LP**—loop
PAT—pattern   **SP**—space

*—starting point for a repeated sequence of steps: When instructions tell you to "rep from *" read back to find the point (*) where you must begin to repeat.

CHECKING THE GAUGE

A stitch gauge precedes all crocheting instructions. This gauge specifies the number of stitches (and often the number of rows) to the inch needed to make the project the proper size. Check the gauge by crocheting a sample swatch before beginning your project. The swatch should measure at least 4 by 4 inches and be made with the yarn and hook recommended in the pattern. If two sizes of hooks are required, measure the gauge using the larger needles. Remove the swatch from the hook, lay it flat and count the stitches to the inch, measuring with a ruler, not a tape measure. If the gauge calls for more stitches to the inch, change to a smaller hook. If the gauge calls for fewer stitches to the inch, use a larger hook. This change of hook size will also alter the row-to-the-inch gauge.

BLOCKING THE FINISHED WORK

Press, or block, each garment. Lay it out flat, then cover with a damp cloth and press lightly with a warm iron. Do not pin the garment to the pressing surface or let the iron rest long in one area lest you leave marks. Enlarge or reduce the size of the garment a little by dampening it lightly, then pushing or stretching it as you lay it out.

CROCHETING THE HOODED CAPE

The following instructions are for crocheting the cape and hood pictured on pages 160-161. The directions are for a 30-inch-long cape that fits all sizes. For a longer cape, add more rows of border trim at the bottom; for a shorter garment, make fewer rows. Basic crochet stitches and techniques are shown in the Appendix; additional stitches used for this project appear at the end of the instructions.

You will need 3 four-ounce skeins of knitting worsted for color A (brown in the pictures on pages 160-161); 3 four-ounce skeins for color B (beige); 2 four-ounce skeins for color C (medium blue); 2 four-ounce skeins for color D (light blue); and 5 four-ounce skeins for color E (deep blue).

Use aluminum crochet hooks Sizes I and K and a large tapestry needle for embroidering. Check the gauge on a sample: 3 stitches and 3 rows to the inch on Size K hook.

The cape: Following the diagram for the Quadrate granny square *(opposite)*, make 18 small squares (Pattern 1). Start with Size K hook and color A yarn. Make a foundation chain of 18 stitches. Single crochet the first row. At the end of the row, chain 2 and turn. Half double crochet *(page 165)* the next row. Chain 1 and turn at the end of the row. Repeat these 2 rows 1 more time. Attach color B on the last stitch of the fourth row; work the last 2 loops on the hook in the new color. Following the diagram for color changes and the instructions for attaching new yarn colors on page 164, work the 18 rows of the Pattern 1 square in this manner. Alternate 1 row of single crochet and 1 row of half double crochet in the established pattern. Note: The side visible when the garment is worn is the side on which the row of single crochet stitches must be worked. Break off all threads no longer used, and weave them into nearby stitches, on the wrong side *(page 164)*.

Still using the Quadrate diagram, make 18 more small squares (Pattern 2). Half double crochet the first row after the foundation chain, then single crochet the next row. (If you alternate the order of the rows on the two sets of squares, you will be able to form the small squares into large ones with all pattern ridges running horizontally.) When you have completed the 36 squares, single crochet 1 row around each square, changing colors as necessary to match the colors in the square. Make 3 single crochet stitches in each corner to form the corner.

Form the small squares into large ones for the cape by placing 2 Pattern 1 squares and 2 Pattern 2 squares together, wrong sides down, with all pattern ridges running horizontally and with all corners worked in color D meeting at the center. From now on, work only in color E yarn. Single crochet 1 row along the 2 sides of each small square that touch the sides of other small squares. Begin to join the squares—first horizontally, then vertically—working a row of slip stitches, as shown on page 164, along each single-crochet row. Arrange and join 28 more small squares in the same manner to form a total of 8 large squares.

The back: Place 4 large squares together, with all pattern ridges running horizontally. Work 1 row of triple crochet, as instructed on page 165, along the 2 sides of each large square that touch the sides of other large squares. Slip stitch the 4 large squares together along the triple-crochet rows; join them first horizontally, then vertically. Work 1 long row of triple crochet along the 2 sides of the back.

The front: Use the 4 last large squares for the front. Place 2 large squares at each side of the back, one above the other. Work 1 row of triple crochet along the side of each large square that will be joined to the side of the large square directly above or below it. Slip stitch each set of large squares together along the horizontal rows of triple crochet stitches just completed. Work 1 row of triple crochet on the side of each front panel where it meets the side of the back.

Now join the two front panels to the back, working a row of slip stitches along the vertical rows of triple crochet stitches at the sides of the panels and at the back.

Begin working the slip stitches at the top of the garment. Work the stitches for about 10 inches—or to a comfortable level for your arm length. Fasten off. Leave an 8-inch opening for the armholes, then start to slip stitch the pieces together again, ending at the bottom of the garment.

The hood: Arrange the 4 remaining small squares into two halves of a large square, with the pattern ridges vertical and the centers of each half square at the front of the hood. Work 1 row of single crochet along the side of each small square that touches the side of the small square directly above or below. Work 1 row of slip stitches along the rows of single crochet to join each set horizontally.

Work a row of triple crochet along the vertical edges of the 2 half squares where they meet to form the center back of the hood. Begin at the bottom of each piece, then continue across the top. Slip stitch the 2 half squares together to form the large square of the hood, joining the rows of triple crochet stitches on each piece.

The neckband: Place the cape wrong side down. Use Size I hook and work along the top edge as follows: Single crochet the first row, decreasing 1 stitch in every stitch across the row. Half double crochet the next row. Single crochet the following row. Work another row in half double crochet. On the next row, work 3 single crochet stitches, then decrease and single crochet across the row, decreasing every fourth stitch. Work the next 4 rows without decreasing, alternating the half double and the single crochet rows in the established pattern. Fasten off.

Finishing the hood: Using Size I hook, work 1 row of single crochet then 1 row of half double crochet around the front of the hood. On the next row, work around the front using half double crochet stitches. On the next row, single crochet around the front and bottom of the hood. Now work only along the single crochet stitches at the bottom.

On the first row, work 1 triple crochet stitch in the first single crochet stitch of the previous row. Chain 1 and skip

1 stitch. Repeat this pattern across the row. At the end, chain 1 and turn. On the next row, work 1 single crochet stitch in each triple crochet stitch of the previous row, and make 1 single crochet stitch in each chain-1 space of the previous row; then chain 1 and turn. Single crochet across the next row, decreasing 10 evenly spaced stitches across the row. Fasten off. Join the hood to the cape with a row of slip stitches.

The finishing touches: For a border around the outer edge of the cape and hood, place a marker at the starting point, then single crochet 1 row around the garment, decreasing 1 stitch every sixth stitch. When you reach the starting marker, chain 2 and turn. Working in the opposite direction now, double crochet a row around the piece. End by chaining 1 and turn. Reversing the direction again, single crochet the next row around the garment. Continue this for 4 more rows, alternating the rows of half double crochet and single crochet and reversing the direction of each successive row. Fasten off. Make the tie with Size K hook and 3 strands of color E yarn used as 1 strand. Make a series of chain stitches approximately 1 1/2 yards long. Fasten off. Weave the tie through the spaces formed by the row of triple crochet stitches at the bottom of the hood. Thread a large tapestry needle with 4 strands of color E yarn used as 1 strand. Embroider large cross stitches, measuring 1 1/2 inches from tip to tip, at all intersecting points on the cape and hood where the triple crocheted edges of the large squares meet at a corner. Make a 1/2-inch fastening stitch at the center of each cross stitch. Block, following the instructions on page 163.

THE SLIPSTITCH FOR JOINING CROCHETED PIECES

Align the edges of the pieces to be joined. Insert the hook from front to back through both loops of the first stitch at the end of each piece. Then attach a strand of yarn as shown in the drawing below, left. Draw the yarn through all 4 loops, leaving a loop on the hook (drawing 1). Insert the hook through both loops of the next pair of stitches. Bring the yarn over the hook and draw it, in one motion, through these stitches as well as through the loop on the hook (drawing 2). Continue in this manner until the pieces are joined.

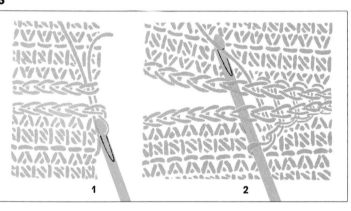

JOINING YARN

Attach a new ball of yarn at the beginning of a row by wrapping it around the hook and drawing it through the first loops of the stitch at the edge (drawing 1). Leave 3-inch-long loose ends. After crocheting 2 or 3 rows, weave the loose ends of the yarn through nearby stitches on the wrong side of the work (drawing 2). When working with more than one yarn color, carry a second color up from row to row, or carry it loosely across the back of the work for a maximum of 5 stitches. Join a new color while you are working the last stitch in the color to be dropped—as follows: attach the new yarn by wrapping it around the hook; then draw the strand through the last 2 loops of the stitch on the hook for single crochet, and the last 3 loops for half double crochet.

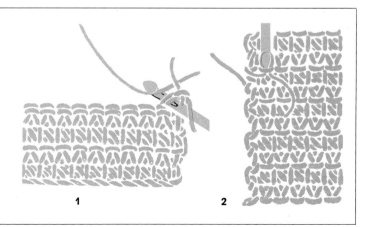

THE TRIPLE CROCHET STITCH

Make a foundation chain of the desired number of stitch-es. Chain 3. *Row 1:* Bring the yarn over the hook from back to front twice. Insert the hook into the fourth chain stitch from the hook *(drawing 1, right).* Bring the yarn over the hook once, and draw it through the loop closest to the tip *(drawing 2).* There are now 4 loops on the hook.

Bring the yarn over the hook again and draw it through the 2 loops that are closest to the tip *(drawing 3).* Bring the yarn over the hook again and draw it through the next 2 loops closest to the tip *(drawing 4).* Bring the yarn over the hook one more time and draw it through the remaining 2 loops *(drawing 5).* These steps form 1 triple crochet stitch.

Repeat these steps in each succeeding chain across the row. At the end of the row, chain 3 and turn. *Row 2:* Bring the yarn over the hook twice, then insert the hook into the first stitch. Continue to triple crochet as instructed in the preceding steps. At the end of the row, chain 3 and turn. Repeat row 2 to complete the pattern.

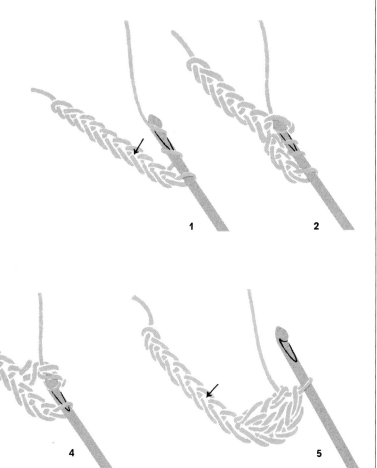

THE HALF DOUBLE CROCHET STITCH

As above, make a foundation chain of the desired number of stitches. Chain 2. *Row 1:* Bring the yarn over the hook from back to front. Then insert the hook through the sec-ond chain stitch from the hook *(drawing 1, right).* With 3 loops now on the hook, bring the yarn over the hook again *(drawing 2).* Catch the yarn under the tip of the hook and draw it through the loop closest to the tip *(drawing 3).* Bring the yarn over the hook again and draw it through all 3 loops on the hook *(drawing 4).* Repeat these steps in each suc-ceeding chain across the row. At the end of the row, chain 2 and turn.

Row 2: Bring the yarn over the hook, and insert the hook into the first stitch. Continue to half double crochet as in the preceding steps *(drawing 5).* At the end of the row, chain 2 and turn. Repeat row 2 to complete the pattern.

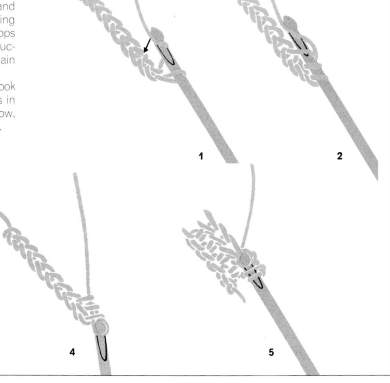

The special elegance of needlepoint

For present-day lovers of needlepoint, few American heirlooms are as precious as a certain chair cushion *(opposite)* in the Washington Museum at Mount Vernon. It is one of a set of 12 worked by Martha Washington—an avid and talented needlewoman her life long—and later cherished by her three granddaughters. She finished the set at age 70, two years after Washington's sudden death in December 1799 and only months before she herself died. The task must have provided both distraction and solace for the bereaved widow.

Shaped to the curve of a Windsor chair, the cushion cover has a design of stylized scallop shells stitched on coarse canvas in mustard yellow and brick red wools, highlighted skillfully with touches of gold silk. The look is tasteful and traditional, as one might expect from the well-brought-up daughter of 18th Century Virginia plantation gentry. But it could never be described as exquisite. Something about the bold authority of Martha's pattern, done entirely in cross stitch, gives it a free, forthright spirit that spells "American."

Martha Washington and ladies like her were the exception rather than the rule: needlepoint was not a widely practiced art in early America. The blunt tapestry needle and the background canvas were expensive items that generally had to be imported from Britain. Yarn itself was costly and scarce enough to discourage needlepoint, which usually required more wool than crewel embroidery did. And needlepoint on an ambitious scale was time-consuming, an art reserved almost exclusively for women of the leisure class.

Even affluent gentlewomen like Martha Washington often had much more urgent assignments that awaited their needles. Mrs. Washington herself spent eight war winters with the General at Continental Army headquarters, and she was kept constantly busy there sewing, mending and knitting to ensure that the clothing of officers and men were in good repair.

But when conditions were right, a few of our founding mothers could and did practice an expert "canvaswork," as needlepoint was then called. A handsome card table cover now in the proud possession of the Pilgrim Society of Plymouth, Massachusetts, was designed and executed by Martha Washington's friend Mercy Otis when she was a young woman in Barnstable, Massachusetts, awaiting her marriage. (Later, as Mercy Otis Warren, she became a poet and historian and a memorable figure in Revolutionary America.) Worked in tent stitch, the cover is a marvel of lively design and sensitively harmonized color.

Needleworkers who were far less talented than Mercy Warren could still find great pleasure in working, say, a man's pocketbook (an accessory much like the modern wallet). Perhaps done in a pleasing flame stitch, which is more familiar to us as the Florentine or Bargello stitch, the design might incorporate the recipient's name, the date and a tender legend: "When this you see, remember me."

That personal touch is one of the hallmarks of colonial and Federal needlepoint. Often laboring under conditions of scarcity, compelled by circumstances to design or adapt her own pattern from English models and to choose the stitches and colors according to her own best instincts, the early American needlepointer inevitably gave her handiwork an individual character.

Sometime around 1820, this rather elegant and private diversion of the leisured gentlefolk began its quite remarkable transformation into what eventually became a Victorian fad. Canvaswork was, and remained for about 50 years, something called Berlin work. The name is traceable to a Berlin print seller who, around 1803, dreamed up the idea of printing needlepoint designs on paper with copper plates etched in a grid pattern. Designs came off the presses automatically marked off in tiny squares, and each square was then painstakingly hand tinted to indicate exactly what colors should be used to make a chair cushion, stool top or pillow cover. It was a labor-saving device that the fad-following ladies of America adopted with alacrity.

Two needlepoint masterpieces—a chair cushion worked by Martha Washington (right) and a card table cover done by Mercy Otis—are among the most treasured stitchery heirlooms from colonial America. The cushion, with a bold scallop pattern, was completed in 1801. The needlepoint table cover, showing the ingredients for a game of loo, is one of the most elaborate designs ever attempted. It was finished about 1750.

Like so many breakthroughs of technology, Berlin patterns opened up a mass market. But in the long run they debased the art. Worked on relatively coarse canvas, usually in tent or cross stitch, they frequently had the look of earnest samplers turned out by superannuated children. Perhaps it was the garish yarns—which acquired harsh hues of brass, magenta, purple and lurid green after mineral and aniline dyes were introduced. Perhaps it was the Victorian subject matter—pet dogs begging a crumb, parrots perched on wreaths, regal-looking lions, herds of deer, bulging cabbage roses smothered in lilies and ivy. Individual works could still reveal inspiration, taste and a personal signature, but the monotonous and slavish copying of mass-produced designs by the uninspired was frequently an artistic dead end—somewhat like the paint-by-numbers kits available today. It was easy to sympathize with Mark Twain's amusing description, in *Life on the Mississippi*, of a Berlin-work picture that hung in the parlor of a riverfront mansion:

"Over middle of mantel, engraving— 'Washington Crossing the Delaware'; on the wall by the door, copy of it done in thunder-and-lightning crewels by one of the young ladies—work of art which would have made Washington hesitate about crossing, if he could have foreseen what

During the Victorian era, needlepoint was popularized, romanticized and hybridized. Blatantly sentimental compositions such as the flower-filled urn at left were made from mass-produced tinted paper patterns. The pattern at right, marked on a grid, shows the placement of stitches and colors for an ornate bird portrait. Needlepoint designs were copied so scrupulously that identical creations appeared in countless homes.

advantage was going to be taken of it."

Today poor Washington crosses the Delaware only in the dark recesses of attics, languishing there with other Victorian excesses like the bustle, the plumed hat and the fringed antimacassar. But though fashions fluctuate, the basics of needlepoint—needle, yarn, stitch, canvas—have changed little over the years. Nor has there been a radical change in most males' attitudes toward the exercise. It is altogether common these days to hear the modern echo of one 19th Century bystander's lament, which was published anonymously as the *Husband's Complaint:*

I hate the name of German wool
In all its colors bright.
Of chairs and stools in fancy work
I hate the very sight.
The rugs and slippers that I've seen,
The ottomans and bags,
Sooner than wear a stitch on me
I'd walk the street in rags.
Oh, Heaven preserve me from a wife
With 'fancy work' run wild
And hands which never do aught else
For husband or for child. . . .

Needlepoint has adapted readily to 20th Century tastes and needs. The picture over the fireplace mantel now is less likely to be a demure shepherdess tending her flock than a copy of Robert Indiana's celebrated rendering of the letters L-O-V-E. And on the shelves of the needlework shops, designs for subtly shaded interpretations of Gauguin's Tahitian paintings vie with boldly patterned copies of Matisse.

Anything from a pair of bedroom slippers to a tennis-racket cover is a potential project for today's needlepointer. One enthusiast, author Russell Lynes, designed and made stereo-speaker covers that are marvels of camouflage. Each rectangular piece of stitchery is an artfully arranged shelf of knickknacks and books real and imaginary. A needlepoint tankard filled with pencils, for example, shares space with a book appropriately called *Trompe l'Oeil.* At first glance the needlework is almost indistinguishable from the books and *objets* that surround it. With this kind of ingenuity, Lynes has contributed his own distinctive chapter to the history of needlepoint.

Other 20th Century needlepoint creations rely more closely on traditional inspirations and motifs. The card-table cover, once the perfect setting for the gambling game of loo, now becomes a 1970s backgammon board *(pages 184-185).* The once-popular man's pocketbook is now more likely to be a woman's catch-all carrybag. Suspenders have returned to favor, but their designs are wildly colorful rather than traditionally subdued. Chair covers are as popular as in Martha Washington's day, but now they are more likely to express personal themes, like a family crest or a family's pleasure and prowess in music *(pages 180-181).* Even the most traditional American motifs—designs originated by the Indians—have found new popularity in needlepoint *(pages 170-171).*

With all its possibilities for inventiveness and adaptation, needlepoint remains what it was for the first First Lady: the enriching art of leisure moments, a skill with which to ornament possessions and create lasting tokens of regard and affection.

A needlepoint tribute to Indian art

The earliest American art of all, created centuries ago by Indian craftsmen, inspired the designs of this contemporary needlepoint fashioned by Nora Cammann. The models are from the collections of The American Museum of Natural History in New York City and include objects that are a thousand or more years old. Like so many other traditional styles, those of the American Indians have proved virtually timeless.

Pre-Columbian bowls unearthed in the Southwest furnished motifs for the round table cover, the turtle cushion and the quail cushion. Baskets woven by the Tlingit of the Pacific Northwest inspired patterns for the belt and the pillow. The needlepoint bag —which can be used to hold unfinished knitting or needlepoint and yarn—is almost a duplicate of a carryall woven by Wisconsin's Winnebago.

To make the patterns, the Indian designs were copied onto graph paper so that the size could be changed to suit the work, and the designs were then transferred to needlepoint canvas with indelible markers. In some of these designs crewel embroidery was used to add extra texture or such fine detail as the feet and feathers of the bird on the quail cushion.

Table-top cover and Southwestern Indian bowl

Whale and Gull belt and Tlingit basket

Pillow and Tlingit basket

Turtle cushion and Mimbres Valley bowl

Quail cushion and Mimbres Valley bowl

Needlepoint bag and Winnebago carryall

A select set of needlepoint stitches

For the creative needlepointer, selecting stitches is as important as choosing patterns. Each new stitch learned offers additional opportunities for variations on the smooth surface produced by the basic tent stitch (*Appendix*).

Among the stitches described at right and on the following pages, the mosaic is the most versatile. The basic single mosaic stitch can pinpoint fine details like flower centers. Repeated horizontally or vertically, it forms precisely regimented rows, which are especially attractive for small geometric designs.

Diagonal mosaic stitches, on the other hand, are useful for filling in the background area quickly and form an interesting pebbled texture. Other decorative stitches are the leaf stitch, with a three-dimensional quality that can give greenery a lush look, and the cushioned Scotch stitch, which has a padded look and may be worked in contrasting yarns for a checkerboard effect.

All of these stitches look well when worked on either fine or coarse monocanvas (single mesh) with 18-inch lengths of Persian yarn—one strand for 18 mesh canvas, two strands for 12 mesh canvas. In all cases, the canvas must be cut with at least a 2-inch border around the area to be worked so that the edges of the canvas can be bound and the finished work can be mounted.

STARTING A PIECE OF YARN

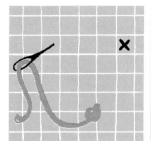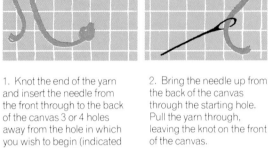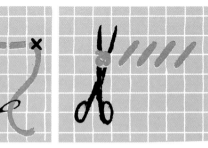

1. Knot the end of the yarn and insert the needle from the front through to the back of the canvas 3 or 4 holes away from the hole in which you wish to begin (indicated here with an X). If your pattern is to be worked from right to left, insert the needle 4 holes to the left of the starting hole; if your pattern is to be worked from left to right, insert the needle 4 holes to the right of the starting hole.

2. Bring the needle up from the back of the canvas through the starting hole. Pull the yarn through, leaving the knot on the front of the canvas.

3. When the pattern stitch you are working reaches the knot, cut the knot off.

ENDING A PIECE OF YARN

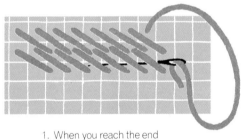

1. When you reach the end of each piece of yarn, or when you finish a pattern, turn the canvas over to the back and weave about 1 1/2 inches of yarn through the finished stitches on the back of the canvas.

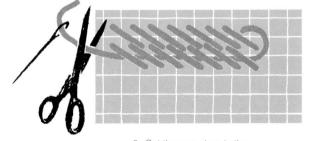

2. Cut the yarn close to the finished stitches, leaving no loose end.

THE SINGLE MOSAIC STITCH

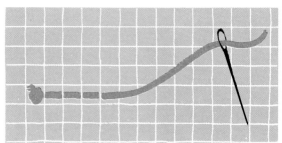

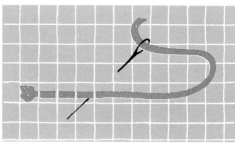

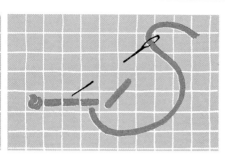

1. Anchor the yarn to the canvas 4 holes to the left of the hole in which you wish to begin, as shown in the instructions for starting a piece of yarn.

2. Insert the needle 1 hole above and 1 hole to the right of the hole from which the yarn emerged in the previous step. Slant the needle downward diagonally and bring it out 1 hole to the left of the hole from which the yarn last emerged. Pull the yarn through.

3. Insert the needle 2 holes above and 2 holes to the right of the one from which the yarn emerged in the previous step. Slant the needle downward diagonally and bring it out 1 hole above the hole from which the yarn last emerged. Pull the yarn through.

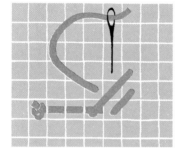

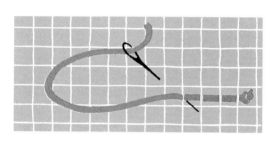

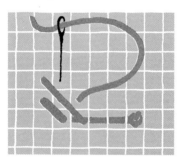

4. Insert the needle 1 hole above and 1 hole to the right of the one from which the yarn emerged in the previous step. Pull the needle through to the back of the canvas without beginning a new stitch. This completes a single mosaic stitch.

IF YOU ARE LEFT-HANDED...

1. Start in the upper left corner of the pattern area and work to the right as shown.

2. Follow the directions given above for working below or above the hole from which the yarn emerged in the previous step, but reverse the right and left directions so that each pattern stitch will slant from upper left to lower right.

THE MOSAIC STITCH WORKED HORIZONTALLY

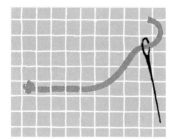

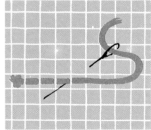

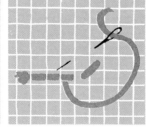

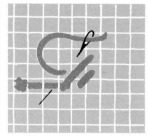

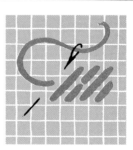

1. Anchor the yarn to the canvas 4 holes to the left of the hole in which you wish to begin, as shown in the instructions for starting a piece of yarn.

2. Follow the instructions for making the single mosaic stitch, Step 2.

3. Follow the instructions for making the single mosaic stitch, Step 3.

4. Insert the needle 1 hole above and 1 hole to the right of the one from which the yarn emerged in the previous step. Slant the needle downward diagonally and bring it out 1 hole below and 1 hole to the left of the one from which the yarn last emerged. Pull the yarn through.

5. Work each ensuing stitch in the row to the left of the previous one by repeating Steps 2-4 as many times as your design requires.

continued

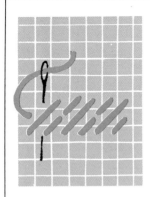 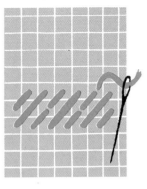 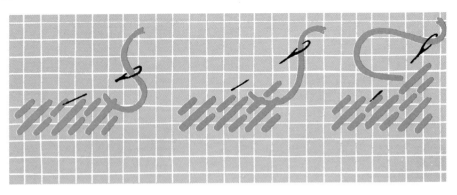

6. On the last stitch of the first row, work only Steps 2 and 3. Then insert the needle 1 hole above and 1 hole to the right of the hole from which the yarn last emerged. Slant the needle downward vertically and bring it out 1 hole below and 1 hole to the right of the hole from which the yarn last emerged. Pull the yarn through.

7. Turn the canvas 180 degrees so that the bottom edge is now on top and the yarn now emerges at the upper right, above the finished row of stitches.

8. Repeat Steps 2, 3 and 4 across the row.

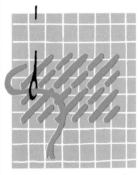 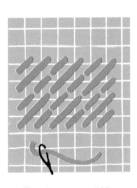 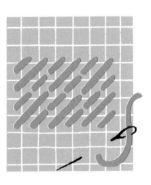 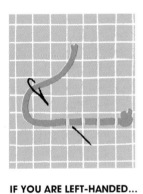 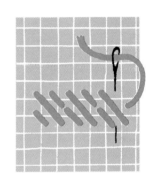

9. On the last stitch, work only Steps 2 and 3. Then insert the needle 1 hole above and 1 hole to the right of the hole from which the yarn last emerged. Slant the needle upward and bring it out 3 holes above and 1 hole to the right of the hole from which the yarn last emerged.

10. Turn the canvas 180 degrees so that the top edge is again on top and the yarn now emerges at the lower right, below the finished rows of stitches.

11. Continue the pattern across the row, beginning with Step 2 as shown.

IF YOU ARE LEFT-HANDED...

1. Start in the upper left corner of the pattern area and work to the right.

2. Follow the directions given above for working below or above the hole from which the yarn emerged in the previous step, but reverse the right and left directions so that each pattern stitch will slant from upper left to lower right.

THE MOSAIC STITCH WORKED VERTICALLY

    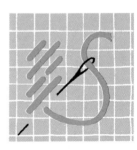

1. Anchor the yarn to the canvas 4 holes to the right of the hole in which you wish to begin, as indicated in the instructions for starting a piece of yarn.

2. Insert the needle 1 hole above and 1 hole to the right of the hole from which the yarn emerged in the previous step. Slant the needle downward diagonally and bring it out 1 hole below the hole from which the yarn last emerged. Pull the yarn through.

3. Insert the needle 2 holes above and 2 holes to the right of the hole from which the yarn emerged in the previous step. Slant the needle downward diagonally and bring it out 1 hole to the right of the hole from which the yarn last emerged. Pull the yarn through.

4. Insert the needle 1 hole above and 1 hole to the right of the hole from which the yarn emerged in the previous step. Slant the needle downward diagonally and bring it out 1 hole below and 1 hole to the left of the one from which the yarn last emerged. Pull the yarn through.

5. Repeat Steps 2, 3 and 4 as many times as your design requires to complete the row.

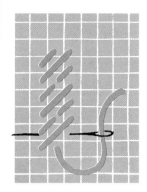 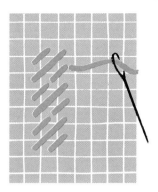 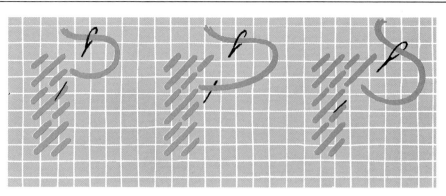

6. On the last stitch of the first vertical row, work only Steps 2 and 3. Then insert the needle 1 hole above and 1 hole to the right of the hole from which the yarn last emerged. Slant the needle to the left horizontally and bring it out 1 hole above and 1 hole to the left of the one from which the yarn last emerged. Pull the yarn through.

7. Turn the canvas 180 degrees so that the bottom edge is on top and the yarn now emerges at the upper right.

8. Repeat Steps 2, 3 and 4 down the row.

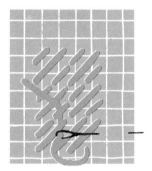 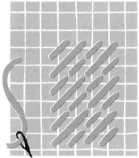 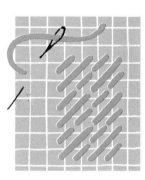 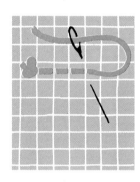 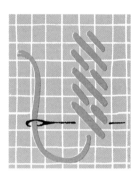

9. On the last stitch, work only Steps 2 and 3. Then insert the needle 1 hole above and 1 hole to the right of the hole from which the yarn last emerged. Slant the needle to the right; bring it out 1 hole above and 3 holes to the right of the hole from which the yarn last emerged.

10. Turn the canvas 180 degrees so that the top edge is again on top and the hole from which the yarn emerges is now at the upper left.

11. Continue the pattern down the row, beginning with Step 2 as shown.

IF YOU ARE LEFT-HANDED...

1. Start in the upper left corner of the pattern area and work to the right as shown.

2. Follow the directions given above for working below or above the hole from which the yarn emerged in the previous step, but reverse the right and left directions so that each pattern stitch will slant from upper left to lower right.

THE MOSAIC STITCH WORKED DIAGONALLY

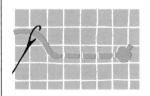 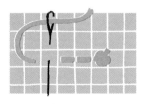 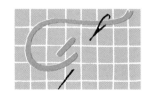  

1. Anchor the yarn to the canvas 4 holes to the right of the hole in which you wish to begin, as indicated in the instructions for starting a piece of yarn.

2. Insert the needle 1 hole above and 1 hole to the right of the one from which the yarn emerged in the previous step. Bring the needle out 1 hole to the right of the hole from which the yarn last emerged. Pull the yarn through.

3. Insert the needle 1 hole above and 1 hole to the right of the hole from which the yarn emerged in the previous step. Slant the needle downward diagonally and bring it out 1 hole below the hole from which the yarn last emerged. Pull the yarn through.

4. Insert the needle 2 holes above and 2 holes to the right of the hole from which the yarn emerged in the previous step. Slant the needle downward diagonally and bring it out 1 hole to the right of the hole from which the yarn last emerged. Pull the yarn through.

5. Insert the needle 1 hole above and 1 hole to the right of the hole from which the yarn emerged in the previous step, and bring the needle out 1 hole below the hole from which the yarn last emerged. Pull the yarn through.

continued

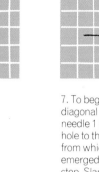

6. Insert the needle 1 hole above and 1 hole to the right of the hole from which the yarn emerged in the previous step. Slant the needle downward diagonally and bring it out 3 holes below the hole from which the yarn last emerged. Pull the yarn through. This completes one downward diagonal row.

7. To begin the upward diagonal row, insert the needle 1 hole above and 1 hole to the right of the hole from which the yarn emerged in the previous step. Slant the needle horizontally to the left and bring it out 1 hole above the hole from which the yarn last emerged. Pull the yarn through.

8. Insert the needle 1 hole above and 1 hole to the right of the hole from which the yarn emerged in the previous step. Slant the needle downward diagonally and bring it out 1 hole to the left of the hole from which the yarn last emerged. Pull the yarn through.

9. Insert the needle 2 holes above and 2 holes to the right of the hole from which the yarn emerged in the previous step. Slant the needle downward diagonally and bring it out 1 hole above the hole from which the yarn last emerged. Pull the yarn through.

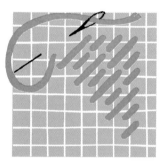
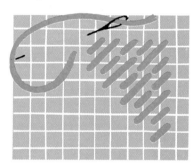

10. Continue working the pattern on the upward diagonal row by repeating Steps 8 and 9.

11. On the last stitch work only Step 8. Then insert the needle 1 hole above and 1 hole to the right of the hole from which the yarn emerged in the previous step. Slant the needle downward diagonally and bring it out 3 holes to the left of the hole from which the yarn last emerged.

12. Continue to work the pattern following the shape of the diagonal. On the downward rows, begin by repeating Steps 2-4 once. Then repeat Steps 3 and 4 as many times as necessary to complete the row, ending with Step 3. At the bottom of the diagonal, work Step 6 once as shown.

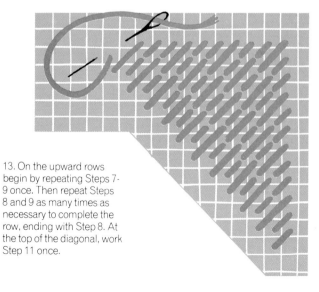
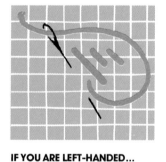
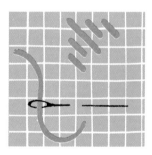

13. On the upward rows begin by repeating Steps 7-9 once. Then repeat Steps 8 and 9 as many times as necessary to complete the row, ending with Step 8. At the top of the diagonal, work Step 11 once.

IF YOU ARE LEFT-HANDED...

1. Start in the upper left corner of the pattern area and work to the right as indicated.

2. Follow the directions as given above for working below or above the hole from which the yarn emerged in the previous step, but reverse the right and left directions so that each pattern stitch will slant from upper left to lower right.

THE LEAF STITCH

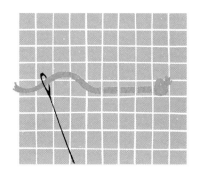

1. Anchor the yarn to the canvas 4 holes to the right of the hole in which you wish to begin, as in the instructions for starting a piece of yarn.

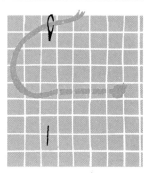

2. Insert the needle 3 holes above the hole from which the yarn emerged in the previous step. Slant the needle downward vertically and bring it out 2 holes below the hole from which the yarn last emerged. Pull the yarn through.

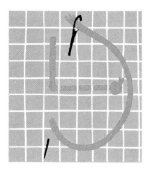

3. Insert the needle 4 holes above and 1 hole to the right of the one from which the yarn last emerged. Slanting the needle downward diagonally, bring it out 1 hole below the one from which the yarn last emerged. Pull the yarn through.

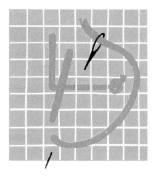

4. Insert the needle 4 holes above and 2 holes to the right of the one from which the yarn emerged in Step 3. Slant the needle downward diagonally and bring it out 1 hole below the one from which the yarn last emerged. Pull the yarn through.

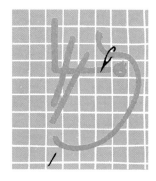

5. Insert the needle 4 holes above and 3 holes to the right of the one from which the yarn emerged in Step 4. Slant the needle downward diagonally and bring it out 1 hole below the hole from which the yarn last emerged. Pull the yarn through.

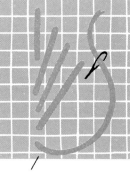

6. Insert the needle 4 holes above and 3 holes to the right of the hole from which the yarn emerged in Step 5. Slant the needle downward diagonally and bring it out 1 hole below the one from which the yarn last emerged. Pull the yarn through.

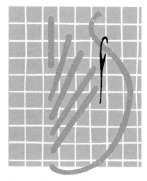

7. Insert the needle 4 holes above and 3 holes to the right of the hole from which the yarn emerged in the previous step. Pull the needle through to the back of the canvas. This completes the right side of the leaf.

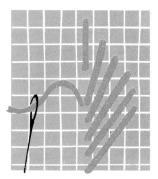

8. Begin the left side of the leaf by bringing the needle up from the back of the canvas 3 holes to the left of the hole through which the yarn entered the canvas in Step 7.

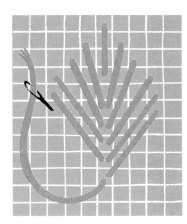

9. Repeat Steps 2-6 with this exception: in each case, insert the needle above and to the left rather than to the right of the hole from which the yarn emerged in the previous step.

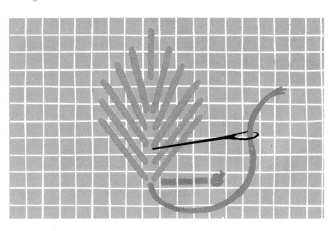

10. To add a stem to the leaf, thread your needle with a new strand of yarn of either the same or of a different color. Anchor the yarn to the canvas as shown and bring the needle out in the center bottom hole of the finished leaf. Pull the yarn through. Insert the needle 2 holes above the center bottom hole and pull the yarn through without beginning a new stitch.

THE CUSHIONED SCOTCH STITCH

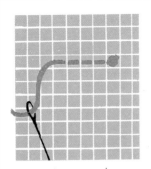

1. Anchor the yarn to the canvas 4 holes to the right of the hole in which you wish to begin, as shown in the instructions for starting a piece of yarn. For this stitch the beginning hole should be 1 hole below the top left hole of the pattern section.

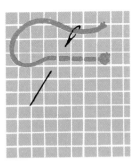

2. Insert the needle into the canvas 1 hole above and 1 hole to the right of the hole from which the yarn emerged in the previous step. Slant the needle downward diagonally and bring it out 1 hole below the one from which the yarn last emerged. Pull the yarn through.

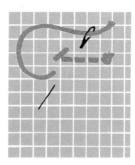

3. Insert the needle 2 holes above and 2 holes to the right of the one from which the yarn emerged in the previous step. Slant the needle downward diagonally and bring it out 1 hole below the one from which the yarn last emerged. Pull the yarn through.

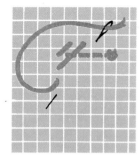

4. Insert the needle 3 holes above and 3 holes to the right of the one from which the yarn last emerged. Slant the needle downward diagonally and bring it out 1 hole below the one from which the yarn last emerged. Pull the yarn through.

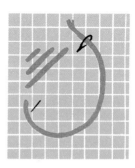

5. Insert the needle 4 holes above and 4 holes to the right of the one from which the yarn emerged in the previous step. Slant the needle downward diagonally and bring it out 1 hole to the right of the hole from which the yarn last emerged. Pull the yarn through.

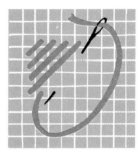

6. Insert the needle 3 holes above and 3 holes to the right of the one from which the yarn last emerged. Slant the needle downward diagonally and bring it out 1 hole to the right of the hole from which the yarn last emerged. Pull the yarn through.

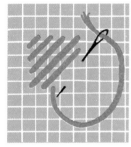

7. Insert the needle 2 holes above and 2 holes to the right of the hole from which the yarn emerged in the last step. Slant the needle downward diagonally and bring it out 1 hole to the right of the hole from which the yarn last emerged. Pull the yarn through.

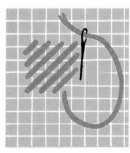

8. Insert the needle 1 hole above and 1 hole to the right of the hole from which the yarn emerged in the previous step. Pull the needle through to the back of the canvas.

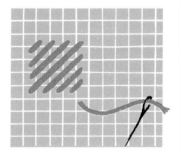

9. To begin the next square, bring the needle up from the back of the canvas 2 holes below the hole through which the yarn entered in Step 8.

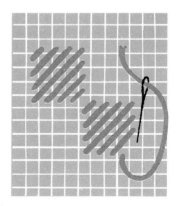

10. Repeat Steps 2-8 to form the second square.

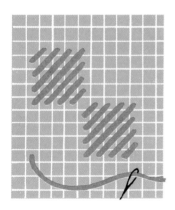

11. Bring the needle up from the back of the canvas 1 hole below and 8 holes to the left of the hole through which the yarn last entered in Step 10. Pull the yarn through.

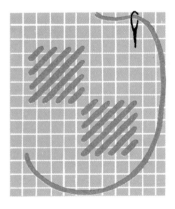

12. Insert the needle 8 holes above and 8 holes to the right of the hole from which the yarn emerged in the previous step. Pull the needle through to the back of the canvas without beginning a new stitch.

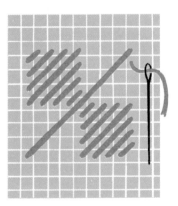

13. Bring the needle up from the back of the canvas 1 hole below the hole through which the yarn entered in the previous step. Pull the yarn through.

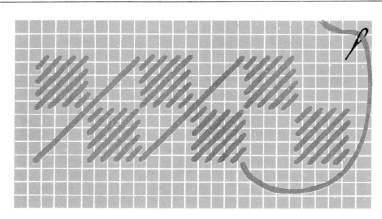

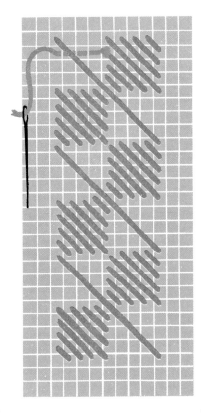

14. Repeat Steps 2-13 as many times as your design requires. On the last square, work only Steps 2-12.

15. Rotate the canvas clockwise 90 degrees so that the bottom edge of the canvas is on the left. Thread your needle with a new strand of yarn of either the same or of a different color. Then repeat Step 1, bringing the needle up from the back of the canvas 1 hole below the hole through which the yarn entered the canvas in Step 12.

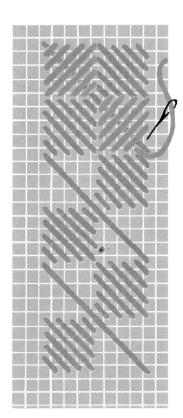

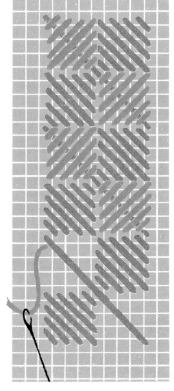

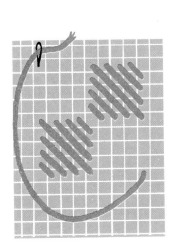

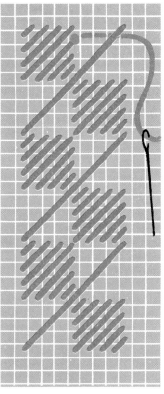

16. Repeat Steps 2-10 to complete the first pattern unit.

17. To complete each ensuing unit in the pattern, bring the needle up from the back of the canvas as shown in Step 15 and then repeat Steps 2-10.

IF YOU ARE LEFT-HANDED...

1. Start in the upper right corner of the pattern area and work to the left as shown.

2. Follow the directions given above for working below or above the hole from which the yarn emerged in the previous step, but reverse the right and left directions so that, as you work it, each pattern stitch will slant from upper left to lower right.

A medley of musical chairs

Among the most traditional of all articles of needlepoint are covers for chair seats. The covers shown here, created especially for this project, bring to mind an earlier day when household furnishings tended to be more unique and individualistic—in fact, frequently made by hand.

The motifs—which were inspired by and adapted from examples of colonial American advertising art —seem particularly appropriate for a musically talented family. But their

bright colors and evocative designs make them equally suitable for almost anyone whose tastes run to traditional decor.

The designs present a challenge; they are large and, in addition, each one requires six different needlepoint stitches as well as yarn of 14 different colors. However, they are more than worth the painstaking and intricate stitchery required to execute them. For designs like these suggest a myriad of other uses, such as throw pillows, covers for footstools or hassocks, or even framed wall hangings. Instructions appear overleaf for needlepointing the two covers seen here as well as for additional instrument designs.

Instructions for needlepointing musical chairs

To make the needlepoint chair covers (each measuring 16 1/2 inches by 19 1/2 inches) shown on pages 180-181, you will need 12-mesh monocanvas, several Size 18 tapestry needles and 2 strands of Persian yarn in the amounts noted on the color chart at right. The instrument, garland and ribbon are separate elements in the design; vary their arrangement as desired.

Preparing the canvas: Cut the canvas 3 inches wider on all sides than the area to be worked. (Add an extra 1/4 inch of background on each side so that no canvas will show when the seat is placed in the chair.) Always cut the canvas in a square or a rectangle so it can be blocked easily. Bind the edges with masking tape to avoid raveling.

Transferring the design: Draw and enlarge each design element to the scale desired (*Appendix*). Position the garland on the canvas; then place the instrument in the garland and add the ribbon. Adjust the elements to form a pleasing unit, eliminating excessive overlapping.

Handling the yarn: If possible, use a different needle for each color. Cut yarn no longer than 18 inches; longer strands will tend to fray. When using a given color of yarn, jump to the next area of that color only if it is less than 1 inch away; if not, finish off and begin a new strand.

Stitching the garland: Work each element with 2 strands of yarn. First stitch the blue trefoils, then outline the blue flowers, using the horizontal tent stitch (*Appendix*). Fill in the blue flowers and work the pink ones in single, vertical or horizontal mosaic stitch (*pages 173-175*). Work the green vines in horizontal tent stitch. Use the leaf stitch (*page 177*) for the medium green leaves first, then the light green ones, followed by the dark green stems.

Stitching the musical instrument and the ribbon: Work with 2 strands of yarn and use the horizontal tent stitch. Stitch the dark colors before the lighter ones.

Stitching the background: Work with 2 strands of yarn in the diagonal mosaic stitch (*pages 175-176*).

Blocking the finished work: Put the canvas face down on a muslin-padded board. Align the edges—with pliers if necessary—and tack them down with rustproof tacks. Rub the back of the canvas with a sponge soaked in cold water and let it dry on the board for 24 hours.

garland and ribbon

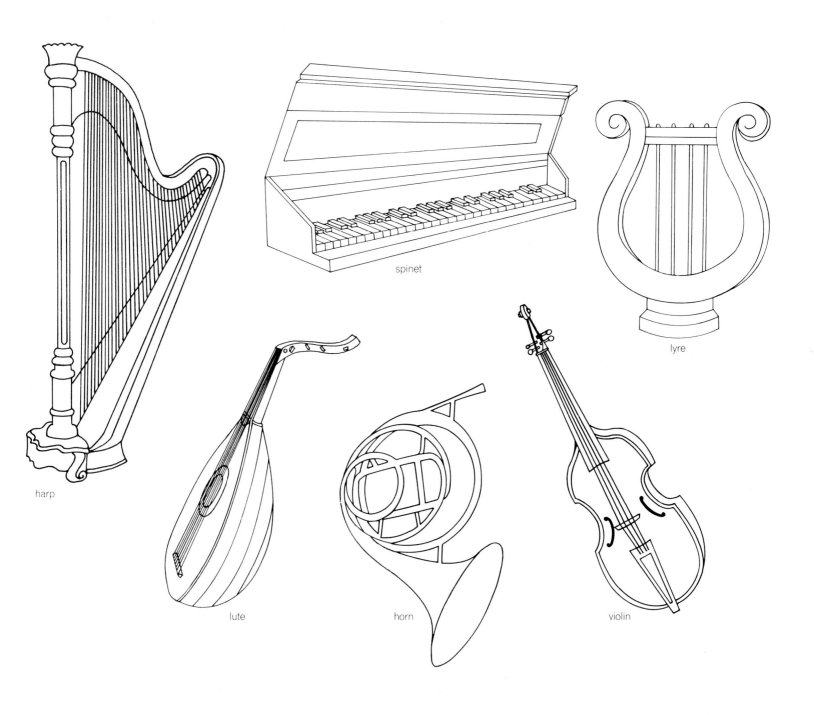

spinet

lyre

harp

lute

horn

violin

light blue—1 ounce

medium blue—1 ounce

dark blue—1 ounce

light pink—1 ounce

medium pink—1 ounce

deep rose—1 ounce

light green—2 ounces

medium green—2 ounces

dark green—1 ounce

light gold—1 ounce

medium gold—1 ounce

deep gold—1 ounce

dark brown—1 ounce

yellow—8 ounces

rust brown—1 ounce

medium brown—1 ounce

chocolate brown—1 ounce

A decorative board for backgammon

Backgammon is as old as Babylon, whose ancient city of Ur has yielded up to excavators at least one playing board 5,000 years old. Today back-gammon enthusiasts are fostering a spirited revival, inspiring creative adaptations of the conventional board, such as the flower-dappled one illustrated at right.

Made with only three stitches —according to the instructions overleaf—this needlepoint board is a demanding project but a rewarding one. The finished piece is elegant enough to deserve prominent display; for example, a carpenter can adapt it to a coffee or end table so that the board may become a permanent fixture in a game room, den or living room. Alternatively, the framed board can serve as an attractive wall hanging.

Instructions for needlepointing the game board

To make the needlepoint backgammon board pictured on pages 184-185, you will need a rectangular piece of 18-mesh mono-canvas (the board illustrated on the preceding pages measures 26 1/2 inches long by 19 3/4 inches wide), along with several Size 22 tapestry needles, and single strands of Persian yarn in the amounts indicated on the color chart at right.

Preparing the canvas: Cut the canvas at least 2 inches wider on all sides than the area to be worked. Temporarily bind the nonselvage edges with masking tape so the canvas will not ravel as you work.

Transferring the design: Follow the instructions that are given in the Appendix.

Handling the yarn: If possible, use a different needle for each color of yarn. Cut yarn no longer than 18 inches; longer strands will have to pass through the mesh so many times that they will tend to fray. When working with any given color of yarn, you can jump to the next area of that same color if it is no more than 1 inch away; if it is more than 1 inch, finish off and begin with a new strand.

Stitching the flowers: Work with a single strand of yarn and use the horizontal tent stitch (Appendix). Shading each flower as desired, stitch the dark colors first, then the lighter ones. Complete all the flowers in the design before beginning any other portion.

Stitching the triangles: Work with a single strand of yarn and use the diagonal tent stitch (Appendix). Stitch the dark colors first, then the lighter ones.

Stitching the border: Work with a single strand of yarn and make a double row of the cushioned Scotch stitch (pages 178-179) along each side of the center strip. Work the dark color first, then the light one.

Stitching the background: Work with a single strand of yarn and use the diagonal tent stitch (Appendix) to complete the background.

Blocking the finished work: Place the needlepoint face down on a board padded with muslin. Align the edges—using a pair of pliers if necessary to grip the fabric—and tack it down with rustproof tacks. Rub the back of the needlepoint with a sponge soaked in cold water and allow the canvas to dry on the board for 24 hours.

ivory beige—13 ounces

gold—2 1/2 ounces

brown—2 1/2 ounces

light green—1/4 ounce

medium green—1/4 ounce

dark green—1/4 ounce

light pink—1/4 ounce

medium pink—1/4 ounce

light blue—1/4 ounce

medium blue—1/4 ounce

light yellow—1/4 ounce

medium yellow—1/4 ounce

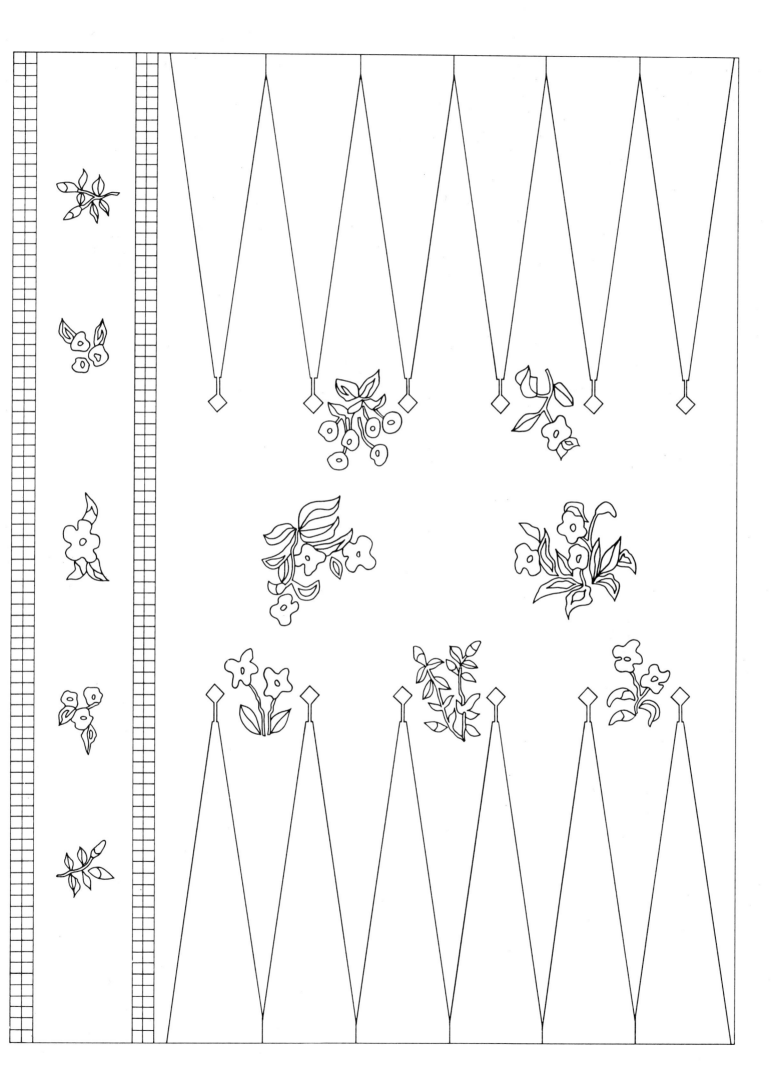

GLOSSARY

APPLIQUÉ: The sewing of cutout strips and shapes of fabric on larger cloth backgrounds, traditionally used to make coverings for bed quilts.

BASTE: To stitch fabric pieces together temporarily, or to indicate pattern markings on both sides of the fabric. Basting stitches can be made either by hand or by machine, generally at 6 stitches to the inch, and are removed when permanent stitching is completed.

BIAS: A direction diagonal to the threads forming woven fabric—the warp and the weft, or grains. The true bias is at a 45° angle to the grains.

BIAS TAPE: A folded strip of nylon, rayon or cotton, cut diagonally to the fabric threads—on the bias—so that it will stretch to cover curved and straight edges of a garment piece. Double-fold bias tape, 1/4 inch wide, is usually called bias binding and is only made of cotton. It is used to bind raw edges.

BLOCK: To shape finished knitting, crochet or needlepoint. For knitting or crochet, lay the work out in the correct shape and press it with a warm iron through a damp cloth. For needlepoint, mount the piece face down on a board with rust-proof tacks, making sure the canvas is taut and the sides are straight. Sponge the back of the needlepoint with cold water and rub it hard to flatten and smooth the work. Let the needlepoint dry on the board. If it is not straight when dry, repeat the blocking process.

CLIP: A short cut made into the fabric outside a seam to help it lie flat around curves and corners.

CREWEL: See EMBROIDERY.

CROCHETING: The process of making fabric by using a hook to knot strands of yarn into a series of connected loops.

DART: A stitched fabric fold, tapering to a point at one or both ends, that shapes fabric around curves.

DRESSMAKER'S CARBON: A marking paper, available in several colors and white, used to transfer construction lines from pattern to fabric.

EASE: The even distribution of fullness, without forming gathers or tucks, that enables one section of a garment to be smoothly joined to a slightly smaller section, such as in the seam attaching a sleeve to its armhole or in the hem of a flared skirt.

EDGING: A strip of decorative fabric such as ribbon, lace, or braid, which may be used to finish a hem or as trim on any part of a garment.

EMBROIDERY: The decoration of fabric with a needle and thread in a wide variety of stitches. When wool yarn is used, the embroidery is called crewel.

FACING: A piece of fabric, frequently the same as that used in the garment, that covers the raw fabric edge at openings such as necklines and armholes. It is first sewn to the visible side of the opening, then turned to the inside so that the seam between it and the garment is enclosed.

GATHERING: Bunching fabric together by pushing it along basting threads to create fullness, as in the bodice section joined to a shoulder yoke.

GAUGE: The number of stitches and rows to the inch in a piece of knitted or crocheted material.

GRAIN: The direction of threads in woven fabrics. The warp—the threads running from one cut end of the material to the other—forms the lengthwise grain. The weft, or woof—the threads running across the lengthwise grain from one finished edge of the fabric to the other—forms the crosswise grain. Only if the two grains are at right angles to each other is the fabric aligned on the "true grain."

JABOT: A fall of cloth, often ruffles, at the front of a collar.

KNITTING: The process of making fabric by using two or more pointed needles to knot strands of yarn into a series of connected loops.

MACHINE STITCH: To stitch permanent seams or finished edges by machine, generally at 12 stitches to the inch. A line of machine stitching is usually reinforced with backstitching at both ends. Insert the needle 1/2 inch in from the beginning of the line, stitch in reverse to the outside edge and then stitch the line. At the end of the line, stitch in reverse 1/2 inch.

MUSLIN: An inexpensive, plain-woven cotton fabric used for making prototypes of garments (called muslins) as an aid to styling and fitting.

NEEDLEPOINT: Designs created by working yarn through the meshes of stiff canvas, covering the canvas completely.

NOTCH: A V- or diamond-shaped marking made on the edge of a garment piece as an alignment guide. It is meant to be matched with a similar notch or group of notches on another piece when the two pieces are joined. Also a triangular cut into a curved seam to help it lie flat.

PEPLUM: A short flounce flowing over the hips from the waist of a blouse, jacket or dress designed to accentuate the silhouette. A peplum does not extend below the bottom line of the hips.

PIECING: The creating of new fabric by sewing together small bits of cloth, one of the traditional methods of making coverings for patchwork quilts.

PIVOT: A technique for making square corners by stopping the machine where the direction of a seam line changes, raising the presser foot, pivoting the fabric and lowering the presser foot before continuing to stitch again.

QUILTING: The sewing together of two layers of fabric with a soft bulky layer of filler between them, traditionally to make coverlets.

RUFFLES: Gathered strips of fabric used to decorate a garment, usually made from the garment fabric. Ruffles may be gathered along one edge or down the center of the fabric strip, and vary in size according to their use.

SEAM ALLOWANCE: The extra width of fabric, usually 5/8 inch, that extends outside the seam line.

SELVAGE: The lengthwise finished edges on woven fabric.

SKEIN: A length of yarn or thread coiled and packaged for knitting or crocheting. Usually the skein is wound into a ball before use.

SMOCKING: An embroidery technique for gathering, used to control fullness without limiting movement.

STAY STITCH: A line of machine stitching sewn on or alongside the seam line of a garment piece before the seam is stitched. Stay stitching is used as a reinforcement to prevent curved edges from stretching, and as a guide for folding an edge accurately.

TRACING WHEEL: A small wheel attached to a handle, used with dressmaker's carbon to transfer markings from pattern pieces to fabric.

TRIM: To cut away excess fabric in the seam allowance after the seam has been stitched. Also, a strip of fabric—such as braid or ribbon—used to decorate a garment.

TUCKS: Stitched-down pleats, arranged either vertically or horizontally, to serve decorative or structural purposes. They may be visible, with the folds sewn directly on the outside of the garment, or hidden, with the folds sewn on the inside of the garment.

UNDERSTITCHING: A line of machine stitching sewn alongside the original seam. It serves to attach the seam allowance to the facing and prevents the facing from rolling out.

ZIGZAG STITCH: A serrated line of machine stitching used as decoration, to prevent raveling of raw edges and for appliqué.

BASIC STITCHES

The diagrams below and on the following pages show how to make the elementary hand stitches, knitting, crocheting, embroidery and needlepoint stitches referred to in this volume.

THE FASTENING STITCH

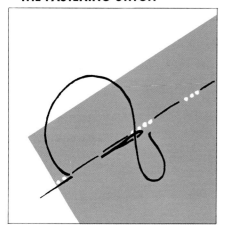

To end a row with a fastening stitch, insert the needle back 1/4 inch and bring it out at the point at which the thread last emerged. Make another stitch through these same points for extra firmness. To begin a row with a fastening stitch, leave a 4 inch loose end and make the initial stitch the same way as an ending stitch.

THE RUNNING STITCH

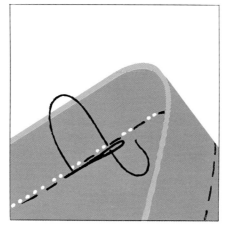

Insert the needle, with knotted thread, from the wrong side of the fabric and weave the needle in and out of the fabric several times in 1/8-inch, evenly spaced stitches. Pull the thread through. Continue across, making several stitches at a time, and end with a fastening stitch. When basting, make longer stitches, evenly spaced.

THE CATCH STITCH

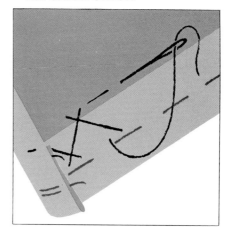

Working from left to right, anchor the first stitch with a knot inside the hem 1/4 inch down from the edge. Point the needle to the left and pick up one or two threads on the garment directly above the hem, then pull the thread through. Take a small stitch in the hem only (not in the garment), 1/4 inch down from the edge and 1/4 inch to the right of the previous stitch. End with a fastening stitch.

THE SLIP STITCH

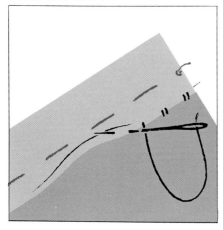

Fold under the hem edge and anchor the first stitch with a knot inside the fold. Point the needle to the left. Pick up one or two threads of the garment fabric close to the hem edge, directly below the first stitch, and slide the needle horizontally through the folded edge of the hem 1/8 inch to the left of the previous stitch. End with a fastening stitch.

THE HEMMING STITCH

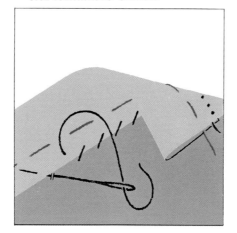

Anchor the first stitch with a knot inside the hem; then pointing the needle up and to the left, pick up one or two threads of the garment fabric close to the hem. Push the needle up through the hem 1/8 inch above the edge; pull the thread through. Continue picking up one or two threads and making 1/8-inch stitches in the hem at intervals of 1/4 inch. End with a fastening stitch.

THE OVERCAST STITCH

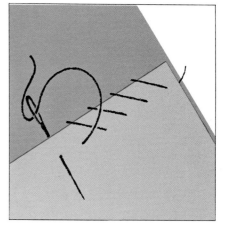

Draw the needle, with knotted thread, through from the wrong side of the fabric 1/8 to 1/4 inch down from the top edge. With the thread to the right, insert the needle under the fabric from the wrong side 1/8 to 1/4 inch to the left of the first stitch. Continue to make evenly spaced stitches over the fabric edge and end with a fastening stitch.

1. Form a slipknot in the yarn, leaving a free end long enough for the number of stitches to be cast on (allow about 1 inch per stitch).

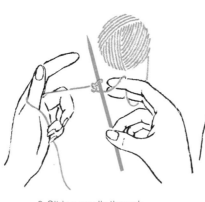

2. Slide a needle through the slipknot and hold the needle in your right hand. Loop the yarn attached to the ball over your right index finger and loop the free end of the yarn around your left thumb.

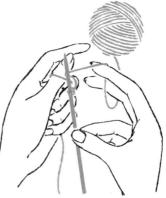

3. Insert the tip of the needle through the loop on your left thumb and bring the yarn attached to the ball under and over the needle from left to right.

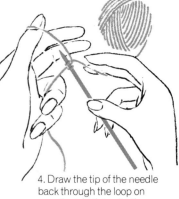

4. Draw the tip of the needle back through the loop on your thumb, then slip the loop off your thumb. Pull the short end of the yarn down to tighten the loop, which is now a stitch. Repeat Steps 2-4 for the required number of stitches.

THE KNIT STITCH

1. Insert the right needle in the front of the stitch closest to the tip of the left needle, as shown. Bring the yarn under and over the right needle.

2. Pull the right needle back through the stitch, bringing with it the loop of yarn. Slide this loop—which is now a stitch—off the left needle and onto the right. Repeat Steps 1 and 2 for each knit stitch.

THE PURL STITCH

1. Insert the right needle into the stitch closest to the tip of the left needle, as shown. Bring the yarn around and under the right needle.

2. Push the needle back through the stitch, bringing with it the loop of yarn —which is now a stitch. Transfer this new stitch to the right needle, letting it slip off the left needle as you do so. Repeat Steps 1 and 2 for each purl stitch.

INCREASING STITCHES

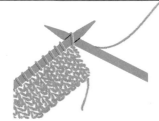

1. On a knit row, insert the right needle through the back of a stitch. Knit the stitch, but do not drop it off the left needle.

1. On a purl row, insert the right needle from right to left through the horizontal loop at the bottom of a stitch. Make a purl stitch but do not let it slide off the left needle.

2. Knit the same stitch in the ordinary way, and transfer the two stitches to the right needle.

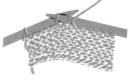

2. Now insert the right needle into the vertical loop above the horizontal one. Purl the stitch in the ordinary way, and slide both loops onto the right needle.

DECREASING STITCHES

1. Insert the right needle into two stitches instead of one, either from front to back as shown, for a knit stitch, or from back to front as for a purl stitch. Proceed as though you were knitting or purling one stitch at a time.

BINDING OFF STITCHES

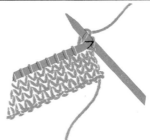

1. Knit (or purl) two stitches. Then insert the left needle through the front of the second stitch from the tip of the right needle.

2. With the left needle, lift the second stitch on the right needle over the first stitch and let it drop.

1. Form a loose slipknot around the crochet hook, about 1 inch from the end of the yarn. Grasp the yarn attached to the ball with the tip of the hook and pull the yarn through the slipknot with the tip of the hook, as shown.

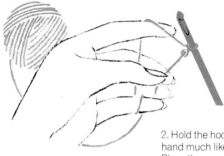

2. Hold the hook in your right hand much like a pencil. Place the yarn from the ball around the left little finger, then up and over the left index finger. Grasp the free end of the yarn between the thumb and middle finger of the left hand.

3. With your left index finger, bring the yarn from the back to the front of the hook and catch it under the tip of the hook.

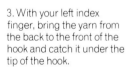

4. Pull the tip of the hook through the loop on the hook, bringing the yarn with it to create the first chain stitch in the foundation chain. Repeat Steps 1-4 to form a chain of the desired length.

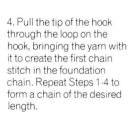

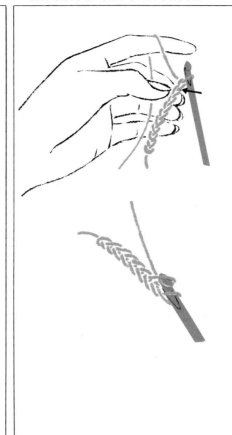

1. To single crochet the first row after a foundation chain, insert the hook through the second chain stitch from the hook (arrow)—do not count the loop on the hook.

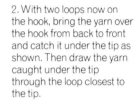

2. With two loops now on the hook, bring the yarn over the hook from back to front and catch it under the tip as shown. Then draw the yarn caught under the tip through the loop closest to the tip.

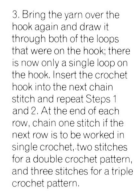

3. Bring the yarn over the hook again and draw it through both of the loops that were on the hook; there is now only a single loop on the hook. Insert the crochet hook into the next chain stitch and repeat Steps 1 and 2. At the end of each row, chain one stitch if the next row is to be worked in single crochet, two stitches for a double crochet pattern, and three stitches for a triple crochet pattern.

4. Turn the work to crochet back across the previous row. Insert the hook through both loops of the second stitch from the edge, as shown, and all subsequent stitches on this and all rows after the foundation chain.

THE DOUBLE CROCHET STITCH

1. To double crochet the first row of stitches after a foundation chain, count back to the third chain stitch from the hook (arrow)—do not count the loop on the hook. Swing the yarn over the hook from back to front, then insert the hook through this third chain stitch.

2. Bring the yarn over the hook again and draw it through the loop closest to the tip. Bring the yarn over the hook again and draw it through the two loops closest to the tip.

3. Bring the yarn over the tip again and draw it through the remaining two loops on the hook. At the end of each row, chain one stitch if the next row is to be worked in single crochet, two stitches for double crochet and three stitches for triple crochet.

4. Turn the work to crochet back across the previous row. Bring the yarn over the hook and insert the hook through both loops of the second stitch from the edge (arrow) on this and all rows after the first.

INCREASING STITCHES

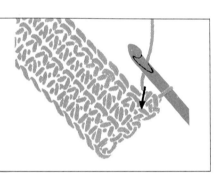

To increase stitches, work one stitch—either a single, double or triple crochet, as called for in the instructions—then insert the crochet hook back into the same loop or loops (arrow) and repeat the stitch.

DECREASING STITCHES, SINGLE CROCHET

1. To decrease in a row of single crochet stitches, insert the hook into both loops of a stitch. Bring the yarn over the hook and draw it through the two loops closest to the tip; this leaves two loops on the hook.

2. Insert the hook through both loops of the next stitch. Bring the yarn over the hook and draw it through the two loops closest to the tip. Bring the yarn over the hook again and draw it through the three remaining loops on the hook.

DECREASING STITCHES, DOUBLE CROCHET

1. To decrease in a row of double crochet stitches, bring the yarn over the hook and insert it through both loops of a stitch. Bring the yarn over the hook again, as shown, and draw it through the two loops closest to the tip. Then bring the yarn over the hook again and insert it through both loops of the next stitch.

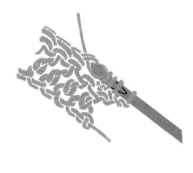

2. Again bring the yarn over the hook and draw it through the two loops closest to the tip, as shown; there are now five loops on the hook. Bring the yarn over the hook again and draw it through the two loops now closest to the tip. Repeat the process until there are three loops remaining on the hook. Then pull the yarn through the three remaining loops.

EMBROIDERY

THE SATIN STITCH

1. Using a knotted thread, bring the needle up from the wrong side of the material held in the hoop; then, at the angle desired, insert it down to the wrong side at a point diagonally across the design.

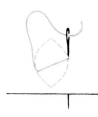

2. Bring the needle straight up from the wrong side just above the first hole and insert it above the hole made in Step 1.

3. Repeat Step 2 until the top is filled. Then bring the needle from the wrong side just below the filled part and make diagonal stitches until the bottom is filled. Secure the last stitch on the wrong side (Ending Off, *below*).

THE FRENCH KNOT

1. Using a knotted thread, bring the needle up from the wrong side of the material held in the hoop. Put down the hoop and loop the thread once around the needle.

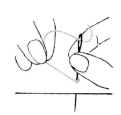

2. Holding the looped thread taut with one hand, push the needle tip into—or just next to—the hole made in Step 1. Slide the loop down to the fabric. Then push the needle through to the wrong side of the fabric.

3. Bring the needle up from the wrong side at a point that suits your design, and repeat Steps 1 and 2. Secure the last stitch on the wrong side (Ending Off, *below*).

THE STEM STITCH

1. Using a knotted thread, bring the needle up from the wrong side of the material held in the hoop.

2. With your left thumb, hold the thread away from the needle. Point the needle to the left, but take a stitch to the right of the hole made in Step 1. The needle should emerge midway between the beginning of this stitch and the hole made in Step 1.

3. Pull the thread through taut and take another stitch to the right the same size as the one made in Step 2. Continue making similar stitches along the design and secure the last stitch on the wrong side (Ending Off, *below*).

THE CHAIN STITCH

1. Using a knotted thread, bring the needle up from the wrong side of the material held in the hoop. Pull it through and loop the thread from left to right.

2. With your left thumb, hold the thread in a loop of the desired size and insert the needle in the hole from which it emerged in Step 1. Keeping the loop under the needle point, bring the needle out directly below. Pull the needle through.

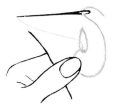

3. Again loop the thread and hold it. Insert the needle in the hole from which it last emerged and bring it out through the loop. Complete the design and anchor the last stitch by inserting the needle below its loop. Secure on the wrong side (Ending Off, *below*).

THE SQUARED FILLING STITCH

1. Using a knotted thread and with the material held in a hoop, bring the needle up from the wrong side of the material in the middle of one edge of the design. Insert the needle down to the wrong side at a point directly across the design.

2. Bring the needle up from the wrong side just to the left of the previous hole on the same side of the design. The distance between stitches should be consistent.

3. Continue making parallel stitches, starting each on the side of the design where the previous stitch ended. Complete the left-hand area, then bring the needle up to the right of the center stitch made in Step 1, and fill the right-hand area.

4. Bring the needle up from the wrong side of the fabric at the center of the far right end of the design, and insert the needle at a right angle across the design to the far left end. Complete the right-left stitches as in Steps 1-3.

5. To lock, bring the needle up in the upper right corner where the 2 stitches cross. Insert the needle diagonally over the intersection. Work 1 right-left stitch at a time. Secure on the wrong side (Ending Off, *below*).

ENDING OFF

On the wrong side of the material, slide the needle underneath the nearest 3 or 4 consecutive stitches and pull it through. Snip off the excess thread.

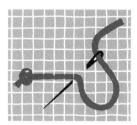

THE HORIZONTAL TENT STITCH

1. Follow the instructions for starting a piece of yarn *(page 172)*. Then insert the needle into the canvas 1 hole above and 1 hole to the right of the beginning hole. Slant the needle downward diagonally and bring it out 1 hole to the left of the beginning hole.

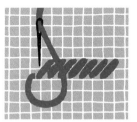

2. Continue, working from right to left, to the end of the row. Then insert the needle diagonally 1 hole above and 1 hole to the right of the one from which the yarn last emerged. Pull the needle through to the back of the canvas.

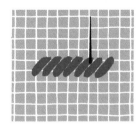

3. Rotate the canvas 180° so the last stitch made is on the right; bring up the needle from the back, 1 hole above the hole through which the yarn entered the canvas in Step 2.

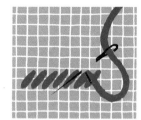

4. Insert the needle 1 hole above and 1 hole to the right of the hole through which the yarn last emerged, continuing as before across the row.

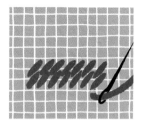

5. At the end of the row, rotate the canvas 180° so the last stitch made is on the right. Bring up the needle from the back, 1 hole below the hole through which the yarn last entered the canvas. Continue the pattern. At the end of each piece of yarn, run the last 1 1/2 inches through the stitches on the back of the canvas.

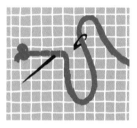

THE DIAGONAL TENT STITCH

1. Follow the instructions for starting a piece of yarn *(page 172)*. Then insert the needle into the canvas 1 hole above and 1 hole to the right of the beginning hole. Slant the needle downward diagonally and bring it out 1 hole to the left of the beginning hole.

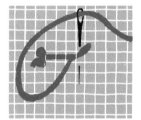

2. Insert the needle into the canvas diagonally, and bring it out vertically 2 holes below.

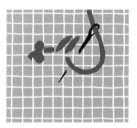

3. Insert the needle diagonally, this time bringing it out 2 holes down and 1 to the left, in the hole below the one from which the yarn emerged in Step 2.

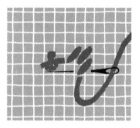

4. Insert the needle diagonally and bring it out horizontally 2 holes to the left.

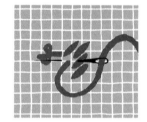

5. Insert the needle diagonally and bring it out horizontally 2 holes to the left.

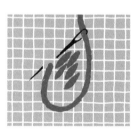

6. Insert the needle diagonally and bring it out diagonally 1 hole to the left of the hole from which the yarn last emerged.

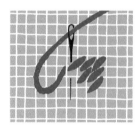

7. Repeat Step 2 three times, inserting the needle diagonally each time, and bringing it out vertically.

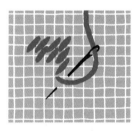

8. At the bottom of the diagonal, repeat Step 3 —*i.e.,* insert the needle diagonally and bring it out at a slant 2 holes down and 1 to the left. Then repeat Step 4 four times, inserting the needle diagonally and bringing it out horizontally 2 holes to the left. Then repeat Step 6.

9. Continue to follow the pattern. Repeat Step 2, working vertically as many times as necessary to get to the bottom of the diagonal. Repeat Step 3 at the bottom. Repeat Step 4, working horizontally back up the diagonal, and then repeat Step 6 once at the top to complete the pattern.

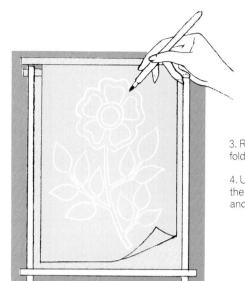

1. Tape the drawing, print or photograph to be traced to a table top or board. Center a sheet of tracing paper over the design and tape it at the top.

2. Trace the design with a fine-tipped black pen. If you are making a tracing for needlepoint be sure the line is strong enough to be seen through the canvas.

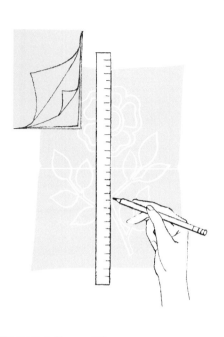

3. Remove the tracing and fold it into quarters.

4. Unfold it and lightly mark the fold lines with a ruler and pencil.

ENLARGING OR REDUCING A DESIGN

1. Trace the design onto a square piece of paper—it must be square to preserve proportions in rectangular designs—and fold the tracing in half across its width, then across its length. Unfold and fold it in quarters and eighths across its width and length to make a grid with eight squares on each side. (For an elaborate design, the paper may be folded into a 16-square grid.) With a ruler and pencil draw lines along the fold marks.

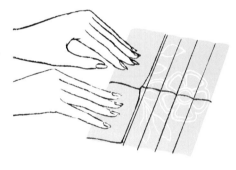

2. Identify horizontal and vertical coordinates as on a map, by penciling letters (A to H) along the top and numbers (1 to 8) down the side.

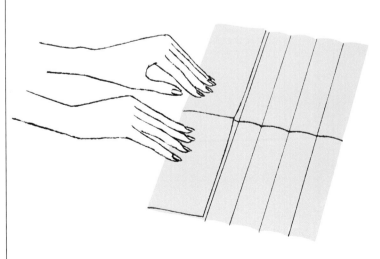

3. Cut a sheet of drawing paper into a square approximately the size you want the embroidery or needlepoint to be.

4. Fold it just as you folded the original and pencil in the same lines and coordinates.

5. Using the coordinates to locate matching squares, copy the design freehand, square by square.

6. Transfer the enlarged or reduced design to the fabric as shown on page 196.

TRANSFERRING A DESIGN TO EMBROIDERY FABRIC

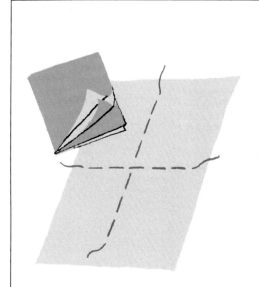

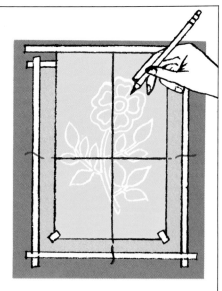

1. Fold the embroidery fabric into quarters and crease the fold lines with your fingers or an iron.

2. Unfold the fabric and baste along the creases, taking long stitches on the visible side for easily followed guide lines.

3. Tape the fabric, wrong side down, to the work surface.

4. Lay the paper tracing over the fabric, aligning its center fold lines with the basting on the fabric, and tape the tracing down along the top. At the bottom corners, put tabs of tape that can easily be lifted as you work.

5. Insert dressmaker's carbon paper, carbon side down, between the tracing or enlarged or reduced drawing and the fabric. (If the carbon paper is smaller than the design, move it as you work.)

6. Trace the design with a dull pencil, pressing hard. From time to time lift the paper and check that the design is coming through distinctly on the fabric. Avoid smudging by working from top to bottom. Remove the fabric and baste around the edges to prevent fraying.

TRACING A DESIGN ONTO NEEDLEPOINT CANVAS

1. Cut a piece of needlepoint canvas at least 2 or 3 inches larger than your design on each side. Fold it in quarters; then unfold it and mark the fold lines with a pencil.

2. Place the tracing under the canvas and align the marked center fold lines on the design with the fold lines made on the canvas in Step 1. Tape the tracing and the canvas in place with masking tape.

3. Trace the design directly onto the canvas with a fine-tipped pen and indelible ink, which will not rub off or stain the finished needlepoint. (You may want to use several colors of indelible ink as a helpful stitching guide.) Minor details may be drawn on the canvas freehand or be stitched in at will. Draw a border limiting the area of the design.

4. Remove the canvas from the design and attach masking tape to the edges to prevent the canvas from unraveling as you work.

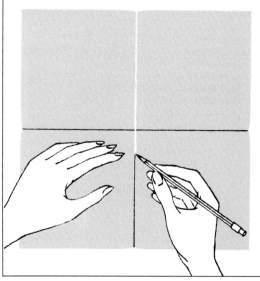

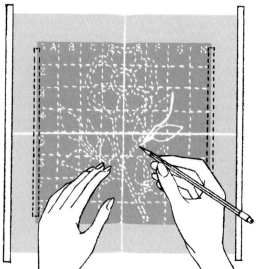

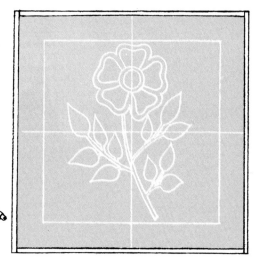

CREDITS

Sources for the illustrations in this book are shown below. Credits from left to right are separated by semicolons, from top to bottom by dashes.

Cover—Design taken from an early American fabric swatch. 6,7—Tasso Vendikos. 10,11—Tasso Vendikos courtesy Collection of Robert Tynes, New York City. 14 through 19—Donald Caýce. 20,21—Tasso Vendikos. 24,25—Paulus Leeser courtesy The Brooklyn Museum. 26—Drawings by John Sagan—Drawings by John Sagan except bottom by Jane Poliotti. 27—Drawings by John Sagan—Drawings by Raymond Skibinski; Drawings by Jane Poliotti. 28,29—Tasso Vendikos, background courtesy The Brooklyn Museum. 30,31—Drawings by Ted Kliros. 32,33—Tasso Vendikos, background courtesy Culver Pictures. 34 through 45—Drawings by Ted Kliros. 46,47—Tasso Vendikos, background courtesy The Bettmann Archive. Smocking by Ginger Seippel. 48 through 51—Drawings by Ted Kliros. 52,53—Tasso Vendikos, background courtesy Culver Pictures. 54 through 67—Drawings by John Sagan. 68,69—Tasso Vendikos, background courtesy The Brooklyn Museum. 70—Drawings by John Sagan. 71—Drawings by Dale Gustafson. 72 through 85—Drawings by Raymond Skibinski. 86,87—Tasso Vendikos, background courtesy The Brooklyn Museum. 88 through 91—Drawings by Ted Kliros. 92,93—Robert Colton. Quilt courtesy Phyllis Haders, New York City. 97—Courtesy Abby Aldrich Rockefeller Folk Art Collection, Williamsburg, Virginia. 98 through 101—Paulus Leeser, drawings by Stephen Cervantes. Quilts courtesy The Quilt Gallery, New York City. 102—Richard Jeffery. Quilt courtesy Phyllis Haders, New York City. 103 through 109—Drawings by Raymond Skibinski. 110 through 113—Drawings by Ted Kliros. 114—Richard Jeffery. Quilt courtesy Collection of Rhett Delford Brown, Great Building Crack-up Gallery, New York City. 115 through 117—Drawings by Ted Kliros. 118—Richard Jeffery. Quilt courtesy The Quilt Gallery, New York City. 119 through 123—Drawings by Ted Kliros. 124,125—Tasso Vendikos. 129—Ken Kay. 130,131—Enrico Ferorelli courtesy Brooklyn Botanic Garden. 132 through 137—Drawings by John Sagan. 138,139—Tasso Vendikos. Embroidery by Lucy Ciancia. 141—Drawing by Carmen Mercadal. 143—Illustration from *People of Eight Seasons—The Story of the Lapps* by Ernst Manker, Tre Tryckare Cagner and Co., Gothenburg, Sweden. 144,145—Herbert Orth. Knitting by Annette Feldman. 146,147—Tasso Vendikos. Knitting by Annette Feldman. 148—Drawings by Carmen Mercadal. 149—Drawings by Walter Johnson except upper right by Carmen Mercadal. 151,153—Drawings by Carmen Mercadal. 155—Drawings by John Sagan. 156 through 159—Herbert Orth. Crochet by Annette Feldman. 160,161—Tasso Vendikos. Crochet by Annette Feldman. 162—Drawings by Carmen Mercadal. 164,165—Drawings by John Sagan. 167—Courtesy Pilgrim Society, Plymouth, Massachusetts; Courtesy The Mount Vernon Ladies Association, Virginia. 168—Courtesy San Antonio Museum Association, Texas; Courtesy Pauline Fischer Needlework Collection, New York City. 170,171—Enrico Ferorelli, with permission of Charles Scribner's Sons from *Needlepoint Designs from American Indian Art* by Nora Cammann, Copyright© 1973 Nora Cammann. 172 through 179—Drawings by Raymond Skibinski. 180,181—Tasso Vendikos. Design by Carolyn Ambuter, needlework by Cecilia Toth. 182,183—Drawings by Penny Burnham. 184,185—Tasso Vendikos. Board design by Mazaltov's Inc. except center strip by Carolyn Ambuter, needlework by Virginia Mailman except center strip by Sondra Albert. 187—Drawing by Carmen Mercadal. 189 through 193—Drawings by John Sagan. 194—Drawings by Mulvey/Crump Associates, Inc. 195—Drawings by Raymond Skibinski—Drawings by John Sagan. 196—Drawings by Raymond Skibinski—Drawings by John Sagan.

ACKNOWLEDGMENTS

For their help in the preparation of this book the editors would like to thank the following individuals: Angela Alleyne; Carolyn Ambuter; Mrs. Elaine Benson, Benson Gallery, Bridgehampton, New York; Karen B. Booth; Penny Burnham; Rhett Delford Brown, Great Building Crack-up Gallery, New York City; Mrs. Frederic G. Cammann; Lucy Ciancia; Audrey C. Foote; Bernie Gold; Rhea Goodman, The Quilt Gallery, New York City; Phyllis Haders; Carol Higgins; Yvonne McCarge; Mrs. Norton Mailman; Carolyn Mazzello; Norma Ponard, Coiffure Naturelle, New York City; Belle Conway Rivers; Mrs. Janet Tiso; Cecilia Toth; Robert Tynes.

The editors would also like to thank the following: B. Altman & Co.; Brooklyn Botanic Garden; Femme Fatale, Ltd.; Fred Leighton Imports, Ltd.; The Gazebo; Henri Bendel Inc.; Jill of Storyhill; LeRoy's Dress Shop; Mazaltov's Inc.; Nonesuch, Ltd.; Paul Stuart, Inc.; Philip Pfeifer Antiques; Scalamandré.

# INDEX

Numerals in italics indicate an illustration of the subject mentioned.